FATBOY SLIM
FUNK SOUL BROTHER

Printed in the United Kingdom by Biddles Ltd, Surrey

Published by Sanctuary Publishing Limited, Sanctuary House, 45–53 Sinclair Road, London W14 0NS, United Kingdom

www.sanctuarypublishing.com

Photographs courtesy of Alexis Maryon, Camera Press, Rex Features, SIN/CORBIS and Redferns

ISBN: 1-86074-430-3

FATBOY SLIM
FUNK SOUL BROTHER

Martin James
Sanctuary

ABOUT THE AUTHOR

Martin James became a music and popular-culture journalist by accident over 10 years ago. Since then he has enjoyed editorial positions at various magazines, including *Muzik* (where he was a founding section editor), *Melody Maker*, *Vox*, *Flipside* (UK) and *Seven* magazine. He has contributed to *The Independent*, *The Guardian*, *Mixmag*, *DJ*, *Select* and US magazine *Urb*. He is also the author of three acclaimed books: *State Of Bass: Jungle, The Story So Far*; *Moby: Replay*; and *Prodigy*.

At the age of 14, Martin left home to follow The Clash and the then-unsigned Siouxsie And The Banshees around the UK. He has subsequently written and recorded music under such aliases as General Seven, Box Disciples and Crunch Bird. He's promoted gigs and raves in pubs and clubs. He's written or commissioned the first music-press interviews with more big names than can be listed here. Iggy Pop once pissed on his shoes. He's been punched by Goldie and kidnapped by an unknown DJ in Italy. He swam across crocodile-infested waters in Indonesia, danced for three days and nights solid in Japan, shared a few drinks with George Best in the pubs of Marlow, Buckinghamshire, and got stoned senseless with Cypress Hill in Amsterdam. He was among the first journalists to cover big beat, supported Fatboy Slim from the first single and lost it on numerous occasions at the Boutique. He also conducted the last ever interview with Dr Timothy Leary by a British journalist – Winona Ryder was at the door, Oliver Stone in the kitchen and Perry Farrell on the sofa.

Martin currently lives in the relative quiet of Brighton and Hove City with his partner, Lisa, and their two children, Ruby Blue and Felix Drum.

ACKNOWLEDGEMENTS

The Fatboy Slim story is about far more than just Norman Cook. Sure, he's the central figure, but his career is inextricably linked to so many artists, musicians, clubs, scenes, etc, that it's impossible to talk about him without mentioning them.

As a result, I interviewed over 50 people for this book, many of whom wished to remain anonymous, for reasons that I will explain later – this unofficial biography, as it turned out, was far more political than I had ever thought possible. Out of respect for these people, many of whom I know personally and like immensely, I have agreed not to list them. So, for all of these people, and you know who you are, thanks for your help. And I hope I represent your contributions accurately.

There are of course a great many people who helped either directly or indirectly that deserve thanks. First of all, Graham Gilbert, one-time boss of Rounder Records; Kevin Stagg of The Esselle Beat Co Studio; Jim Carmichael; dancer Michael Gier (who was in the video for 'Praise You'); Steve Philips; Nick Smash and all at Skint/Loaded, the Boutique crew; Dan, Ed and Tammy at the Darling Department; Garry and Bally at Anglo Management; various members of Freakpower and Beats International; all of the wonderful journalists whose work I read in the name of research (the UK should have more pride in its music-journo talent!); and all of the photographers whose work appears here, especially Alexis Maryon. Thanks also to Mary Anne Hobbs (as always), Annie Nightingale and half of Brighton, all of whom had a story, few of which could be repeated! I'd also like thank Norman and Zoë. All I can say is, I was too far gone to turn around. I hope you like it!

Respect and thanks are also due to the Sanctuary team, Iain, Penny, Michelle, Dan, Alan and super subs Yvonne and Gill. I would also like to thank good doctors everywhere and the staff at The British Library.

Finally, as ever, my love goes out to friends and family (both the Thomas and the Tansey branches) and eternal love to my beautiful little clan: Ruby Blue, Felix Drum and Lisa.

Martin James
Brighton, August 2002

CONTENTS

To Lis, Ruby Blue and Felix Drum

THE BIG BEACH BOUTIQUE

BRIGHTON BEACH, 6 JULY 2001

'Ladies and gentlemen, this is a public safety message. All people to the right of the stage by the sea must move back towards the West Pier. In the interests of safety, please follow the stewards and police advice and we'll start the show again as soon as possible. Thank you.'

It could be Ibiza. The air is balmy with mid summer heat. A sunset bleeds its brilliant heady hues across the horizon. The waves lap the beaches with gentle invitation while the sea plays host to a multitude of yachts and pleasure cruisers. People drunk with enjoyment wade into the waters, cooling blood and washing away the daily grind of real life while all across the mile-long stretch of pebble beach people dance like they're a part of the greatest party on Earth. Smiles spread contagiously, encouraging people to lift their feet and jump to the adrenalised music, which is busy challenging the sunset for impact.

Throughout the town pubs lie nearly deserted while off-licences fight off the avalanche of customers all seeking supplies for the perfect beach party. But the cans of beer ran out hours ago; not a drop can be found within a mile of the seafront. Some off-licences are almost stripped bare of all alcohol, and are declaring all-time record takings.

Back on the beach some of the more enterprising locals wander around the crowd selling shots of tequila and overpriced warm lagers to the thirsty masses. Behind them, at one end of the beach to the east, the Palace Pier flickers with fairground lights, while far in the west the silhouetted shapes of the Hove beach-side houses – known as Millionaires' Row to the locals – can just be seen. It's here that our host calls home.

On a stage set in the middle of the beach the Fatboy Slim effect is in full flow. Breakbeats collide with pulsating house grooves, disco *a cappellas* float over muscular techno funk and all the while Norman Cook jigs behind the decks, raises his hands to the crowd, laughs, shouts, screams. He's having the time of his life. It's the moment he was born for. He lifts vinyl from his boxes and scribbles notes on the labels for the benefit of the huge screen behind him.

'Are you from Brighton?' he writes and the crowd roar with appreciation. Tonight all 40,000 of us are. The local clubbers, the kids too young to go clubbing yet and the older one-time clubbers; unemployed beach bums, middle-aged businessmen and young-at-heart pensioners: gay, straight, black, white; all people united for an evening of pure celebration.

Between the back of the stage and the derelict yet stunning West Pier, a similar story unfolds as young families dance with their children. The acid house generation – now parents – wave their arms like it's 1987 again as kids copy every move, waving fluorescent light sticks for added fun.

Overhead searchlights pick out the decrepit West Pier, sending wave upon wave of birds into a panicked yet majestic flight around the old structure. And then fireworks explode as the whole of Brighton is lit up in a lysergic pyrotechnic display like the fourth of July multiplied by a thousand.

And then it's all over. A night of unparalleled joy. A celebration of everything that Brighton publicly stands for. Togetherness, tolerance and full-throttle hedonism.

A free party like this could only have happened in Brighton. The English city situated on the south coast has long been the favoured destination for pleasure seekers and hedonists from all walks of life.

In the late 18th century, one Doctor Richard Russell bought acres of land around the fishing village called Brighthelmstone and decided to turn the place into a spa for the fashionable elite of London to enjoy the healing elixir of the local waters. Brighton then became a place where the elite few could enjoy rest and relaxation. Hotels sprang up all along the coast as people came to improve their health by imbibing as much seawater as their aching stomachs could handle.

The lazy relaxation of the spa was quickly turned into a thrill-seeker's paradise when, in 1783, the Prince Regent (later crowned King George IV) was advised to take his pleasure away from London's royal court. In fact, he was advised to take his wild parties and even wilder private life as far away as possible so that his nocturnal habits didn't become the subject of society gossip. So the would-be patron sinner of Brighton decamped to the seaside and built a stunning pleasure palace in the shape of the Royal Pavilion, with its Indian domes and minarets and its Chinese-style interior. And society quickly followed him.

Since the days of the Prince Regent, Brighton has enjoyed a double life. On the one hand a town of great wealth, with its grand Regency-period houses, and on the other hand a magnet for the seedy side of life. Indeed the Prince Regent himself notoriously had a tunnel constructed between the Pavilion and the red-light area of the North Lanes.

'I think the era with the Prince Regent was interesting,' Norman told *Select* in October 1998. 'Back then, Brighton was the Ibiza of Britain – a hedonist's playground, with all the young beauties and gay guys. It's still like that, really. It's just that it's gone from people necking invigorating bottles of spa water and bathing to people necking E and sitting in the sun.'

In the years since the Prince Regent's patronage, Brighton has been the chosen weekender destination for London's hedonists. It was host to the Mods and Rockers battles made famous by *Quadrophenia*. It's been the gay capital of Britain for as long as anyone can remember. It's had a club scene for just as long. It was one of the first places to choose house as its soundtrack, and has been a stronghold for the free-party generation since the earliest days of acid house.

It's no wonder that Brighton has long been the chosen home for musicians, DJs, actors, artists and writers. From Radio 1's first-ever female DJ, Annie Nightingale, to indie-dance-turned-electro-punk anarchists Primal Scream, global house hero John Digweed to gothic-shanty overlord Nick Cave, Brighton has been home to them all.

Local entrepreneur David Courtney (who wrote and produced some of local boy Leo Sayer's biggest hits in the 1970s and the man behind Brighton's Walk of Fame, which will feature Norman when it is unveiled in 2003) has described Brighton as 'the Hollywood of Britain', thanks to its relaxed attitude towards the rich and famous. In no other place in the UK could you expect to see ex-Spice Girls Emma Bunton and Geri Halliwell soaking up the sun on the beach, Paul McCartney strolling along the promenade, comedians Steve Coogan and Mark Little sipping pints at beachside bars, Prodigy main man Liam Howlett shopping for full Samurai Warrior uniform, glamour model Jordan getting her hair done and world-champion boxer Chris Eubank knocking around town on his motorised microscooter. The list is endless. And no one gets hassled. Brighton's laid back, you see.

And then there's Norman and Zoë: a couple whose constant appearances in celebrity gossip magazines haven't stopped them from enjoying the city. On any given day you're likely to bump into them walking their dog on the beaches of Hove, doing their shopping in Sainsbury's supermarket, relaxing at the lagoon near their house (where Norman has publicly supported the construction of a skate park). And, of course, despite international fame, you can still find Norman popping up behind the decks in the city's local clubs.

This is Norman's town. He's Brighton's favourite adopted son. And since he married TV presenter Zoë Ball, it's been her town, too. That's why, when she first moved to Brighton, the locals didn't go up to her to ask for her autograph but went and welcomed her to the party. Why Norman's name graces the front of the 7A bus. Why newsagents throughout the city have posters of Norman reading local paper *The Argus*. Why Brighton boasts a hairdresser's called Fatboy Trims, while Hove has one called Right Hair Right Now.

Brighton is Norman's town. And only *he* could have pulled off a party like Normstock.

THE WEEKEND STARTS HERE

'I used to tell people I was a Quaker. That was much simpler than explaining this obscure religion, practised by about 300 people around the world, that I belonged to.'

– Norman Cook

Catholic, Church of England, Muslim, Buddhist – there is no such thing as a one-size-fits-all religion. In a world seemingly hell-bent on focusing on difference rather than similarity, the list of religious faiths is fittingly endless. From extreme fundamentalists to the liberally minded, there are religions for everyone. Few global faiths, however, can claim quite such a miniscule flock as the obscure Kosmon faith, of which Norman Cook is a follower.

Often described as a new-age religion, the Kosmon faith is based on a book entitled *Oahspe* (pronounced 'Oh-ahs-phee'), which was written by Dr John Ballou Newborough (a practising dentist with a consuming interest in spiritualism and a trustee of the First Society of Spiritualists of New York City in the 1850s) and published in New York in 1882.

Oahspe, meaning 'earth, sky, spirit', was purported to have been channelled through Newborough by spirit guides. He'd been experimenting with automatic writing some years earlier, when early one morning in 1870 he claimed he was awakened by a striking vision: 'pillars of soft light…great numbers of beautiful spirits and angels' flooding his room.

One of the spirits asked him to perform a mission for Jehovah (or 'Jehovih' as it is spelled in *Oahspe*). Through the medium of automatic writing, Newborough was chosen to produce a book which would herald a new era of mankind. This new era would be the seventh age, characterised by non-violence – it was called the 'Kosmon era'.

As Newborough would have it, as he sat at his typewriter, angels spread a ray of light over his hands and wrote through him. The angels subsequently appeared an hour before dawn for the next 50 weeks, during which time *Oahspe* was written.

The first edition of *Oahspe* was published in 1882. A second edition was published some 10 years later and featured portraits of great spiritual teachers, painted by Newborough while in a trance.

Oahspe purports to be a revelation that supersedes all previous ones, including the Bible. It claims that Jesus was actually the Jewish teacher Joshu who was 'a law-giver of sub-cycle ranks'. *Oahspe* also states that the word 'Christ' means 'wisdom, knowledge [and] education'. But it is a word which is also synonymous with a 'warrior'. Christians, or Kriste, were a brotherhood of warriors. The name Kriste, given them by the Hebrews, meant 'one who rushes into a multitude of rioters and, with a sword, enforces peace…'

Oahspe states that angels work intimately with mankind, but that this harmony was disrupted by the appearance of a Beast which divided itself into four Heads. The names of the Heads were Brahmin, Buddhist, Christian and Mohammedan. Each Head commanded its own army and their main purpose was killing mankind.

To end the violence perpetrated by the four heads of the Beast, Jehovih sent His angels to Earth. He proclaimed that, 'The four Heads of the Beast shall be put down; and war shall be no more on the Earth. Thy armies shall be disbanded. And, from this time forth, whosoever desireth not to war, thou shalt not impress; for it is the commandment of thy Creator.'

One of the many things that *Oahspe* charges the Christian faith with is the claim that it denies the reality of spirit existence. The 'new religion' proposed by *Oahspe* encouraged not only spirit communication but also social reform. The latter of these was implemented both in an *Oahspe*-based community located near the Rio Grande in New Mexico (called 'Shalam', meaning 'land of peace and plenty') and in a New York orphanage. According to the teachings of *Oahspe*, Shalam was a place where no one person ruled over another. However, Newborough and his associate Andrew Howland attempted to impose autocratic control over the members, which subsequently created friction and numbers started to dwindle. Newborough died at Shalam on 22 August 1891. The community continued to decline and the property was sold on 30 September 1907. Several further communities were founded, but none survived.

The original manuscript for *Oahspe* was destroyed by a flood, thus avoiding close scrutiny, but half a century later, in 1936, the Kosmon Press in California acquired a number of sheets of the second version of the book and issued a new edition, which is now obtainable in America and England. As a result, the concepts contained in the book were made freely available to a wider range of people and the Kosmon Faithists slowly grew in number around the world. However, even today these numbers are so few that the religion remains almost unknown.

Ros Cook was raised in a Kosmon household. When she married Ron, he also took the faith, openly embracing the ideologies. It was into this little-known faith that Quentin Cook was subsequently born on 31 July 1963. He was named Quentin after the Latin *Quentus*, meaning 'fifth', because he was the youngest of three kids, and so the fifth in the family. It was an educated, middle-class gesture that was typical of the Cooks. Quentin wouldn't become known as Norman until he was 22.

Ros and Ron were, by their own admission, a liberal couple. Years later, their youngest son would sum them up in interviews as 'sort of middle class, sort of liberal vegetarian types'. She was a teacher, while he ran a glass business before turning ecologist and introducing the first bottle banks into the country, which he promoted by dressing up as a character called Ali Jam Jar. Ron was later awarded an MBE for his efforts. A photograph of Ron receiving the honour from Prince Charles sits on the couple's fireplace to this day.

Like all Faithists (as followers of Kosmon are called), Ron and Ros were staunch pacifists who forbade their children from playing with toy guns or any other objects that glorified war. The Kosmons considered war to be a by-product of the major religions and that their own beliefs were based on a global unity through spiritual awareness. The young Quentin, however, would later get round this by playing with a stick that he would pretend was a gun.

At the time of Quentin's birth, the Cooks lived in the middle-class

Kent suburb of Bromley. This town became infamous in 1976 thanks to the notorious Bromley Contingent, a group of friends who would become embroiled in the punk era's best-known televised incident – The Sex Pistols swearing on air at *Tonight Show* host Bill Grundy. Central to this outburst was Grundy's suggestion to Bromley punkette Susan Ballion that they meet after the show. She would become better known as Siouxsie Sioux, while fellow Bromley punk and participant in the *Tonight* débâcle Steve Bailey would change his surname to Severin and take up bass guitar. Together with an ever-mutating line up, Sioux and Severin would eventually achieve world fame as Siouxsie And The Banshees.

Quentin Cook was born in a suburb of some subcultural notoriety. However, while he was still only a toddler, his family moved to the much less inspiring suburban idyll of Reigate in Surrey. 'It's suburban hell. Everything revolves around garden centres. It probably has the highest incidence of garden centres per capita in the country,' he would later explain.

When Quentin started school at the local Holmsdale Road Primary, he was forced to endure constant teasing from other kids. It was something that continued when he went to Reigate Priory Middle School. The reasons were simple: his name and his religion. The latter he got around by telling everyone he was a Quaker, because it was easier to explain. 'Every time I tried to explain it at school, everyone would go, "What? Are they cosmonauts? Or Moonies?"' he told *The Observer Magazine*'s Chris Heath in 1999. 'There's only about 40 people in England who do it. There's some in Nigeria. A lot in India. Unity. That was the overriding watchword of the church. It was all about guardian angels protecting you, and to do with karma. What you put out, you'll get back. You've got your own personal guardian angel that looks after you rather than some kind of God'.

The Cooks weren't obsessive Faithists, they would only go to church four times a year at the equinoxes, so it wasn't as if Quentin was noticeably different from his friends. Like any kid of his age he was more interested in how to get out of going to any kind of family event, especially those related to church.

Perhaps a more pressing problem for him was his name, which

inevitably drew ridicule from other children, not least because of the famous homosexual Quentin Crisp, whose books *The Naked Civil Servant* and *How To Become A Virgin* turned him into a notorious celebrity.

'Two years after I was born, Quentin Crisp became the most famous homosexual in the world and people at school seemed to think that was really funny,' explains Cook.

The taunts about his namesake calmed down a bit when politician Quentin Hogg was in the news a lot. However, as his career faded, the other famous Quentin came back to the fore. Quentin Cook quickly adopted the nicknames of Q or Cookie, while his brother and sister called him Finky or Finx. Or even Julie. 'Because I looked like Julie Andrews,' he explains.

Ironically, Quentin would later consider that having a name which singled him out ended up having a positive effect. It forced him to stand up and be counted.

'Me being who I am, I was probably influenced by having had a daft name through my formative years,' he told *The Observer* in 1999. 'I either had to live up to it or make people get over it. It meant I was always the focus of attention, so I showed off to live up to my name.'

Quentin Cook wanted fame from a very young age. He recalls watching pop stars on television as a child and dreaming of being just like them. One of the earliest influences came from seeing Donny Osmond and his brothers performing 'Crazy Horses' on television. 'He had a piano with lights that flashed up when he played it, and a leather jacket with his name in studs on the back, and I thought, "That's what I want to do,"' he told Chris Heath. 'I always liked music, but that was when I started to think, music plus girls plus glamour. You get to travel in jets with your name on the side! Being a pop star sounded like a great job.'

At the age of seven he even started practising his autograph. In the mid 1970s, when he was 11, Quentin was enrolled in the local Reigate Grammar School. Cook described it in Nick Swift's biography of The Housemartins, *Now That's What I Call Quite Good*: 'Our school was seen as a posh one. We were always getting beaten up by the lads from the comprehensive. We were seen as the swots of the area.'

Although the book is clearly written and dictated from The Housemartins' left-wing perspective, it was obvious that Norman wasn't happy in this school. As an adult playing the pop game, he was able to add political meaning to this unhappiness, but it was more likely that his interests were diametrically opposed to those of the school.

It was one of the few areas to still possess the old grammar school system (another was Buckinghamshire), and the emphasis was on the traditional public-school values. Rugby was the main sport, Latin was still taught, school uniforms were compulsory. Since he had been brought up by a liberal family, Quentin was bound to react. Furthermore, his obsessions couldn't be further removed from academia.

The first records that Quentin bought were 10cc's 'I'm Not In Love' and Suzi Quatro's 'Devil Gate Drive'. Then, at the age of 11, thanks to the influence of his Uncle Derek, he had a brief affair with heavy metal. It was the time of AC/DC, The Sensational Alex Harvey Band, The MC5 and 1,000 other bands obsessed with loud, anthemic, foot-stomping music. The natural follow-on from the heavier end of glam rock (The New York Dolls, Alice Cooper, etc), heavy metal proved particularly attractive to the UK's middle-class, Home Counties youths. The same kids who would, in turn, champion punk rock.

Quentin Cook discovered punk rock at the age of 13 after his brother brought home the debut album by The Damned. The youngster felt an immediate affinity with the album, even finding his own voice within its songs.

In February 1977, *Damned, Damned, Damned* was the very first album to be released by any of the UK punk bands. This fact caused much consternation in both the Sex Pistols and Clash camps, where rivalry between the two blinded them to many of the other bands on the scene. One of the first wave of punk outfits, The Damned originally formed in London in May 1976. Their debut gig wasn't in the capital, however, but in High Wycombe's Nag's Head, where the attendant crowd included Mark Riley (who would become better known as 1980s pop artist Matt Bianco) and *GQ* editor Dylan Jones, who at this time wore his hair long and his trousers very flared. He dropped this look very quickly when he went on to launch *i-D* magazine a few years later!

It's little surprise that The Damned's debut album caused such excitement with Quentin Cook. The band were always one of the more wayward punk groups. Their look verged on the ridiculous while their songs offered adrenalised stabs of pop joy. 'Neat, Neat, Neat' remains one of punk's golden moments, while 'New Rose' is an essential in any punk compilation.

To a youngster living far enough away from the London scene but still avidly reading the music press (and fanzines like the legendary *Sniffin' Glue*), The Damned were easy to identify with. In many ways they offered the perfect antithesis to The Clash's polemic and The Pistols' fury. The Damned simply offered a no-strings-attached good time for all. It was an ideology that would surface again and again in Cook's own music over the years.

Ironically, The Damned were the last to realise what people loved them for, and on their follow-up album, *Music For Pleasure*, they attempted to take their music deeper by employing Pink Floyd's drummer Nick Mason in the producer's seat. Among their follies on this album was the use of avant garde jazz saxophonist Lol Coxhill. Sadly, the album was a disaster, seemingly embracing all that punk had stood to destroy and losing the essence of the band in the process.

The punk phenomenon happened at an important time in Quentin's life. According to the teachings of the *Oahspe*, followers become free to choose their own path at the ages of 12, 13 or 14. It's at this point that the child is emancipated from the promises made by parents on their behalf. Quentin chose to leave the Faithist path entirely, although it is arguable that many of the concepts and ideologies presented in the Kosmon faith would have an influence on many of his future life decisions. At this point, however, music was more important to him. 'My parents realised I probably wasn't going to follow the path of worship, especially as I'd just discovered punk rock,' he has said.

Quentin had a much more pro-active involvement in punk than most of his peers. Like them, he would dye his hair on Friday nights and then wash it out for Monday-morning school. Like his friends, he would get involved in the tomfoolery associated with being a young punk. He would even take the customary beatings from those kids (the vast majority) who hated punks. He just rolled himself up in a ball until they got bored of kicking him. 'I always wanted to look tough, but I've got photos of me leaning up against the wall, sneering with my mates, and I just looked so cute. My sister said I was the most endearing, cuddly punk she'd ever seen. There was nothing I could do about it apart from disfigure myself. I was angry. Underneath, I was seething rebellion waiting to happen.' (*The Observer Magazine*, 18 April 1999, Chris Heath.)

This rebellion manifested itself in numerous ways, and one of them was petty theft. Cook was arrested for shoplifting at one point – much to his mother's personal shame; she blamed herself for any failings in her children. Unlike his friends, however, Quentin became actively involved in the creative processes of punk culture by starting up his own fanzine, called *Peroxide*. Through the magazine he was able to interview a number of his heroes, including a *Dirk Wears White Sox*-era Adam And The Ants, of whom he was a huge fan. In fact, a number of years later, he would become an extra in the video for Adam And The Ants' 'Goody Two Shoes' single, playing the part of a porter. In 2001 he revived this look for a Fatboy Slim photo shoot.

In 1978, at the age of 15 Quentin teamed up with a friend to set up a mobile disco to play at weddings and private parties. He was already an avid record collector and loved being the centre of attention, making people laugh, so becoming a DJ was an obvious choice. This way he was able to remain at the centre of things, play his favourite records and make people dance into the bargain. Even at 15 he was aware of the power of being able to create a good party.

One of the other motivating factors in his decision to become a DJ was the pulling power it gave him. Girls would come to him to ask for records and he would take the opportunity to use his impish demeanour and cheeky grin, practising his chat-up skills.

It was little surprise that the attention-seeking youngster jumped at the chance to appear in girls' magazine *Jackie* a couple of years later. At the time, the magazine was a bible for young girls (and some boys), as it featured most of the most popular bands of the day being asked the kinds of questions no serious paper would ask. In many ways, the success of *Jackie*'s interview style opened the doors for the obsession of trivia in today's magazines. Clearly contemporary publishers were deeply influenced by *Jackie* when they read it in their youths!

Quentin was used in a photo-love story. However, despite his every effort, he only appeared in the few of the final pictures, and then not centre frame. Even now he admits that he was upset by this, but he did earn the princely sum of £21 for two hours work, which was very good money at the time.

The *Jackie* experience happened while Quentin was studying for his A-levels at Reigate Sixth-Form College. He had hoped to remain at Reigate Grammar to study for his A levels, but the school asked him to leave instead, although he had gained nine GCE O-levels.

Once at Reigate Sixth-Form College, his antics with girls became notorious, and to this day they are fondly remembered. One afternoon the common room was stage for a pretend marriage between Quentin and his then-girlfriend, Ciara. Their friends were the witnesses.

It was while studying for his A-levels that Quentin formed his first band, Disque Attack. Sporting a blonde quiff, he initially took up drum duties, later changing to lead vocalist. Although a pretty average band whose sound could have been described as poppy punk, Disque Attack built up a reasonable following, regularly playing at the local Railway pub.

As he became ever-more embroiled in both the local scene and with his band, Quentin's school work suffered and, perhaps not surprisingly, he failed his A-levels. In an attempt to make amends, he decided to retake them at another college, so he enrolled at the North East College of Technology in Ewell, where he would eventually pass the exams.

In the meantime, his band had been invited to play a date at the college with local punk outfit Tools Down, who had developed a name for themselves on the local pub circuit with their brash songs and a singer who would read lyrics from a school exercise book while on stage. They released an unremarkable track called 'All I Want' as a part of a local compilation called *Surge Of Sound*. The most notable thing about the band was that it featured brothers Adi and Paul Heaton, the latter of whom would become internationally known as songwriter and front man for The Housemartins and The Beautiful South.

Paul had moved to Surrey from Sheffield at the age of 14. The move proved to be very unsettling for the lad, who was showing an obsessive side to his personality by insisting on writing everything down. After he was expelled from the local Nork Park Secondary School for bending the rules too far on the last day of term (setting off fire alarms, throwing bricks, shouting obscenities and wearing punk sunglasses!) he was enrolled at Redhill Technology College.

Here Paul professes to have attempted to rob the school disco. After stealing the student safe, he and a friend (Raymond 'Trotsky' Barry) spent hours trying to smash it open, to discover it contained only 35p!

Paul became something of a legend at Redhill Tech thanks to his wayward behaviour and Modish clothes. He even rode a Lambretta for that added Mod touch. When Paul and the drummer-turned-vocalist from Disque Attack met on the night of their gig, they instantly hit it off, talking at great length about music.

As would always remain the custom with Paul Heaton, he gave his new friend a nickname, Quintox, because he thought he looked like an ox! The two quickly became good friends with a shared passion for punk. Paul would also introduce Quentin to the soul and blues music that would become such a feature of his later career.

Soon Paul convinced Quentin to form a new band with him, trumpeter John Laurenson and drummer Chris Lang. Together they were known as The Stomping Pond Frogs and would quickly establish a reputation for their impromptu performances on Reigate Heath, where they would park their cars in a semicircle with headlights on and perform.

'We'd busk for cash at the weekend outside the Market pub in the town centre,' Cook would tell Mike Pattenden in his biography of The Beautiful South, *Last Orders At The Liars' Bar.* 'We called ourselves an "international beach band" and wore horrible Hawaiian shirts. Paul played Trombone very badly. It sounds a bit cabaret but it was Dexy's Midnight Runners meets The Monkees. It was a kind of a prototype for The Housemartins, but cheery instead of angry.'

The Stomping Pond Frogs played covers of tracks like 'Tequila', as well as a few original numbers. Among these was a song about nuclear testing called 'Bikini Beach', which was written by Quentin. It proved to be a crowd favourite and displayed an early example of the songwriter's ear for a strong melody and catchy hook line. Already he was playing to the people.

Just as The Stomping Pond Frogs were starting to attract regular audiences upwards of 200 people, the various members announced they were leaving. Lang went to RADA and would later become a respected actor while both Laurenson and Cook packed their bags for university, leaving Heaton behind with dreams of becoming a pop star, but with no band to help him along the way. He was, to say the least, disappointed.

'Paul was really pissed off because we were getting a reputation and you can tell he had something,' Cook told Mike Pattenden a few years later.

Quentin, however, had a new horizon in view. He had been accepted into Brighton Polytechnic to study for a BA in English, Politics and Sociology. He hadn't been attracted to the Poly for the superiority of its teaching, or the courses it offered; rather he had been drawn to the nightlife. Oh, and possibly the fact that one Stuart Goddard (aka Adam Ant) had been a student there!

Always the gregarious party animal, Quentin threw himself into the social side of Brighton with fervour. An early favourite clubbing venue was Sherries, where on Wednesday nights he would be found 'listening to Depeche Mode, "Planet Rock", early electro, James Brown, Culture Club, drinking, drugs, girls, realising that this was my world.'

Quentin immediately fell in love with his new home town. Such was the depth of his enthusiasm, he would eventually use the place as the subject matter for his end-of-degree thesis. Called 'From Bathing Huts To Space Invaders', it was an in-depth study of local urban development.

The Brighton that Quentin first encountered was, musically at least, walking in parallel with the trendy New York discos like the Paradise Garage and the Red Zone, where the electro-pop records of artists like New Order, Divine and new romantic artists like Depeche Mode and Visage would be fused with the post-disco, pre-house sounds of Hi-NRG and techno funk, as epitomised by Harlequin Fours' 'Set It Off', Hanson And Davis's 'Tonight' and Colonel Abrams's 'Trapped'.

Much of this soundtrack to clublife in Brighton owed a debt to the influence of the town's well-documented gay scene. As was often the case in the UK in the early 1980s, the better clubs were the gay clubs. However, since the new-romantic era, these clubs had been adopted by straight people in search of good music and good vibes. As a result, the DJs of the time were in a unique position to expose more and more people to music previously only enjoyed by the gay scene. In many ways it was here that the some of the seeds of the late 1980s club scenes of Balearic, acid house and Rave were sewn.

Among the more influential Brighton DJs was the simply named Rory, a hugely flamboyant Scotsman who held a residency at the now-defunct Coasters. Although Coasters was a gay club (which had hosted performances by, among others, the legendary disco performer Sylvester), Rory's Saturday-night sets became a huge draw for the South Coast's straight clubbing crowd. He didn't tailor the mood or rhythm of the set to the non-gay punters; he did exactly what he always did, presenting a blistering, sweat-soaked night of sex-fuelled metronomic dance music. Eventually Rory would be among the first DJs in England to play Chicago-house music (the first was Nottingham's Colin Curtis, who would subsequently inspire Graeme Park).

Although Quentin would openly reject the stylings of house music in interviews in later years, there was little doubt that the atmosphere of nights like those at Coasters had instilled in him an even deeper love of dance music and the positive effects it could have on a crowd of people.

However, it was Quentin's love of the stylings of hip-hop and electro that really came to the fore and he soon struck up a friendship with a breakdancing crew from Manchester called Broken Glass. Among its members was a lad called Kermit, who would go on to be a pivotal member of legendary UK hip-hop crew Ruthless Rap Assassins before eventually teaming up with a post-Happy Mondays Shaun Ryder for the flawed Black Grape project.

It was through Kermit that Quentin had an early brush with mega-stardom. When Broken Glass were invited to travel to Newcastle to appear on 1980s music show *The Tube* (presented by Jools Holland and the late Paula Yates), the crew found themselves sharing a dressing room with an unknown US singer. Quentin chatted with this new-found friend for ages and when she took to the stage in what was to become her trademark black string vest, he even stood behind her throughout the performance, clearly in the frame of the camera for the whole song. It was to go down in history as Madonna's first ever UK television performance.

Cook's involvement in the nightlife of Brighton increased through an ever growing list of DJ dates. One of his regular slots was at the Brighton Belle (a long-closed-down club in Brighton's Oriental Place), where he would offer a very eclectic mix. The style of music was apparently not as important as whether or not the tracks actually worked. He also teamed up with DJ Jez and became known collectively as Tequila Disco. The vibe for this venture was based more around beat mixing, so less old soul and funk was played in favour of more electronically produced tracks.

By 1983 Quentin had taken a job working behind the counter at Brighton's Rounder Records. It was inevitable that he would gravitate towards the record shop. Since he spent most of his spare time scouring shops for new vinyl, it made perfect sense to go and work in what was (and still is) Brighton's finest record shop. Once working there, he quickly made an impression with his passionate knowledge of music. Furthermore, he impressed Graham Gilbert, the proprietor between 1982 and 2000, with his willingness to skip college in order to work in the shop. 'At the time, we had a pool of people like Quentin who would work for us,' recalls Gilbert. 'Thing is, whenever anyone was ill, we could guarantee that Quentin would come in. It didn't matter if that meant missing lectures.'

Gilbert explains that the experience of working in the shop gave Cook the chance to directly affect the biggest-name DJs in the area at the time, thanks to his knowledge of music and his informed suggestions: 'He was quite shy at the time really, but he was shy in an odd way because he had a kind of brashness about him. Working at Rounder gave him a great introduction to the DJ fraternity. Basically the shop had a saturation point of 99 per cent for DJs from Brighton and the south coast. Which meant that every known DJ from the area would come in. Which meant that he was getting exposed to loads of different types of music all of the time.'

One day in late 1985, Cook received a call from an old friend which would have a huge and lasting effect on his life. Paul Heaton invited him to join his latest band. They had already been signed by Go Discs! and were about to put out the single 'Flag Day', so the band was already on the first rung of the ladder. Furthermore, they had a UK tour booked in for the next few weeks.

The chance to be reunited with his old friend and sample the euphoria of touring and playing with a signed band proved too much for Quentin. The next day he went into work and announced that he was leaving.

'I remember it had been talked about for him to join in February, so it didn't come as a shock to Norman,' recalls Gilbert 'Then the other bass player left suddenly and the date was brought forward. It was just before Christmas so you can imagine it wasn't the best time to lose a member of staff. But to be fair on Quentin, he was worried about leaving me in the lurch. He actually came back and played our Christmas party a couple of weeks later.'

Two days after handing in his notice, Cook moved to the north-east port town of Hull and jumped aboard the good ship Housemartins. It was November 1985 and the 22-year-old Quentin had become bassist with what was to become one of British pop music's most notorious bands. His first act was to change his name, 'To make me seem more working class!'

The name he chose was perhaps the most un-star-like moniker imaginable: Norman – by which he's been known ever since.

BRIGHTON 0 HULL 4

'I wouldn't have listened to the band if I hadn't been in them. I wouldn't have gone near them.'
– Norman Cook on The Housemartins, 1990

The Stomping Pond Frogs had lasted less than a year. However, their no-thrills, nitty-gritty approach to busking had translated into notoriously raucous gigs and a solid fan base. When three of the four band members disappeared to start new lives, you might have expected the remaining Frog to hang up his ambitions and retire to the nearest job centre. Not Paul Heaton. He had other ideas, which would eventually take him to the international stage as a member of The Beautiful South.

Paul was born on 9 May 1962 in Bromborough, Merseyside. The youngest of three sons, he was moved from house to house in his early years because of his father's work. When Paul was four, the Heatons settled in Sheffield and then, 10 years, later they moved south to Surrey, where fate eventually brought Paul and Quentin together.

Heaton had been deeply affected by the move south and quickly turned into a disruptive influence in school. He developed an overriding sense of not belonging and increasingly started to cling to his working-class roots. He doggedly refused to lose his northern accent and took every opportunity to promote the north–south divide. It was a 'them and us' theme which was to resurface throughout his songwriting career.

Following the break-up of The Stomping Pond Frogs, Heaton had taken a job at the Royal School for the Blind in Leatherhead. However, he quickly found that his humanitarian approach to disability was at complete odds with the State's perception. He was asked to leave after he was discovered teaching a student how to ride a bike, after they'd been on a drinking session together. Not one to do things by halves, Heaton decided a move was in order. Rather than go to another English city, he left the country entirely and went to Norway. This started a travel bug which was to last for the next few years.

In 1981, while he was busking in Germany, he was befriended by a group of people from Dietkirchen. One of them offered to put Paul up in what was essentially a commune. It was an experience which was to have a profound effect on him, and he was immediately impressed by the way they lived the politics they preached. Quite simply, their approach to socialism amounted to far more than the usual lip service that Heaton had previously encountered. Here the ideologies were very real.

Other trips abroad further opened his mind to socialist politics and on his return to England, he vowed to put what he'd learned into practice. While showing a friend from Dietkirchen around the sights of England, he stumbled upon Hull for the first time. He immediately decided to set up home in the depressed port, along with fellow travelling companion Raymond 'Trotsky' Barry.

They took a run-down house on Grafton Street and the pair immediately set about running a comic fanzine called *The Saturday Elephant*. When this failed, Paul decided to return to busking, and it was then he met Ian Cullimore, who had read one of Paul's adverts for fellow musicians, and walked into the Grafton Street house demanding to meet whoever it was that had put the ad in the front window of the house.

The seemingly eccentric Cullimore hailed from Cambridgeshire and was a Maths student at Hull University. Already a veteran of a few local bands, he was always on the lookout for fresh musical adventures and Paul's 'trombonist seeks street musicians' plea struck just the right chord with him.

Paul and Ian hit it off immediately and soon the duo were writing together and pulling huge crowds when they busked in the town centre's Whitefriargate. They even made it into the local paper, *The Hull Daily Mail*. Soon they were gigging under the name of The Housemartins while, in an act which would hold a resonance for Quentin Cook a couple of years later, they changed their names. Paul became known as simply PD and Ian was renamed Stan.

Throughout this period of furious songwriting and gigging the band dispatched tapes to anyone they thought would appreciate what they were doing. Among these people was Brighton resident Quentin Cook, who, although not particularly into the music, would find suitable ways of showing his appreciation. 'Before I joined The Housemartins, when they were just a duo of Paul and Stan, they used to send me demo tapes to listen to and I could never resist the temptation to cut them up, slip in a rap beat and send them back. If I wasn't doing this sort of thing for a job I'd most certainly be doing it for a hobby,' he told *Melody Maker* journalist Push (who would go on to found *Muzik Magazine*) in 1990.

Doubtless Paul and Stan would have been horrified at such appropriation of black music forms being associated with their earnest indie guitar tunes. It's fair to say that they quickly had the last laugh when fledgling independent label Go! Discs offered them a recording contract. Their advance? £3,000 and a set of shirts for local youth footie team Dane Villa FC (who duly changed their name to Housemartins FC).

Go! Discs was founded by Andy Macdonald in 1983, a mere 11 months after he joined Stiff Records as a press officer. The first release on the label was the debut offering from The Box, featuring ex-members of Sheffield act Clock DVA. Fronted by Adi Newton, Clock DVA were at the vanguard of the arty end of the punk funk movement. Their first two albums, the cassette-only *White Men In Black Suits* and the vinyl offering *Thirst*, offered stunning examples of the genre.

The debut by The Box, however worthy, was hardly likely to set the charts alight. Luckily for the imprint, success came with the release of political singer/songwriter Billy Bragg's debut album *Life's A Riot With Spy Vs Spy*.

Bragg had supported The Stomping Pond Frogs back in the days when he was known as Spy Vs Spy, so Paul started bombarding the label with letters and tapes. Go! Discs' Macdonald was impressed (while many others, including Stiff, weren't) and eventually signed the band.

Not, however, before Paul and Stan had stood at local elections, released their own cassette album – *Themes For A Well Dressed Man* – and extended the band line-up to record a demo with the inclusion of ex-Pond Frogs Chris Lang playing drums and Quentin Cook on bass. The demo was recorded in Surrey to the satisfaction of all concerned, even though Stan got food poisoning and vomited all over Quentin's car. 'I don't think he liked me at first,' says Cook, 'but after he'd been sick over me, he changed his mind. He had to, really.'

The inclusion of the southern rhythm section could only be temporary, however. For starters, Quentin had only agreed to do the demo as a favour. By this stage he was deeply entrenched in dance music and was making a name for himself in Brighton as a DJ of some renown. Quite simply, the music his mates were making just didn't float his creative boat. Furthermore, The Housemartins wanted to remain a Hull-based band. They wouldn't consider for a second moving to Surrey and neither would they have dreamt of settling down in Brighton.

There was a strong reason for the latter, though: Paul held a hatred for Brighton (which remains strong to this day) thanks to the reaction he got at a gig they'd played in the town's Brighton Belle club. At the time Paul and Stan had started to augment their show with a series of political sermons under the banner 'Left Wing Gospel'. More than simply a different angle for the live gig (and an obvious way to express the duo's politics), the Left Wing Sermon was, they jokingly suggested, 'a serious challenge to the accepted Christian Church'.

In an interview with Hull-based Viking Radio in 1985 Paul and Stan explained:

STAN: 'The left wing gospel is enthusiastic and optimistic.'
PAUL: 'Yeah, it's grown out of belief and optimism; we want The Housemartins to be the light at the end of the tunnel.'
STAN: 'It's like we're bringing good news. It's got sincerity, power and belief, gospel music, and that's what we want to achieve, for the audience to feel it and get involved with us.'

The audience in Brighton were either bemused or plain disinterested and their old friend Quentin was even less impressed. Since he had organised the date for them at one of the venues where he had a regular residency, he couldn't believe that they would treat the crowd in such a way.

It was a moment which showed an early difference of values between Quentin and Paul. For the DJ, audience enjoyment was all. Opinions and beliefs were one thing, but for them to get in the way of a good night out was another. Paul, on the other hand, saw everything to do with music as being inherently political and the stage as the natural place to express ideologies, no matter how intrusive.

The solution to The Housemartins' line-up problems would have to lie in the Hull music scene. They didn't have to go far, however. The Gargoyles were a band that they'd played alongside a number of times and, although they weren't big fans of their music, Paul and Stan did rate their bassist. So they drafted Ted Kaye in. As luck would have it, he brought with him the final part of the jigsaw: drummer Hugh Whitaker.

With the band's eventual signing to Go! Discs, The Housemartins finally delivered their first single in November 1985. Called 'Flag Day', the advert for the single simply declared, 'This exceptional record is available now,' while promotional copies were mailed out with badges that read, 'The Housemartins are quite good.' Further promotion came from the label 'buying' the top slot in adult comic *Viz*'s pop chart. (The Housemartins would even eventually sponsor Fulchester United's shirts in the *Viz* comic strip 'Billy The Fish'.)

'Don't flush the toilet before you've stopped pissing,' urged Paul Heaton to *Melody Maker* – who had awarded the record with the coveted Single Of The Week status – in the 14 December issue. 'In other words, don't dismiss the single before its gone. Listen to it again and again because its a slow starter. But it could be a fast finisher.'

It was clear from the start that the Hull band were not interested in the ego-driven aspirations of the music industry. Their clothes were a mixture of flat caps, tanktops and student anti-chic recycled from charity shops, while they sported imageless haircuts. This was in the era of the spiky bleached barnets, diamanté and crushed velvet of The Eurythmics, Howard Jones and Simple Minds. Even U2, the most politically motivated rock band of the time, would melt a hole in the ozone with their hairspray usage. Musically, The Pet Shop Boys were making headway with the techno pop of 'West End Girls' while arch politicos The Clash were about to collapse with their post-Mick Jones album, the terrible *Cut The Crap*.

'Flag Day' was released only a few months after Live Aid and it seemingly contained a dig at charity organisation in its lyrics. In an era when charitable gestures seemed motivated by self-promotion, such a blatantly opinionated single went completely against the grain.

Paul also offered some barbed comments on the subject of charities in the *Melody Maker* feature. 'I can see The Housemartins turning into a charitable organisation,' he exclaimed. 'Like if we're successful in a couple of years time, I could easily see Housemartins Oxfam shops and it would be a highly ironic state of affairs. We would emphasise the education behind charity – why do we have to do it – which is one of the things groups like Oxfam don't really do. They do occasionally print leaflets saying that these things are not an act of God, and that it's the Western world who have got far more money than we need. Oxfam is there simply to get money out of people and give it to the Third World. They've done their bit, have Oxfam. It's just, how long do they have to keep on doing their bit? That is the question.'

With their political and ideological leaning well and truly laid out and the single receiving a good, if slow, reaction, the scene seemed set for the band to gain huge popularity and even sell a few records. Margaret Thatcher's Conservative government had alienated many people through their doctrines, and The Housemartins echoed the sentiments of a huge number of people who were sick and tired of Thatcherite politics.

The Housemartins' first tour had been set up in support of 'Flag Day' (then nestling in the glorious position of 124 in the UK charts), and so the next step in that journey to chart domination seemed easy. Except for one thing – there were already problems within the band.

There had been ill feeling from the first day that Ted had joined the band. Essentially he had aspirations to being the main focus of the band's songwriting, which was naturally a cause of major consternation with Paul. However, when Ted started dating Paul's ex-girlfriend, the singer saw his way of engineering a solution.

Knowing that his ex was very possessive and had hated it in the past when he went away on tour, he announced that they'd been offered a major support slot with Madness (which never materialised). Naturally this would have meant that Ted would have been away from his girlfriend for a long time. Ted refused to tour.

Paul and Stan offered Ted ownership of the band van and songwriting credits on three tracks in a legal document they'd had drawn up in order to formalise his departure. Ted simply threw the papers in the bin and threatened Stan. In response, Paul went after Ted with an iron bar, smashing every window in the van in the process.

So, faced with the problem of losing their bassist just before a national tour, Paul resorted to his original option. He picked up the phone and called his mate in Brighton. Quentin immediately snapped at the offer. He handed in his notice at his day job (realising that he could still keep a lot of his DJing activities going) and headed north.

As we have seen, Quentin had in fact already been approached to join the band the previous February. In fact, the earliest recorded instance of the new Housemartins bassist dates back to the last week in November 1984, when Quentin appeared in a performance of the Gospel classic 'We Shall Not Be Moved' and their own 'We're Not Deep' for *The Tube*. Interestingly, both were recorded in the steam baths at Newcastle United's legendary St James's Park ground. (Not that the Toon Army would be singing about a band from Hull in return.)

Talking to Nick Swift, long-time friend and official biographer of the band, Quentin explained how the appearance came about: 'When they went into the studio to record these tracks, Ted wasn't available for the session so he left them in a bit of a dilemma. I had been told to be prepared to step in soon so I had already been learning some of the material and I did OK in the studio. *The Tube* would only film with the musicians who recorded the songs, so obviously Ted couldn't do it.'

When Quentin joined the line-up, he brought with him another problem. One of the reasons why Quentin changed his name when he joined the line-up was because the previous bassist had possessed a fine northern working-class name in Ted. Quentin just wasn't right. Paul had been calling his friend Quentox since their first meeting. Following his induction into the band, however, he was given the unassuming moniker of Ernest for a while. But Paul didn't like it and a few days later Norman entered in its place. And even this wasn't enough for the band who were apparently obsessed by nicknames. Soon Norman found himself renamed Sporty Norman.

Norman Cook's decision to join The Housemartins has to be questioned. Since Heaton had first introduced him to forms of black music, and during his time in the club scene in Brighton, he had become almost entirely devoted to hip-hop, funk and other black music. The post-punk guitar scene left him almost entirely cold, while the pop scene that had flourished in the wake of the futurism, or new romantic, movement turned him off entirely.

Yet here he was, about to forsake his adopted hometown for the comparatively bleak Hull, which at the time was deeply affected by the economic slump and the negative aspects of Conservative politics, such as the closure of shipbuilding yards, mines and steelworks, all mainstays of the local economy. Not only that, but he was also leaving to join forces with a band whose stock in trade was jangly guitar music tempered by biting politicism. The latter may have been of interest to Cook, but he would surely have ridiculed the former had he not known the band's leader.

Knowing Heaton would surely not have offered a big enough incentive to embrace the band. Despite the success of The Stomping Pond Frogs, Cook had still felt enough of a pull to leave the band for college in Brighton. Surely if his intentions with the band had been serious he would have forsaken college for a while to give Heaton and co a chance?

The Stomping Pond Frogs were, in Norman's own words, 'a kind of a prototype for The Housemartins', and he felt happy to leave. Here he was, however, a few years later, joining The Housemartins. A few years later, Norman would be lambasted again in all quarters for his apparent betrayal of the indie cause in favour of the dance bandwagon. However, if he has ever been guilty of betrayal, then it surely came at this point.

The Housemartins' sound represented white English working-class folk music. Lyrics concerned themselves with the working-class struggles of politics and love, rich and poor, us and them, while the music stuck to the Tin Pan Alley mode of standardised structures, including singalong choruses. They were about as white as pop music could get, despite any allusions to soul that they would eventually offer.

Furthermore, despite their claims to be Marxist, the music they created couldn't stand up to a Marxist critique. They offered nothing that was oppositional, nothing that broke the monotony of the production line. Indeed, The Housemartins even played on the mechanics of the industry with their self-effacing slogans: 'The Housemartins are quite good' are the words of the beaten-down and subservient rather than belligerent opposition. It was an attitude which was actually the antithesis of British folk and US soul's 'stand tall and fight for what you believe in' belief systems.

So what exactly was the motivation for Norman Cook to cross the tracks into a world which was almost the diametric opposite to the one he loved so much? Friendship can't have been enough, but the lure of immediate success, without the frustrating struggle, may have been. As a youth, Norman had always dreamed of being onstage, touring the country, releasing records and generally playing the rock 'n' roll game. With Heaton's offer, he would be able to sample it for himself. Within weeks, he would be touring and recording an album. The media were already behind The Housemartins, so chart success seemed a possibility.

On the face of it Norman had nothing to lose – except perhaps his credibility. Indeed, as he would find in his post-Housemartins career, he would be tarnished with the indie brush for a very long time. In fact, it wouldn't only be the indie kids who would accuse Norman of jumping on a bandwagon, but the more snobbish elements of the dance arena would be similarly scathing. Despite his past. 'All I was doing, really, was helping out a mate,' he declared a few years later. 'Paul bribed me with a promise of free beer and travel, so I joined. And we had an excellent time.'

Rounder Records' boss Graham Gilbert has a different understanding of his ex-employee's motivation in joining the band: 'He loved so much music that it just wasn't a surprise that he joined an indie band. Just because his main thing was dancey stuff didn't take away from the fact that he was once a punk – he still loved The Clash, still enjoyed guitar music. He was obsessive about music, to the detriment of other things in his life. At the time, Brighton had junk shops on every other street and each one would have a record section. You would always find him scouring these shops for different stuff. So I can see why he might have actually liked The Housemartins' music.'

HE RE C OME S T HE HAPPY HOUR...AG AI N

Norman Cook arrived in Hull in November 1985, just in time for the release of the 'Flag Day' single. It is interesting to note that, during the band's debut interviews in the British weekly music press, only three band members were present.

Had Norman hoped to slot in unnoticed at his hastily arranged debut Housemartins gig at Goldsmith's College in London's New Cross on 22 November 1985, however, he had another think coming. At the time he hadn't learned all of the band's songs, so they played the first part of the set without a bassist before announcing his grand entrance to the audience: 'Norman, come on down.' Norman duly ran onstage and fell flat on his face!

'At the audition, I was read the rules,' recalled Norman to Mike Pattenden, 'which were basically no hats and no drugs. Paul had this passion thing, a bit like Dexy's, but instead of jogging we all went drinking religiously. It was like, we're all in this together. He forged this tight-knit bond and he was very professional.'

The aim for a 'tight-knit bond' gives an insight into the flipside of the question as to why Norman had joined the band – namely, why exactly would Paul Heaton want in his band a southern DJ with a love of hip-hop, funk and soul and a history of cutting up Housemartins' demo tapes with a breakbeat and scratches? There was no way that this old friend could share the same musical vision.

The answer was quite simply that he was a friend. And, in order for The Housemartins to operate as a closed community, friendship was all-important. With friendship came respect and trust.

Norman's first full gig with The Housemartins came on 5 December 1985 at Bradford University, while in a strange twist Ted would play his farewell testimonial show two days later in Hull's Wellington Club. Despite the backstage politics that had forced him to quit, both Ted and his now ex-bandmates kept up the façade of friendship. It was as if iron bars had never been brandished.

The following night, Norman played his second gig at the Bull and Gate in London's Kentish Town as a part of the Go! Discs roadshow, with His Latest Flame and William The Goat (a pseudonym of Billy Bragg's). Immediately after this show, the band went out as support to waning electronic pop outfit Blancmange. The gigs were a disaster, as the bands were desperately mismatched. However, Rounder Records' boss of the time recalls, 'I didn't really know too much about The Housemartins, but Quentin invited us to see the band supporting Blancmange. They blew the main act off the stage. A really entertaining band. I could see the appeal then.'

New Year's Eve 1985 saw The Housemartins finish on an absolute high, as support to Madness. The north London ska pop band had come to be typified by their trademark 'nutty' sound and behaviour. They would in turn become a constant reference point for reviews of The Housemartins in the future.

The band's first full headlining UK tour hit the roads in February 1986. Called the Twisting Rainbow Roadshow, it would visit 23 venues in as many days, eliciting rave reviews from the press and cementing their standing as a potent live force. 'These boys have put the wit and the wisdom back into political songwriting and some much-needed soul into what's left of the punk dynamic,' wrote *Melody Maker*, surprisingly detecting an influence from black music.

The tour was notable for more than just the shows, however. In order to keep costs to a minimum, the band instigated the 'adopt a Housemartin' scheme, in which they would ask punters at each venue to put the band and entourage up for the night. Invariably, the people doing the adopting would end up being girls.

It was a surprisingly exploitative thing to have done, considering their political stance. Essentially it not only offered an easy solution to their accommodation needs but also opened up the band to the possibility of sex with their fans. Perhaps naïvely, the band hadn't considered that their following would include fans cast from the obsessional mould.

On one occasion, Norman went home to a girl's house only to discover his picture all over her bedroom wall. Another time found Paul and Norman staying with two girls who were tape-recording them to prove to their friends that The Housemartins had stayed. The potentially abusive situation wasn't ideal.

Go! Discs' Andy McDonald did, however, see the advantage. After the story was leaked to the press, thus eliciting the inevitable sensational response, he went a step further and told the *NME* that a burglar had posed as a fan of the band and took them to a house to which he had the key. In the morning, according to McDonald, the band woke up to find themselves in a stranger's home, confronted by the real owners, with all of the music and video equipment gone. The band quickly wised up and knocked the idea on the head.

As the tour drew to a close, The Housemartins released their first single with Norman on bass duties. Called 'Sheep', it reached the heady heights of number 54 in the UK charts. However, the band attained a greater level of notoriety during the promotional work for the single than the music could ever have achieved.

In the band's second feature in UK weekly *Melody Maker* – which had given away a free single featuring The Housemartins, Marc Almond, Cactus World News and The Men They Couldn't Hang a month earlier – journalist Will Smith enquired about the band's feelings on the monarchy. Given their outspoken nature and their ability to spout forth a theory on anything, the monarchy was an obvious target. Add to this their supposedly Marxist leanings and the topic was potentially incendiary. Smith wasn't disappointed – the second Heaton opened his mouth, brilliant, tabloid-media-baiting copy just flowed.

'You know there's Buckingham Palace,' exclaimed Paul, 'and the next thing round the corner around Soho there's fuckin' people lying in the street without any fuckin' shoes. It's disgusting. I still can't get over that, I just can't, emotionally. It's so backward, so backward. Even if it's making money, it's such a glorious example of everything that's wrong that it should be scrapped, it really should. Or put in a museum – you know, stuff 'em. Kill them, stuff them, and put 'em in a museum. That's what I'd like to do with them.'

'Yeah, it'd be a far better tourist attraction if you could show the heads of royalty rotting away on the spikes of Buckingham Palace gates,' continued Stan. Norman was notable for his absence from this section of the interview, although it has dogged him ever since.

Perhaps not surprisingly, the British tabloid press were outraged, most notably *The Sun*, which declared the band's view as a 'sinister secret' while going on to eventually 'out' Norman's middle-class background and name – apparently a crime in the light of the band's working-class aspirations!

As if these attempts to undermine the success of The Housemartins weren't enough, the tabloid press also started a rumour that the band were all gay. This in itself wasn't particularly offensive to the band, but to a largely homophobic, anti-leftie public, the idea of an openly gay left-wing band was. In the end the band chose to ignore it, although Norman was jeered at the time.

'In The Housemartins, when I first got recognised, I thought it was brilliant because only people who like you recognise you,' Norman explained to Stuart Maconie in 1998. 'Then you go on telly and everyone recognises you whether they like you or not. You end up with taxi drivers throwing you out of their cabs for being gay, treacherous, royal-bashing, pretend-socialist, and it hurts.'

If the band's earlier royalty-bashing quotes had been aimed at getting column inches, then they had worked. In reality however both Paul and Stan held deeply anti-royalist views. And although Norman wasn't heard adding to the comments, he also wasn't quoted as arguing against them.

In September 2001 Norman would be quoted in *Q* as saying, 'These days I wouldn't behead the royal family – a year's redundancy pay and a carriage clock would do,' thus confirming his belief in Paul's heartfelt stance. Ironically, by this time support for the royals would be at an all-time low in Britain.

Among the other aspects of The Housemartins that were gaining notoriety was their decision to support themselves as an *a cappella* outfit, The Fish City Five. In the routine, which would include them walking offstage and then reappearing through the venue doors still singing, they did a number of gospel and soul-tinged tracks which drew on Paul and Norman's love of black music.

Ironically, the act didn't inject a sense of 'blackness' into their sound so much as underline their 'whiteness'. Despite obvious love and reverence for the songs they sang, everything from their delivery to their accents was attacked from that white northern working-class perspective.

It was definitely not an act that could be perceived as racially motivated, but it would put into question any suggestions Paul may have had that Norman was appropriating black music for his own gain later in his career. Arguably, it's exactly what The Housemartins were doing.

The media were less interested in this aspect of the band, however, focusing far more on their apparent spiritualism. The *a cappella* versions naturally drew a direct line with gospel music and the oral tradition of the so-called 'Negro spirituals' of the days of slavery.

In the same *Melody Maker* interview that drew the infamous attacks on the British royalty, Norman – who had previously embarrassed the rest of the band by asking a waitress to turn up the radio when 'Sheep' came on – expressed his respect for the spiritual aspect of music. 'I'm not a very religious person,' he exclaimed, despite his religious upbringing, 'but the time when I first started really thinking was when I saw Al Green describing how one day he found God, and he was nearly crying, so happy about it, and I thought, "I wonder if that'll ever happen to me?" Imagine if we were doing a gig and all of a sudden a light shone down.'

'It may happen,' replied Paul. 'We're always trying to make the light shine on stage!'

This reference to spiritualism actually echoed an interview with *NME* from the previous November, in which the journalist Cath Carrolls referred to a window sticker in the band's van declaring 'I Love Jesus'. When asked if this represented a genuine sentiment, Paul replied in a nervous manner, 'Can I say, "I'm not saying"? It just comes from a love of gospel music. When I'm listening to Al Green singing "Belle", I think

I'm missing out on something here. And "Jesus, You've Been Good To Me" by The Keytones. It's literally fantastic. I don't know what Jesus has done for them but it must be something big. They are singing something special. That's what the Labour party should be doing, sending round a sort of "Jesus" fan saying "Marx Saved You!"'

The band's big breakthrough happened in June 1986, when they released the cheekily catchy 'Happy Hour', aided by an animated video featuring choreography reminiscent of that from Madness's earliest videos. The featured 'dance routine' would be another aspect of The Housemartins which would dog Norman for years to come. Its goofball banality hit a chord with a generation which was at the time hooked on the allegedly anarchic comedy of television sitcom *The Young Ones*.

A month later, The Housemartins' debut album was released. Called *London 0, Hull 4*, it hit the number three slot, beaten only by Madonna's *True Blue* and *Invisible Touch* by Genesis. *London 0, Hull 4* captured much of the band's live energy with its fast tempos and frenetic guitar strumming, while the inclusion of a lyric sheet left no confusion as to the band's political leanings.

Any fan of the band's pop melodies might have been a bit surprised by the general themes of poor against rich, commoners against gentry, but the album hit a general mood in the country, which was about to enter its last period of youth-orientated political activity. *London 0, Hull 4* remains the finest documentation of 1980s agit-pop ever released.

In response to the album's success, the BBC broadcast a documentary on the band in the series *Rock Around The Clock*. The film featured performances of various tracks in a live situation and one mimed take that found the band sauntering along the river. Cut into the programme, however, was the first real public hint as to where Norman's true allegiances lay.

Each member was featured in their own solo vignette. Norman chose to display his deck skills by cutting up a couple of records on the decks in his bedroom. It was, we were reliably informed, the kind of noise with which he woke the rest of the band each day.

On 2 October of that year, The Housemartins were once again causing a stir in the media thanks to Paul's onstage remarks. This time, the controversy surrounded an anti-Thatcher comment during their gig at Liverpool Playhouse, which was being simultaneously broadcast live as a part of the *Eurorock Show* across the full independent network. Paul had suggested that Thatcher might be better engaged in some kind of sexual activity involving husband Dennis than running the country. In the resulting furore, there was a call for live shows to be banned from being broadcast.

In response to the situation, the Independent Broadcasting Authority issued a statement which read, 'We deplore obscenities and the irresponsibility of the band. We believe artists have a certain responsibility to behave, especially in front of live and potentially underage audiences. We are looking at ways to avoid this in the future.'

Not ones to let others to get the last word, The Housemartins released the following statement: 'We would like to apologise to anybody offended by any language that might have been a little down to earth, but we've been picked up on obscenities, and obscenities to us are the real obscenities of poverty, racism and sexism, etc. People are constantly talking about the responsibility of people in the privileged position of being heard on the radio, but there's only two sets of privileged people in this country – Tories and the Royal Family.'

In the media outburst that followed, most bands would have been forced to lie low. Hull's self-styled fourth-best band had no intention of doing this. Instead, a month later, they would release the single which would place them at the number one position immediately before Christmas. The coveted position on the big day would go to Jackie Wilson's reissued 'Reet Petite'. Given the band's love of this era of soul, it was an honour to have been able to keep the number one position warm for a hero like Wilson.

The Housemartins' single was an *a cappella* remake of The Isleys' 'Caravan Of Love', which came as a part of an EP which included renditions of 'We Shall Not Be Moved', 'When I First Met Jesus' and 'Heaven Help Us'. It was this moment when the band fully lived up to their promise of bringing the light of evangelical music into their sound.

The religious imagery now reached fresh heights with all four band members pictured with crosses shaved into the napes of their necks.

'The crosses in the hair was something Paul stumbled on,' recalled Cook in *Last Orders At The Liars' Bar*. 'He wanted to start a new religion really. He had this character Bob Christ who was like Jesus, but he drank more. The joke was "Bob Jesus, Bob Christ, Bob Hope."'

Throughout this manic year with his new band, Norman kept returning to Brighton for the occasional DJing date, and to go clubbing with his friends. His desire to make dance records had also increased. Prior to leaving Brighton, he had mucked around with a basic sampler, tape and record decks, creating raw cut-and-paste tracks. Nothing serious, but he knew that this was where his future lay.

In early 1988, Norman approached his old boss at Rounder about recording one of his tracks properly. Graham Gilbert already had a production partnership with Mike Roberts under the name Keep It In The Red Productions, and the duo jumped at the chance of working with Norman. They duly booked into Brighton's Esselle Beat Company studio, on Dyke Road. The recording was quick, with Norman cutting up some of his favourite tracks and lifting oddments for samples. 'He was painting with sound at this time,' says Gilbert.

The production duo then created a backbeat for Norman's collage to sit on and added a few keyboard hooks, courtesy of Adrian Thomas. 'Adrian also worked at Rounder,' recalls Gilbert. 'He was a bit of a 1980s new romantic. In fact, there's a load of graffiti on the toilet door at the shop which is basically an argument about Levi's between Adrian and Norman. He was a bit of a perfectionist with the music and didn't understand the DJ ethic at all. So he did this hookline and made a mistake, but we all loved it and said, "Keep it." The next day we came into the studio and he'd over-dubbed it to correct the mistake. We were horrified.' Not unduly affected by the experience of working on the track, Adrian Thomas is now musical director with Mike Oldfield.

The subsequent single was called 'The Finest Ingredients' and went under the dubious moniker of DJ Megamix. Although the A-side was an instrumental cut-up which echoed Double Dee And Steinski's 'Lessons' series (notably 'Lesson 1: The Payoff Mix'), the flipside actually featured a rap by Norman and Brighton rapper Wildski – a cherished moment in Norman Cook's recording history.

'It was one of the earliest records of its type, really quite naïve by today's standards, but ahead of everyone else,' recalls Gilbert. 'We actually tried to get the track released officially. We played it to Danny D at Chrysalis, who liked it but thought it would be a nightmare to handle because of the amount of samples in it.'

When the avenue of an official release closed down, Gilbert and Roberts looked into the idea of putting it out as a bootleg. They had already played the track to Champion Records' Mel McGally and the label's A&R man, Paul Oakenfold (who would go on to become one of the biggest DJs in the world). He also felt that the sample-clearance issue would be too difficult with the track. However, Gilbert and Roberts suggested that they simply manufacture the record and get it put out as a bootleg.

The idea got as far as sending the masters off to the pressing plant in the US, but in the process someone else picked up the track and bootlegged it. So the intended bootleg was now being bootlegged!

When the track started to filter through, Paul Heaton and the rest of The Housemartins were furious. They demanded that Norman should distance himself from the track as it undermined the band's own image and ideology. To Paul, 'The Finest Ingredients' represented the sound of black music being appropriated for a white musician's gain. 'The band were up in arms,' Norman exclaimed. 'We shared tons of fans with The Smiths. It was a hanging offence!' (The Smiths had famously declared 'hang the DJ' in their hit 'Panic'.)

In James Hamilton's column in *Record Mirror*, the record was lambasted, and so too were Rounder, who received the lion's share of the blame for the track. They were apparently guilty of cashing in on the success of The Housemartins.

Years later, the single remains one of Norman Cook's lost classics, although it has been bootlegged on numerous occasions since. Interestingly, co-producer Mike Roberts would later attain huge success as the main sound engineer for urban percussion dance troupe Stomp!

In retrospect, the actual creation of 'The Finest Ingredients' offered the first glimpse into the demise of The Housemartins. Following the band's number one single, friction started to appear in the ranks. This would initially result in the departure of drummer Hugh Whitaker, who had become increasingly exasperated at the dilution of the band's political stance in favour of hit records. Hugh would subsequently lose all of his money in a bad business venture with a car dealer called James Hewitt. His reaction was to attack Hewitt's home by pouring petrol through the letterbox and firebombing the building on the following day. He then attacked Hewitt with an axe, causing him to lose the use of one arm. Whitaker was sentenced to six years' imprisonment.

With the replacement drummer Dave Hemmingway now in residence, Paul and Stan started work on the band's second album. However, it was here that cracks really started to show in the band's previously impenetrable armour.

Stan had been listening to a lot of stuff by The Smiths and wanted to take the album in a more guitar-orientated direction, while Norman wanted the recording to feature loops and samples, much to the abhorrence of his bandmates.

'It was one of the reasons why we split up,' Norman explained to UK style magazine *Deluxe* in 1998. 'I was getting sick that all my mates like Dave Dorrell and CJ Macintosh were having hits doing the sort of stuff I was into.'

Increasingly Paul Heaton took the position of bandleader and saw it as his job to decide on the direction the album would take. In his mind, the new stuff would be more influenced by his ever-growing love of gospel music. The resulting album, *The People Who Grinned Themselves To Death*, was a far more assured recording. Much of its predecessor's rawness had gone, while the previously overbearing frivolity (which often overshadowed their political nature) was stripped to a bare minimum.

Once again they wore their ideologies on their lyrical sleeves. Among the album's many targets was agricultural capitalism (there is a caustic attack on 'Me And The Farmer'), the trendy metropolitan types who made up the majority of the music business ('Five Get Over-Excited') and even property developers ('Build').

The internecine friction eventually boiled over in an Irish TV interview in which the band launched into a full-blown argument, and the writing seemed truly on the wall. During the making of the video for the single 'Build', this metaphor found a physical realisation. In the film, the band were shot performing as a house was built around them. As an act of pure frustration at Paul's increasingly domineering attitude, Stan and Norman daubed the words 'Housemartins RIP' on one of the walls.

'I was a megalomaniac,' Paul explained to Mike Pattenden, author of *Last Orders At The Liars' Bar*. 'I wouldn't let people do what they wanted. Norman sat me down during the video shoot for "Build" and told me I had become a control freak. He said, "You're power mad and you're grinding me and Stan into the dirt..." I never meant to behave like that, but I had become obsessively dictatorial. Norman was right, but the truth hurt me.'

The dissatisfaction within the ranks of the band was glaringly obvious to everyone around them. At one point they even sat down and discussed the reason why everyone was so unhappy in order to try to sort things out. True, they still respected each other (to this day Norman rates Paul Heaton as a great songwriter), and their politics were still similarly ensconced in the outer edges of the left wing, but they were faced with the usual band problem of musical differences and an unavoidable reality that they'd painted themselves into something of a stylistic corner.

The public had certain expectations of the band and when they didn't live up to them, people stopped buying the records. In order to return to the heights, they would have to turn back into the Monkees pastiche of early days. But they didn't want to do this.

In an attempt to avoid this straitjacket, they even considered disappearing, changing the band's name (and probably even their own) and just returning with a different set of songs. But that would have taken too much organisation. And the record company would have objected – after all, they were being bankrolled by the band's sales during these years.

The eventual demise of The Housemartins was marked by two press releases. On the eve of the release of 'Build', they issued a statement that underlined their strength of opinion when it came to politics. When they heard about Status Quo's decision to play at South Africa's notorious

Sun City, they declared, 'In playing Sun City, an artist is fully embracing the South African Apartheid system. Status Quo's fans should realise that the band's decision to play is based purely on a mixture of greed and ignorance, a mixture so potent with Botha himself. The Housemartins would never agree to these murdering white South African bastards.' (This anti-Apartheid stance would be continued on Norman's later Beats International records, which would all carry the statement, 'For moral reasons, this record is not on sale in South Africa.')

If that Housemartins press statement presented a band unified by a common cause, then the band's final statement shows just how far they had gone down the road of no return. Despite Norman's heartfelt plea for Paul to face up to himself, it would appear that he hadn't yet started. In one final act of megalomaniacal control, he wrote the band's declaration to split up to the press without telling the band or the label.

In the statement, Paul was aided and abetted by roadies Sean Welsh and Nick Swift. The press release read: 'The Housemartins' contract expires in spring 1988. From that point on, The Housemartins will cease to exist. They believe that, in a world of Rick Astley, Shakin' Stevens and The Pet Shop Boys, quite simply they weren't good enough.'

Although The Housemartins will not go down in the rock 'n' roll pantheon as one of the great bands, they did offer a fresh alternative to the manufactured pop of the day. Indeed, their naïve polemic wouldn't go amiss in the post-millennial mood of apolitical apathy. If nothing else, their albums capture the other side to the 1980s never-had-it-so-good arrogance. Love them or hate them, The Housemartins were a much-needed antidote to yuppie culture. However, with the country moving into a huge economic decline, unemployment about to reach all-time highs and homes throughout the country being repossessed in a housing crash, people living the period directly after the band's split didn't need a group of four lads stirring the political stew; they needed a soundtrack to help them forget.

That music was already filtering into the UK from Chicago. Acid house was about to be what Tony Wilson would call 'the last great working-class movement in the UK'. And almost unwittingly, Norman Cook was about to position himself in the very centre of the dance revolution. 'I'd like to make a record that will always get put on at parties and to have won the game without foul play but with some good tackles on the opposition,' he told Nick Swift immediately after the demise of The Housemartins.

Clearly, Norman's career path was set on a completely different trajectory to those of his ex-band mates. It was almost inevitable that he would reject the guitar culture of the time and develop a hatred for indie music: 'I was a punk. I loved punk, and I also liked a lot of the bands that came immediately afterwards, bands like Cabaret Voltaire and The Human League, but I simply couldn't get into the indie stuff which had become popular by the mid 1980s. A lot of the bands simply wanted to relive 1977 and those that didn't wanted to relive 1967, which was even worse. I've always loved people like Roddy Frame and Elvis Costello, but people like that are few and far between.'

What of the rest of The Housemartins? Paul would reappear a year later with his new outfit, the now internationally huge The Beautiful South. Stan recorded an album for Go! Discs which duly sank without a trace, moved to Bristol to open a wholefood shop; became an author (*How To Become A Pop Star* and children's tale *Grumpyguts*) and started a film-production company, making animations like his biggest success for Nickelodeon, *Spider And Fly*.

'I was too far in the beat direction, and Paul and Stan were too much against drum machines and sequencers,' Norman explained to *Melody Maker*'s Dave Jennings in April 1990. 'At the end of The Housemartins, we were going to do "Always Something There To Remind Me" with a drum machine and sequencer playing the bassline to get it really choppy, but certain members of the band couldn't cope with the fact that we'd release a single and there'd only be two of us on it. And I think it's a bit of an old-fashioned attitude.

'Basically, I was stuck in this band, playing music that I didn't like, but wasn't able to do anything about for fear of letting the others down. When we split up, I felt like a heavy weight had been lifted from my shoulders.'

With his Hull exile finally over, Norman packed up his record collection and returned to Brighton. It was June 1988.

BL AME IT ON THE BAΓΓLI Nε

'This is what I want to do in life, whereas The Housemartins were
something good to do when you were young.'

– Norman Cook, 1989

When Norman Cook walked away from the Hull base of The
Housemartins and back into the welcoming arms of his adopted home
of Brighton, he could hardly have been able to predict what lay in store.
It was 1988, only three years since his departure, and in that time huge
changes had occurred in the dance terrain.

For the kid known as Quentin, dance music had been a mélange of
styles ranging from the funk of James Brown through the soul of Otis
Redding and onto the groove of old-skool hip-hop cut-ups like Double
Dee And Steinski's 'Lesson' series and electro grooves as delivered by
Soul Sonic Force. Despite hearing the soundtracks to Brighton's gay
clubs, Hi-NRG, electro funk and early Chicago house, his heart lay in
the funky sounds that would inform all breakbeat music to come.

Throughout his time with The Housemartins, Cook had continued
his obsession for dance culture and DJ mixing, but as the final weeks of
his day job drew to a close, a dance revolution was in full swing. A few
years earlier, Chicago had delivered the blueprint for house music, and
by 1988 the young clubbers of Brighton (like those in many areas of the
UK) were hooked. Indeed, it was in this year that the legendary Zap Club
opened its doors, boasting among its regular DJs Carl Cox, Paul
Oakenfold and Gary Clail's Tackhead Soundsystem. (Gary would score
a huge hit with his agit-rap/house crossover 'Human Nature' in 1989.)

In 1988, then, Brighton had turned *en masse* to house music – with
the exception of one Norman Cook. He just didn't get the house thing.

Its metronomic rhythms didn't move him. Indeed, like so many artists and DJs who would become influential over the next 14 years, from Liam Howlett to Goldie, Massive Attack to The Chemical Brothers, the earliest days of the acid-house sound were just a diversion from the dance sound of hip-hop, electro and their funk roots. 'When I joined The Housemartins, they were an anti-drug band,' he recalled a few years later. 'We were up in Hull and all I knew about acid house was what we read in the *Daily Mirror* and the *NME*. Then when I moved back to Brighton I saw all my mates were wearing bandannas and smiley T-shirts and I thought, "What's happened here?" At first I wasn't keen on it. It just obliterated every other kind of music. I used to run a night billed as an "acid-free zone".' He even declared to *The Face* in an early interview, 'I hated that shit. It held a pillow to the face of every other kind of music.'

Norman Cook was enamoured with an earlier age of dance culture, albeit an age that had only come to any real vinyl fruition in 1987 and 1988, hitting the UK charts in the process. Indeed, 1988 was the year in which Bomb The Bass went top five with 'Beat Dis' and S-Express delivered the chart-dominating 'Theme From S-Express', while M/A/R/R/S had scored a number one with seminal DJ record 'Pump Up The Volume' in late 1987.

Although all three may have been inspired by early Chicago house, they represented a very English take on that sound – or, to be more accurate, an England-via-Ibiza take on dance culture. These singles drew heavily on the so-called open-mindedness that many of the UK's nascent club front-runners had witnessed on their first trips to the Balearic Islands.

Essentially, the British spin on Ibiza's eclectic soundtrack involved the appropriation of the DIY stylings of hip-hop, the subversive elements of disco, tons of cult kitsch references and just a hint of punk attitude – exactly the same reference points as on Norman's own 'The Finest Ingredients' single, in fact.

'I remember when he first came in to record that track,' recalls Kevin Stagg, owner of the Esselle Beat Company studios, where Norman would record all of his material until 1996. 'We were all aware of him being involved with The Housemartins, but he just came in with a load of records. Thing is, it didn't seem strange that he was doing a dance track.

And the thing that really stuck with me was just how nice he was as a person. Really genuine. A lovely bloke.'

It was little surprise that Norman would have been drawn to the Balearic approach to beat production. The first wave of Island revellers came from the UK's Home Counties, the very area where Norman had grown up. As a result, he would have been the among the first to take the influence on board.

In the mid 1980s, clubbing in the UK had been divided into the glitzy, dress-to-impress corporate venues like the Ritzy's chain and any of the Bass Leisure outlets, or it was represented by the cliquey rare-groove scene. The latter existed on a constant air of elitism, with the DJs copying the early hip-hop DJs (Kool Herc, Grandmaster Flash, Afrika Bambaataa) by sticking tape over the labels of their records. The intention was to obliterate the source of the breaks that they were playing so no one could copy their style.

In hip-hop, this method of subterfuge was encapsulated by the 'challenge' or 'battle' mentality. However, rare groove came with a very different set of values. This was the arena of the affluent British youth, where flash clothes were of ultimate importance. Essentially, everything was about status, from the records played through to the clothes worn and cars driven.

Tellingly, the rare-groove events, or 'floorshakers', had a firm stronghold in the economically booming south-east of England: the Home Counties, where the mid 1980s brought the kind of financial rewards that would seem alien to the rest of the country, particularly the north, where industry was being stripped and closed down.

This is not to say that the rare groove didn't have a very important place in the creation of club culture as it is known today. It was at the infamous all-dayers at Prestatyn in Wales and Nottingham's Rock City that many of today's leading DJs would cut their teeth. Furthermore, it was at one of these that house music was first played in the UK, although the rare-groove DJs did treat the house sound as a passing fad, while many of the punters rejected it as being the music of 'gay' clubs. Essentially, it was regarded as another form of disco by all but a very few.

There was a suffocating aspect to this scene. The soundtrack was as limited as the style codes. However, it is an era fondly remembered by many. Among them, perhaps surprisingly is Prodigy's frontman Maxim. 'There was a bug crew of us who would go along to these soul all-dayers,' he recalls. 'When we did Prestatyn we'd drive down with a boot-load of booze and weed. That was our thing, just getting mashed up good and proper.'

Given the elitist nature of the rare-groove scene, it was perhaps doomed to failure from the start. A revolt from the apparent style fascism was inevitable. The first seed of this reaction came in 1985, when a group of Home Counties DJs, promoters and party people arrived on Ibiza's idyllic shores and discovered the local hippy approach to dance music in Ibiza Town. Among this group of people was Paul Oakenfold and Trevor Fung, who would open the doomed Balearic Club the Funhouse in South London soon after their return.

'Balearic' was the term given to the eclectic approach to music employed by Ibiza DJ Alfredo Fiorillo. Rather than explore one particular sound, he discovered the hidden grooves in disparate artists from Chris Rea to U2. Coming from the closed mentality of London into this open approach, it was little wonder that Oakenfold was affected. Sadly, however, he was unable to convince anyone else about the value of listening to indie artists The Woodentops or the early output of Simple Minds ('Themes From Great Cities' was a favourite) when all the in-crowd wanted was James Brown.

The turning point came in 1987. After two years of talking about the Ibiza effect, Oakenfold hired a villa on the island and invited a few friends to come and sample the delights for themselves. Among them were Danny Rampling, Nicky Holloway and Johnny Walker. Together they experienced the intoxicating mixtures of the two essential Es in Ibiza: eclecticism and ecstasy.

On their return, Oakenfold revitalised his Balearic parties when he opened an after-hours event at the Project Club in Streatham, south London. It quickly became a favoured haunt of the hundreds of other youngsters who had discovered the Ibiza vibe that summer. Instead of bringing back stories of thuggish behaviour, as usually happened on Spanish package holidays, these people brought back an attitude of inclusivity and even a whole new style of dress. Suddenly the main thing wasn't owning the right status symbols; it was about dancing for the sheer thrill of it all.

In November 1987, just as Norman Cook was entering the final few months of The Housemartins, Danny Rampling and his wife Jenni opened the doors of the legendary Balearic club Shoom. By 1988, just when Conservative leader Margaret Thatcher was entering the record books as the longest-serving Prime Minister of that century, the Ramplings would appropriate the hippy emblem of the smiley badge for the ever-expanding Shoomheads. It was an image that would become important to Norman Cook in the years to come.

Shoom may have represented a new, inclusive attitude among British clubs, but in reality its family spirit of togetherness relied on a door policy every bit as strict as the most exclusive New York club. Jenni Rampling knew exactly the type of people she wanted in her club and alienated those whom she regarded as hangers-on. Only the originals and their guests were welcomed through the doors with open arms.

This apparent state of double standards – the proclamation of openness tempered by an over-riding sense of exclusivity – would present a dichotomy that would resurface time and again in British club culture. Indeed, it would, despite claims to the contrary, re-emerge in the late 1990s with the big-beat explosion, as championed by Norman Cook in his Fatboy Slim guise.

As with any success story, the secret would quickly break in the wider marketplace. With the opening of Paul Oakenfold's Spectrum in London's 2,000-capacity gay club Heaven and Nicky Holloway's the Trip, the doors were finally flung open to the next generation.

While Balearic eclecticism reigned supreme in the soundtrack to Shoom, both Spectrum, and especially the Trip, focused the music on the hard, metronomic sound of acid house as typified by the frenetic 303 pulses and sparking ambience of Phuture's 'Acid Trax'. 'Unless Colin Faver was playing Shoom, it was generally namby-pamby sort of stuff, lightweight gear,' explained DJ, club runner and producer Mr C to Simon Reynolds in his book *Energy Flash*.

With acid house now driving the sound, the other avenues of house culture quickly found a new audience. The techno sounds of Juan Atkins, Derrick May and Kevin Saunderson started filtering through. House anthems by people like Fingers Inc, Farley Jackmaster Funk and Jamie Principle became regulars in the DJs' sets, while the more soulful sound of garage (named after the renowned New York club Paradise Garage) also found new favour. No longer was house culture seen to be 'gay' disco music.

Norman Cook was totally against the house sound, considering that the beats all sounded the same – a common complaint from people who hadn't learned the new language that this music presented. Norman was still mainly influenced by the hip-hop approach to DJing, although the Balearic vibe had certainly had an effect on him. So had his friends CJ Macintosh and Dave Dorrell, the main people behind 'Pump Up The Volume'.

Aspects of the UK hip-hop underground were equally affected by the Balearic touch at this time. Where the over-riding obsession with British MCs had been either the gangsta rap of artists like Ice-T or the aggressive production techniques of Public Enemy's Bomb Squad, suddenly a mellowing out started to occur. Although obviously inspired by the nascent daisy-age movement of crews like De La Soul and 3rd Bass, these crews were more musically open, drawing on a huge variety of musical sources in order to create their beats.

In Bristol, perhaps the most significant development in the UK hip-hop story was developing – a development that would directly coincide with Norman's own beat excursions.

Since 1985, Bristol rap outfit The Wild Bunch Posse had operated as a collective, which initially included in its ranks legendary producer Nellee Hooper and long-standing soundsystem DJ Daddy G. They were later joined by rapper and renowned graffiti artists Rob Del Naja, aka 3D (encouraging the band to lose the 'Posse' in the process), and DJ-turned-producer Mushroom.

It was into the impoverished arena of UK hip-hop that The Wild Bunch unleashed their first single, 'The Look Of Love', on Island Records. It bombed and The Wild Bunch went into an almost inevitable collapse. Nellee Hooper teamed up with Jazzy B to put into action the Soul2Soul game plan, which would deliver the template for New Urban Soul in 1987. 3D and Mushroom were hired to work with Neneh Cherry on her classic *Raw Like Sushi* album. It was during these sessions that the Massive Attack plot first appeared in 1987.

3D joined forces with Daddy G and Mushroom to demo a few ideas with the intention of being a part of the Soul2Soul family. Among these tracks was the debut Massive Attack single 'Any Love' (released on their own imprint) and a loose-limbed lyrical jam based around a poorly sampled fourth-world jazz funk loop by one Wally Badarou. The resulting track provided the band not only with their trademark up-close, smoke-drenched vocal sound (the vocals from this recording ended up on the finished version) but also with the perfect introduction to the range of influences at play in the Massive Attack arsenal.

In essence, the Bristol trio used the musical inclusivity of Balearic, added the production technique of house and then drew heavily on dub soundsystem, jazz grooves and hip-hop to create the chilled-out sound that some would come to describe as 'trip-hop'.

Although seemingly disassociated with the Norman Cook story, the truth is that the approach of the Bristol scene was far more in keeping with Norman's own vision of the breadth of sound that dance music should encompass. Furthermore, it was significant that both Massive Attack and Soul2Soul were exploring the outer edges of the contemporary club culture while still avoiding the four-to-the-floor house beat. This was far more about the breakbeat – which was Norman's language.

So the dance arena that Norman returned to was, despite his efforts to remain involved throughout the Housemartins years, in a very different space to the one he'd left behind. Rather than feel inspired by the new possibilities he was now faced with, he was suddenly overtaken by depression. 'I thought I'd had my 15 minutes,' he once said. 'I knew I wanted to make dance records, but I was white, and in those days white people didn't really make black music.'

Despite his reservations about his own credentials to make dance music, his first post-Housemartins venture would be a remix of old-skool hip-hop outfit Erik B And Rakim. It was late 1988 and Norman had spent a few months tinkering around in the studio, creating grooves, when he got a call from an old friend at Chrysalis dance offshoot Cooltempo. They wanted a remix of Eric B And Rakim's 'I Know You Got Soul' but didn't have permission from the artists. The track wasn't owned by them, so they didn't even have the master.

'So I just said, "Look, there's an *a cappella* on the B-side – I'll spin that and put a groove under it,"' Norman recalls. The groove itself was lifted from The Jacksons' 'ABC'.

'I Know You Got Soul' was engineered by Cooltempo A&R man Danny D, who would soon after enjoy success with D-Mob's commercial acid-house anthem 'We Call It Acieed'. 'Danny taught me a lot,' recalled Norman to Dave Robinson in *Future Music* 'When we started, we didn't have a sampler, so we used to retrigger things off a Bel delay. In those days it was quite exciting, because they hadn't invented all the stuff that's around to do things for you. You had to work things out for yourself.'

Soon after this track was recorded, Norman would team up with Simon Thornton in the engineering seat. He's remained in that position ever since.

'Simon used to work here as an in-house engineer,' explains Esselle Beat Company's Kev Stagg. 'Him and Norman just hit it off very quickly. I think they were very in tune with each other so Simon would understand what Norman was after immediately. I don't know when he became employed by Norman. Throughout this time, and the first album, I definitely paid him, but then one day I was told that he was working for Norman now. I wasn't bothered really. He's a very talented guy and deserves recognition.'

The resulting remix was a post-Balearic remake of hip-hop. It immediately went to number five in the British charts, supplying him with his first solo hit, with a version of a track for someone else, starting a pattern that would continue throughout his career.

This action of taking the *a cappella* to create a brand new remix of the original without the artists actually knowing is something which had now become commonplace in hip-hop's dealings with the mainstream music industry. Soon after, Afro-centric Native Tongues outfit The Jungle Brothers would score a hit with the track 'I'll House You', while a few years later they'd find their tracks being given the jungle treatment by Aphrodite and Mickey Finn. Similarly, in 1998 Run DMC would discover their old-skool classic 'It Ain't Like That' being reworked for the dance scene by Jason Nevins, creating a massive worldwide hit in the process.

Norman Cook's reworking of 'I Know You Got Soul' may not have achieved such global success, but it does have the honour of being the first of these remixes to appear on the shop racks!

In July 1989, Norman Cook emerged with his first post-Housemartins single. Called 'Won't Talk About It', the track was built around a guitar loop taken from Billy Bragg's 'Levi Stubbs' Tears'. If the source of the loop seemed a little strange for a DJ track, then the song's origination would prove to be equally strange. The song was actually written by Billy Bragg, who also supplied falsetto vocals.

'About a year ago, when The Housemartins were splitting up, Billy phoned me up and said "I've got this song knocking about. It's a dance song and I don't know how to make a dance record – can you come and dance it up for me?"', Norman said to *NME*'s Andrew Collins in July 1985. 'So we worked on it odd days here and there while he was doing his album, and we never got it finished.'

However, when Norman began to make his first solo album, he rediscovered the track and asked Bragg if he would mind if Norman finished it for release. Bragg had no objections at all.

'Won't Talk About It' featured many of the sounds which came to be Norman Cook trademarks over the coming years – a loping beat, an old-skool walking funk bass, brass stabs and even a guitar solo which could have come direct from an Isley Brothers track. The vocal line was drenched in old soul, while the scat rapping in the middle-eight was influenced directly by the *Wild Style* movie, with its array of rappers all battling for supremacy. Elsewhere the piano break was reminiscent of 1980s Brit-funk acts like Shakatak. Overall, the single sounded as if it had been compiled in another age, and yet the production was remarkably contemporary.

The single's B-side was perhaps a stronger indication of what could be expected of Cook in the future. 'Blame It On The Bassline' took a standard hip-hop break, a programmed drum machine and a bassline that was similar in feel to the A-side, and added samples from The Jacksons' 'Blame It On The Boogie', Chic's 'Good Times' and Afrika Bambaataa's electro template 'Planet Rock'.

To this brew was added the rapping of Brighton MC Wildski and turntablist cuts and transforms from DJ Streets Ahead. Overall, the track owed more to Coldcut's 'Say Kids, What Time Is It?', from a year earlier, than to house culture. Again, however, it had a resonance in the contemporary climate.

Now-defunct British weekly music magazine *Sounds* was first to come out with praise for the single. In their 1 July 1989 issue, Richard Cook declared his support for what he considered to be experimental dance music, also making the connection between the music that Norman was creating and the post-Wild Bunch output of Soul2Soul: 'Soul2Soul have taken the lead in restoring structural power to experimental dance tracks: it looks like plenty of others are prepared to follow it up. This ex-Housemartins bassist sounds like a fair candidate. The first track is someone sticking together old Philly soul tricks and getting Billy Bragg to do the basement vocals. "Bassline" finds Norm taping other stuff off the radio, asking a few pals into rap while beating out a bonus rhythm on a couple of tin drums. Funny, exuberant record making.'

Funny, exuberant record making perhaps, but the single hid another unfolding story. In the months that followed The Housemartins' demise and his reappearance as Eric B And Rakim's remixer, Norman had been furiously recording what was to become his first solo album at Esselle Studios in Brighton. The plan had been to put the album out straight after the single, but his record label, Go! Beat, refused.

The main reason was that they recognised that the album would be likely to disappear in the musical climate of the time. Norman's own brand of funky beats were increasingly out of vogue in a country hungry for house beats. In order for him to have a chance of any longevity, he needed to have a big single.

'Slow, funky beats rather than house beats – I've never really been able to get into that,' he explained of the album's sound. 'That's why I haven't been releasing anything, because the only way you could get stuff played in clubs was to have a house beat behind it.'

Furthermore, Norman faced what was a very real form of inverted racism at the time. He was a white person playing black music, a fact which worried him immensely. 'I don't want to be The Beatmasters saying, "I am a white person who does dance music," but I still want to have a reputation with those sorts of people,' he said at the time.

In the UK at this time, it was more accurate to say that this was a situation which applied more to the hip-hop and funk scenes. In both, white people would be criticised for not having enough soul to create that kind of music.

And yet, even as Norman was obsessing over the problem, the 'can a white man sing the blues?' issue was already being ridiculed by the house scene, which found white kids adopting what were initially black musical forms to equal effect.

It is possible that Norman's sensitivity to the issue stemmed from his own immersion in hip-hop. However, what is more likely is the fact that his political views were still very left wing, and he'd just spent the last few years working closely with Paul Heaton, who was very outspoken on the subject of the white appropriation of black music, although Norman has claimed that being in The Housemartins had the opposite effect on him: 'If I hadn't have joined The Housemartins, I'd probably have formed a Simply Red type white soul band or something quite terrible,' he told *Melody Maker* journalist Push, once again underpinning the colour divisions that he perceived in music. 'No, I don't regret it. It was a good experience. It helped to give me confidence to do what I'm doing now and it made me less wary about the idea of being a white bloke trying to make black music.'

'Does that matter?' asked Push, who himself was already deeply immersed in the free-party acid-house scene and its attendant ideologies.

'Not now perhaps, but a few years ago it did. It's a question of doing it for the right reasons. There's nothing worse than a white guy pretending to be black and I try to make sure that I'm not pulled into clichés like going round shouting 'Yo!' to everyone and wearing a cap back to front, trying to make out that I'm street-wise. I can't possibly be street-wise because I live in a road!'

The issue of race division in music had become a calling card for numerous white musicians who were enamoured with black musical forms. In a raw reading of history it would often be pointed out that rock 'n' roll was a black form, appropriated and diluted by white musicians. As a result, any other musical form that had emanated from black musicians was deemed out of bounds for white artists. Thus the terms 'white soul' and 'white reggae' came to be derogatory, suggesting that all white musicians would inevitably bleach out the original form and supply an inferior version.

History has subsequently shown us that this form of inverted racism hasn't always been accurate, especially with house and techno. Ironically electro made moves in the 1970s to throw such perceived prejudice out of the window. Afrika Bambaataa's Soul Sonic Force had found inspiration for their seminal 'Planet Rock' (a snippet of which had been used on the outro of Cook's 'Won't Talk About It') in the most soul-less white European band, Kraftwerk. Furthermore Bambaataa had been motivated by the new wave sounds of British musician Gary Numan.

'Planet Rock' quite literally was the sound of two worlds colliding – the New York punk and hip-hop worlds orbiting the Roxy Club in the mid to late 1970s. Afrika Bambaataa was a regular DJ at the club, and through it the one time Bronx gang-banger (he'd run with both The Black Spades and Seven Immortals) came face to face with the burgeoning punk-rock movement in all of its safety-pinned glory. Naturally for a DJ who first spun the wheels of steel at the age of 10, Bam felt the need to create a sound that would complement both crowds.

It was during one of the Roxy nights that Bam would come face to face with rookie producer Arthur Baker. Bam and Baker talked about working together on the project. Little happened for months until one day Bam heard someone playing Kraftwerk's 'Trans-Europe Express' on a boombox. As legend would have it, he knew there and then what the record was going to sound like – although it has also been suggested that Baker brought the concept to Bam, introducing him to The Yellow Magic Orchestra, Kraftwerk and Gary Numan along the way.

'Gary Numan. Man he was dope. So important to us,' recalls Bam. 'When we heard that single, "Are Friends Electric?", it was like the aliens had landed in the Bronx, you know what I'm sayin'? We were just throwing shapes to this tune, man. It just blew up at the Roxy. More than Kraftwerk, Numan was the inspiration. He's a hero. Without him, there'd be no electro.'

Just as the intention of the 'Planet Rock' was to speak to people from wildly different backgrounds, so too the team behind the single couldn't be more disparate. On Bam's side were his compatriots in the self-styled Zulu Nation, in particular GLOBE, who introduced rap's voice-popping technique on the record. Sitting in with Boston-born club DJ Arthur Baker were keyboard player John Robie and Jay Burnett, who would later go on to work with UK imprint Hydrogen Dukebox.

The resulting record sent shockwaves through the music world when it eventually arrived in 1982. Baker's fusion of programmed arcade game beats and Babe Ruth's 'Mexican' break created a rhythm bed that was at once synthetic and organic. The interplay between pulsing bass and bleep percussion only added to the sensation of otherworldliness, while the keyboard refrain and string stabs seemed to have come from another dimension.

Even the vocals sounded like they had been beamed from a distant galaxy, thanks to the liberal use of metallic reverb. 'Party people, party people, can you all get funky?' sang the Soul Sonic Force, and for one brief second you could be forgiven for thinking that aliens had landed.

If it's been electronic dance music's aim to always peek into the future, this record represents one of the few tunes that can claim success. The impact of 'Planet Rock' can never be underestimated. From here, electro was born and the concept of the programmed break became a part of the dance language.

In taking black music and recreating it in a contemporary setting, Norman Cook actually had similar aims to Bambaataa. His intention was to speak to two worlds: he wanted acceptance with his peers in the UK dance scene and he wanted respect from the people he was influenced by. Essentially, his intention was to transcend preconceptions of colour. However, it is possible that his own worries about the issue revealed deep-rooted preconceptions about white, or black, limitations within music. 'I grew up thinking white people had no soul and that the only good funk was made by black people,' he would reveal a few years later.

In 1989, his perception was already outmoded. Indeed it showed him to be out of step with the wider dance culture and the mood of the times in the UK, although his perception was still strongly evident in the divisive music and media industries of the US. However, he would later claim that he came to terms with any race-motivated fears when he went to a predominantly black club night at Brixton's the Fridge. When he heard his remix of the Erik B And Rakim track he was shocked to note that no one stopped dancing. 'They didn't go, "Hang on! This sounds like a white bloke,"' he told *The Face* in 1998.

The album that Norman had already completed was perhaps underpinned by many of these race concerns, but above all he wanted to make an album of party songs that would hold the listener's attention over the course of 47 minutes. Initially he had intended to produce a collection based around dub versions of the tracks he'd recorded with other people. However, when he listened back to Billy Bragg's contribution, he realised that the album would be strong enough with a series of guests, with him taking the role of producer. 'The trouble is, I'm not a very good singer, which put me in a bit of a pickle,' he told *NME* in 1989. 'I'm more like a producer. This way I get the thrill of working with other people's ideas, and also you're your own boss – you can decide when you want to release things, when you want to get married...'

The latter comment revealed friction between Norman and his old band which had previously been hidden behind the 'musical differences' declaration. In the last few months of The Housemartins, Norman had told the band that he was going to marry his girlfriend Pippa. The band were less than overjoyed with the idea at first, as this could have affected their lads-together image. Furthermore, their schedule was so hectic that finding time for Norman and Pippa to marry really was a major issue.

In an interview with *NME*, Norman revealed the problem in even more detail: 'With The Housemartins, it was like a marriage where you could never go off and do anything else without feeling you were cheating on them. Even when I wanted to get married, it was like, "You haven't really got enough time" or, "You can get married but you can't have a honeymoon." Things like that.'

In the end, the couple got hitched in the grounds of a stately home on the borders of Sussex and Kent. 'She was a nurse, not a rock 'n' roll person. But lovely all the same,' recalls Graham Gilbert.

Rock 'n' roll person or not, it was Pippa who would save Norman from being imprisoned following a warehouse party in 1988. Cook was DJing at the illegal event in Brighton when the police stormed in. 'The police were breaking up the party, and they were being a bit rough with people,' he told *Melody Maker* in 1998. 'I moaned at them and they said I was obstructing them. In the end they said, "Go away or we'll nick you," and I said, "Go on then, fucking nick me!" So they did! Then I forgot to turn up for one of my court appearances! I was out shopping, and my wife knew I'd be in the local record shop, so she phoned me up and said, "Get down to court 'cos there's a warrant out for your arrest." My fault for being naïve enough to believe that the police had any essence of humanity about them, I suppose.

'In the end, I got done for breach of the peace and bound over. I haven't done parties since they started getting like that. They've been going for 10 or 12 years in this country, only they weren't called raves; they were called blues parties. But when the tabloids started writing about acid house, the police stated closing them down. The parties were about late drinking and all-night dancing, but as soon as drugs – or the reputation of drugs – took over, there was too much hassle. There's no point in carting all your records down there knowing you're only going to get them confiscated, nicked or something.'

By the end of the summer of 1989, Norman Cook had completed his debut album and delivered it to Go! Beat with the tongue-in-cheek title of *Let Them Eat Bingo*. A release date was set for early the following year, but they'd decided that they needed to launch the album off the back of a big single and a full UK tour.

The live show went under the title of Norman Cook's International Roadshow Versus The Real Sounds Of Africa and toured the UK's universities. The shows were a success in that they helped Norman focus his ideas and increased the working relationship between himself and the musicians involved in his own recordings. However, it was, as he openly admitted at the time, a financial disaster, thanks to the size of the band and the low turn-out at many of the gigs: 'Having 22 people on your tour costs a fortune. I honestly don't particularly rate dance music as a live phenomenon. It's just far too much hassle and effort, and the end result isn't particularly mindblowing. It worked as a show. Some nights we only got 50 or 60 people, but we still got two encores at the end. But considering the three weeks of rehearsal and the amount of money I lost on the tour, I don't want to do it again.'

In the same interview with *Melody Maker*, Norman also hinted at the possibility of his personal relationships suffering from the demands of touring: 'Also, I'm married and I don't want to spend six moths of every year away on tour if I can avoid it. Indie bands have to do countless gigs in shitty little clubs around England, and I did that for three years. I'm sure if they had a nightclub scene like dance has, they wouldn't bother! In dance music, you put out a promo, the track gets played around the underground nightclubs, and that's your version of doing gigs!'

A few years later, Norman would re-address his anti-touring stance when he formed Freakpower, who would tour endlessly throughout their career.

On 21 October 1989, the second Norman Cook solo single was released. Called 'For Spacious Lies' it placed Norman's musical and political agendas clearly in the picture. Musically, the single took its influence from a wide array of sources. The bassline echoed the techno-funk of artists like Cameo, while the beats once again came directly from the old-skool hip-hop lexicon. Voice samples featured numerous duck calls and hooklines lifted from electro. A brass line had seemingly been lifted directly from London's early-1980s soulboy club scene, while Spanish guitars and pianos picked out melodies reminiscent of mid-1980s Brit-funk outfits like Freeeze. Added to this mélange of dance sounds was a melody line that could have come from 1980s pop artists such as Haircut 100 or even The Housemartins.

The overall effect was strangely nostalgic, as if Norman was pointing himself and his listeners at a time when dance music was a more open and, in his eyes, more fun option. Essentially, 'For Spacious Lies' was a party record. Ironically, if Norman's major concern at the time was being perceived as a white kid doing black music, the single was strangely devoid of any of the nuances that you would have associated with black music of the time, despite the fact that the single was created from samples of tunes by, largely, black artists.

It was, of course, the coupling of melody lines and the horn refrain which created this soul-less veneer. Instead of conjuring images of wild block parties in the New York projects, it was drenched in the styles of Wham! and Spandau Ballet.

Lyrically, however, the single showed Norman defiantly waving his left-wing ideologies. Throughout the track, he put forward the concepts of freedom as another form of bondage, democracy as an unreal notion and all corporate industry being built on a bed of lies. 'Our army fights for money but we fight for peace,' sings syrupy vocalist Lester Noel before a defiant chorus declares, 'You won't put out this flame that burns so bright, through any wind any rain/You'll never put out the fire of a dream that will burn on and on.'

Despite the overall lyrical tone of the record and its echoes of The Housemartins' polemic, 'For Spacious Lies' was an insipid record which showed Norman to be out of step with the musical climate of the time. In attempting to make a great party record, he actually created a retro-pop anthem.

Dave Jennings of now-defunct UK weekly music paper *Melody Maker* also felt that the political agenda of the record displayed the producer going against the grain of the gatekeepers of pop culture at the time, so this was a pop record which wouldn't find its market. 'He may just have been too brave for his own good this time,' he wrote. 'For Spacious Lies' is an ambitious sonic collage that employs an unlikely combination of noises to make its point, from an irritating quacking bassline to an elegant Spanish guitar.

'Essentially a defiant we-shall-not-be-moved shout from the left, it may be too radical for both dance floors and radio – it's too thoughtful for most of the former, and the latter's notoriously nervous producers will quake at the coke reference, the raw polemic and the 12-inches closing curse. I'm impressed by the intentions and have some sympathy with the sentiments; rather like Siouxsie, Norm's attacking the men with "10-gallon hats and seven-pint heads". But somehow – maybe it's this grey Thursday morning – the unshakable optimism that Cook expresses via his new creamy-voiced mouthpiece doesn't convince me. He and I are obviously reading different newspapers.'

'I want to keep upsetting people and doing benefits and things, but I don't feel like we did with The Housemartins, that every single song has to have a political message,' said Norman at the time of the single's release.' We [The Housemartins] were just paranoid that, if we did a love song, people would accuse us of selling out. To a certain extent, I think that's still true – like when I hear some of The Beautiful South songs I think, "Where's the twist coming? Where's the political bite in it?" So I'm not interested in everything I do being political, but I still like to get the odd dig in with song titles, or whatever.'

'For Spacious Lies' peaked in the UK chart at number 48 and only remained in the top 100 for four weeks – hardly the great lead-in single that the record company had hoped for.

Throughout this period, Norman's career was marked by two major occurrences. The first would be his growth in status as a remixer. Following his success with Eric B And Rakim, he had been called on to rework artists as diverse as Digital Underground and James Brown – all to varying degrees of success, but all executed with the remarkable speed which had already marked out the recording process for the album.

'He obviously had an incredible talent,' recalls Kevin Stagg. 'The great thing about him, what I did realise at that point, was that he really did work fast. A lot of people don't realise how quick he is and how good he is. I often get people try to slag him off through jealousy, or whatever, but you couldn't slag him, really. In all the years that I've had the studio, I've never seen anyone make tracks as quickly as him. I think it comes from his love of music.'

Thanks to his high speed in the studio environment, Norman had been able to reintroduce himself to a fresh audience. In dance circles, his Housemartins roots were becoming increasingly forgotten.

'I thought people might think I was jumping on the bandwagon moving to dance,' he said at the time. 'I didn't know how people were going to take me. But then, when I started doing lost of remixes, most people buying the records didn't know I'd been in The Housemartins, or didn't even know who they were. I'm a white bloke moving into dance music, but this is what I've been interested in ever since I was 14. And after a while doing the remixes, and seeing people dance to them, I realised I'd almost rebuilt the whole tracks, and that gave me the confidence to do my own records.'

The other key development for him was the Norman Cook backlash which had started to rage in the letters pages of the UK music press. In an act which underlines the extent to which a divide existed between rock and dance music, fans of The Housemartins declared Norman as a traitor to real music thanks to his move into dance music and a number of his off-the-cuff remarks about indie bands (most notably The Smiths). In *NME*'s 'Angst' column he was variously described as an 'arsehole', an 'offensive little twat', a 'bandwagon jumper' and an 'indie sell-out'. Far from being embraced by the nation's indie-loving hordes, he was rejected for creating what was apparently throwaway disco music. To read many of the letters, you could be forgiven for thinking that this music was the spawn of the Devil himself! 'I was tempted to reply, but I thought I'd do it here,' he told *NME*'s Roger Morten in 1990. 'When people slag me off about my supposed sell-out, and for things I'd said about hallowed indie bands, I just think they take it too seriously. I'm just someone doing a job, which is to make people smile, dance or listen. And if I did that, everything else is immaterial.

'I'm not saying Morrissey's got it wrong. I don't think I'm any better than him because I slag him off. I'm just saying I found him boring. But to Morrissey fans that makes me a traitor. It's treason to slag off Morrissey, but I think someone should. Someone should bring him down to earth. He's blown it now. The Stone Roses have got it, but he was in the position where he was spokesman for a whole generation. And what did he say? He waffles, basically. He waffled on about Oscar Wilde, Sandie Shaw and ludicrous 1960s figures. Obviously he has a suss about politics and about life, but did he stand up and encourage people to change the world? No. He said, "Sit in your bedrooms and write poems to Oscar Wilde and worship James Dean," who was a knob-head actor who was stupid enough to kill himself... You know, I don't think it's responsible.'

If Norman's concerns about being seen as a white musician making black music revealed some of society's inverted racist attitudes, then the reaction against Norman's disco music revealed just how intolerant British society was at this time.

Disco (as all dance music was viewed by the rock audience) was considered to be black, or gay, music founded on a frivolous agenda, its very immediate and physical sound reducing it to the level of being merely temporary. 'On several occasions I can recall being asked what sort of music I liked to listen to and whenever I said it was soul or funk or rap the reaction would always be, "*What?* Disco music?", Norman once explained to *Melody Maker*, recalling the friction his love of dance music caused in The Housemartins. 'It made me feel terribly alienated, and even though Paul was the first person who introduced me to black music by playing me his old blues and Stax records when we were 15 or 16 years old – everyone else around us were into The Smiths – backstage there would often be conversations about bands that I'd never even heard of.'

The success of disco in the late 1970s had resulted in quite extreme reactions from snobbish white rock-music fans. Most notably, in the US this resulted in the infamous 'Disco Sucks' campaign. At the height of this anti-disco movement, DJ Steve Dahl invited the people of Chicago to bring their unwanted disco records along to a baseball game at Comiskey Park between the Chicago White Sox and the Detroit Tigers. During the intermission, some 100,000 records were piled up into a huge mound and then blown up with dynamite. A full-blown riot followed. As a result of the vinyl fall-out, the match was postponed and the game was forfeited by the White Sox.

As Simon Reynolds pointed out in his excellent history of dance music *Energy Flash*, 'The "Disco Sucks" phenomenon recalls the Nazi book burnings, or the exhibitions of Degenerate Art. Modern-day spectacles of *Kulturekampf* like Comiskey were impelled by a similar disgust; the belief that disco was rootless, inauthentic, decadent, a betrayal of the virile principles of the true American *Volkmusik*, rock 'n' roll. Hence T-shirts like "Death Before Disco", hence organisations like DREAD (Detroit Rockers Engaged in the Abolition of Disco) and Dahl's own Insane Coho Lips Antidisco Army.'

Disco may have gone into total creative decline by the time that Norman had started making dance music, but the anti-disco attitudes carried on into the rock and alternative scenes of the 1980s, despite artists like The Clash doing their best to introduce dance themes into their sound.

Norman Cook then took the full force of this intolerance with letters from the fans of his old band declaring him to be a white kid who wanted to be black and – in an echo of earlier rumours about The Housemartins published in the tabloid media – that he was obviously gay. The concept that a straight, white male would be capable of loving dance music was apparently beyond many of these people.

There were two ironies about this backlash. The first was in the fact that Norman himself had already crossed the rock/dance divide when he went to join his friends in Hull. If any treachery had existed, it came with Norman's initial defection – although this concept is ridiculously outmoded now. The second irony was that Norman's involvement with The Housemartins actually made him more noticeable in a scene that was noted for its faceless producers and DJs. 'I'm in a privileged position because of The Housemartins, which is nice,' he said at the time. 'I was recognised by Matt Black from Coldcut the other day. It made my year. That and Arthur Baker – he knew every mix I'd done.'

With the Norman Cook moniker receiving negative press and his continued lack of success as a solo artist he came up with the notion of creating a collective of musicians. The recording process for the album had brought a constant stream of people through the doors of the studio and although a band wasn't on the cards, a loose family of people was. Through this process he would also be able to tackle his solo material on the road as more than just a DJ.

DUB BE GOOD TO ME

Towards the end of 1989, Norman came up with the new name of Beats International, under which his solo material would now be released. The first single from this new so-called collective would be a version of The SOS Band's disco classic 'Just Be Good To Me'.

The idea for the song had initially come from vocalist Lindy Layton, whose management company had approached Norman with a view to him producing their new protégée. Belinda Kimberly Layton (born 7 December 1970 in Chiswick, London) had already reached a level of fame through acting in the British children's soap opera *Grange Hill*, which followed the fortunes of a group of schoolkids.

When Lindy first came to Brighton to discuss ideas with Norman, the notion of a cover of The SOS Band's best-known song came up. Although Lindy had been inspired by the free-party scene that was hugely popular in London at the time, she had her sights set on a more poppy dance sound, and 'Just Be Good To Me' encompassed much of the atmosphere she was after.

Typically, Norman approached the track more like a remix, taking the melody and completely recreating the structure of the song. He added a hip-hop flavour to the cut-ups, but most notably he built the track around a reggae bassline lifted from The Clash's 'Guns Of Brixton'. 'The bassline of the single, that's an affectionate tribute to The Clash,' he explained to *NME*. 'It's like tipping my cap to them because they were a huge influence on my growing up, both musically and politically.'

Perhaps one of the highlights of The Clash's third album, *London*

Calling, 'Guns Of Brixton' was actually written by bassist Paul Simonon after he discovered that the lion's share of band royalties went to main lyricists and songwriters Joe Strummer and Mick Jones. Simonon decided he wanted to earn more money and so penned the track, presenting it to the band as a *fait accompli*.

According to Marcus Grey's exhaustive biography of The Clash, *The Last Gang In Town*, Cook changed his mind about the source of the infectious bassline after Paul Simonon approached him for royalties: 'Norman changed his tune (or, at least, the source for his tune), claiming he had lifted the bassline from an obscure reggae track.'

Given Simonon's well-documented love of reggae, which had been with him since childhood, it is conceivable that his original source for the bassline was buried in an old and obscure reggae dub plate, forgotten by all but the most ardent lover of reggae. And with Cook's similarly obsessive love of music, it is possible that he would have known of the original record. However Norman's version is so close to Simonon's bassline in tone, feel and energy that there is little doubt that his inspiration came from The Clash. Any claims that the bassline was recreated, vinyl scratches included, seems far-fetched given his magpie nature on releases thus far. Furthermore, Norman Cook had a love of The Clash that went back to his youth. The original suggestion that the song was an 'affectionate tribute' seemed more likely.

In an interview with *Melody Maker*'s Dave Jennings in 1990, Norman seemed to contradict any claims that he'd lovingly recreated the sample. 'I could go back and re-record everything, just make it sound like it was sampled, but I prefer to use the original stuff – I prefer not to worry about some greedy lawyer,' he exclaimed. 'It's only money. And the stupid thing is, it's only the lawyers and publishers who win – the actual artists don't, by the time the lawyers fees are taken out.'

However, he later conceded, 'The original idea for the music was as a personal tribute to The Clash. As far as I'm concerned, they were probably the greatest band ever, not only for what they did for rock but also for the way they weren't afraid to experiment, particularly with black music. They were the first white band to pick up on reggae and rap, and although a lot of people laughed at them and dismissed their ideas at the time, they were way ahead of their time. What they were doing with tracks like "The Magnificent Seven" is exactly what The Stone Roses are doing now [back in 1990]. The difference is, The Clash did it eight years ago.'

The situation was eventually rectified with an out-of-court settlement. Far from being angered at the appropriation of what was his finest hour, Simonon felt inspired enough to commission one-time Hayzee Fantayzee vocalist and renowned DJ Jeremy Healey to remix the original 'Guns Of Brixton'. However, it failed to reach anywhere near the same level of success as 'Dub Be Good To Me', stalling instead at number 57 in the UK charts.

There was an underlying irony in Cook's use of a Clash bassline, one that relates again to notions of blackness in music. In attempting to create a reggae feel to the track, he looked not to the sounds of Jamaica but to a white punk-rock group who had themselves been accused of appropriating black culture.

Such accusations were rejected out of hand by The Clash, as at least two of them (Jones and Simonon) had grown up in strongly black communities in London, and that's where their influences came from. Furthermore, the punk scene found unlikely allies in reggae's Rastafarians, as both took an oppositional stance against the system. This relationship was subsequently celebrated in Bob Marley's 'Punky Reggae Party' record.

Norman, however, had grown up in a very white suburban enclave in the affluent Home Counties. He could never claim any allusion to otherness, but he could boast a deep love of black music – a fact that filtered through the pop tones of 'Dub Be Good To Me'.

In the 3 February 1990 issue of *Melody Maker*, Simon Reynolds' tone was entirely positive in his review of the single: 'I really enjoyed Norman Cook's "Blame It On The Bassline". It was witty and nifty and funked up like a mutha, and his reincarnation from jangle pop drummer to dancefloor maestro is wonderfully bizarre. This is a traffic, deep-dub version of The SOS Band's fabulous "Just Be Good To Me", the heartquake synths of the original replaced by soaring bleeps, ocean-bed alarms, lugubrious horns and a lonesome *Midnight Cowboy* harmonica. Just fine.'

'Dub Be Good To Me' debuted in the UK charts at number 29 on 10 February. In the next two weeks it crept up to number four and number two respectively until it finally displaced Sinéad O'Connor's MTV-conquering 'Nothing Compares 2 U' from the top slot. After a couple of false starts as Norman Cook, the ex-Housemartin had finally arrived under the moniker Beats International, with a song originally intended for Lindy Layton's solo career.

The track itself would also pre-empt the summer of 1990's soundtrack to Ibiza, which found things becoming more relaxed, with cuts like St Etienne's 'Only Love Will Break Your Heart' and tracks from The Grid and The Bocca Juniors pushing this more chilled vibe. Indeed, a Channel 4 documentary about that year's Ibiza scene would be aptly called *A Short Film About Chilling*. A year later, the Ibiza soundtrack would once again be uptempo as the influence of Italian House was felt.

Ironically, Norman hadn't been convinced that 'Dub Be Good...' would make a good single at the time. As Kev Stagg recalls, 'When they did "Dub Be Good To Me", I said to Norman, "That is a massive record, it's going to be a hit," and he said, "Nah, it's only an album track." I even had a little bet with Norman on that one that it would go to number one. And I won. Back then, getting a number one was a massive thing. I think it surprised Norm, 'cos he wasn't convinced that it was. And it was great for the studio as well, because the track was completely recorded and mixed here.'

With the huge success of 'Dub Be Good To Me' came the writs. Not only did Simonon make an issue of his bassline being used but other artists also claimed royalty rights for use of everything from a snare sample to lyrical lifts.

Norman explained at the time: 'As things stand at the moment, we are giving away 250 per cent of the money from 'Dub Be Good To Me'. We are in a position to lose 150 per cent on every copy sold. We've got people who I never sampled claiming 50 per cent, not just of the songwriting but of the entire record. Publishers are so greedy that they don't say, "OK, you used one snare drum of ours, so we want two percentage points." They always want 50 per cent of royalties. And obviously I can't give away 50 per cent for snare drum, 50 per cent for kit drums, 50 per cent for a note on the bass and so on – that's why I just won't talk about the samples.

'The easiest thing to do is keep quiet. And some of the samples on the album are so distorted that even the people who did do them originally wouldn't recognise them – you know, they're chopped up into little pieces or played backwards. That's half the fun of sampling.'

On of the key lines of questioning around this time was the reggae atmosphere of 'Dub Be Good To Me'. One *NME* journalist suggested that Norman had purposefully written the track in order to get reggae back in the charts again. Given his success rate so far in creating hit singles, however, the notion was half thought out to say the least.

Norman's reply was telling: 'I have this love/hate relationship with reggae because it's not progressed in 10 years, not musically. I mean, the toasting and dancehall side has, but the only time reggae gets into the charts is when they do lover's [rock] covers of well-known songs. During the 1970s and Bob Marley, it was like the next big thing, but it never really lived up to expectations. I'm more into ska.

'I wanted to do something different. I suppose it was a reaction against the pun "from Housemartins to housemaster" because I don't like house music. Also, it was a reaction to the ravers' scene, which as a DJ I find boring, you know? Because I've spent years building up a collection of what I think are brilliant records, and now everyone wants to hear records all night that sound the same.

'I went to the Hacienda on a Friday night, the big house night, and it sounded all the same all night. I mean, maybe I'm getting old and that's what the kids are into, but not me. I'm sick to death of all these bleedin' Italian records. And it was definitely an attempt not to do that. Reggae's about the most unhip form of black music at the moment. And that appealed to my rather perverse sense of humour.'

Perverse sense of humour or not, what is certain is that in 'Dub Be Good To Me' Norman displayed his uncanny ability to conjure perfect pop moments from the most disparate sources. In many ways this single showed Norman accidentally colliding with the mood of the times. The dance arena may have turned to the narrower sound of rave, but the influence of dance culture had also spilled over into indie. The result came with bands like The Stone Roses and Happy Mondays, who would take their decidedly retro approach to guitar music and add dance rhythms to create the blueprint for a sound described as 'baggy' in the UK media.

'I think it's funny that the same people who were slagging me off for liking dance music while I was in The Housemartins are now going out and buying their remixes. I try not to be too smug about it,' explained Norman at the time, when it seemed that indie kids (and bands) were suddenly 'defecting' to the dance scene.

Extremely influential at this stage (and to this overall movement) was Andrew Weatherall's Balearic-inspired remix of Primal Scream's 'Loaded', in which the 1960s Rolling Stones wannabes were given a complete makeover which would change the course of their careers entirely. The single would change the course of music history into the bargain.

Also instrumental in this sea-change were positive soul outfits like Soul2Soul, who had introduced the unity of rave aesthetics into their post-hip-hop eulogies.

'Dub Be Good To Me' profited from this albeit short-lived open-mindedness, which came with the defection of indie kids to the dance arena. People were hearing new music and discovering a world outside the traditional gig, and the excitement that went with this resulted in the embracing of all things dance. Above all else, this was a period of mass exploration.

When this wide-eyed excitement was combined with the effects of ecstasy (which would hugely affect people's judgement), a huge number of very average records filtered through into the charts. Among these, however, were the odd classics. 'Dub Be Good To Me' was one of them.

In an interview in *Record Mirror*, however, vocalist Lindy Layton wasn't quite so supportive of the single's claims to be a 'classic'. 'Let's face it,' she said, 'there was nothing original about "Dub Be Good To Me". Someone else's song, someone else's bassline. In fact, the only original thing about the song was my vocals.'

At least one Italian production team felt the same, as a white label surfaced at the same time with a progressive Italo-house version of the track, courtesy of the *a cappella* on the original's 12" version. Naturally, Norman approved of the DIY sampling ethic behind the version, even though it was terrible.

Although the original idea had been Lindy's, she and Norman remained on good terms. Not only did she become a semi-permanent member of the Beats International collective for the next year, she also moved into Norman's Dyke Road Flat (from where the band's information service, Pig City, was also run) and would remain a close friend through thick and thin.

Sadly, 'Dub Be Good To Me' would prove to be the last time that Beats International were in tune with the culture of the times. Indeed, it would be the last time for almost four years that Norman Cook would walk hand in hand with the music of the time. It is arguable that what happened was a result of Norman's perverse sense of humour, or it could have been due to his inability to embrace the changes in dance culture. Whatever the reason, the pattern that followed is one that has been repeated throughout his career. Certainly the final release of *Let Them Eat Bingo* in April 1990 displayed the extent to which Norman's anti-house perversity was prepared to travel. Through the album's 11 tracks, he explored hip-hop, disco, salsa, Burundi beats, soul, funk, electro – anything in fact apart from house!

Thanks to both Norman's (ironically) narrow-minded approach and Go! Beat's inability to adjust their way of working to suit the speed at which the dance scene was changing (*Let Them Eat Bingo* was almost a year old), Norman's debut album already sounded out of date.

The title to the album itself was a play on Marie Antoinette's pre-French Revolution dismissal of peasant hunger. When told 'The peasants are revolting, they have no bread,' her reply, as legend would have it, was, 'Then let them eat cake.' By changing the adage to read 'Let them eat bingo!', Cook both used the quote to represent his approach to music (taking something which already exists, and then altering it to suit his own vision) and also translated it into the vernacular of British tabloid media.

'I think tabloid newspapers have got this attitude of keeping people in their place by offering one of them £1 million as a bingo prize,' he said at the time offering an unsophisticated Marxist reading of the media. 'Everyone else just hopes for it and that's the way people, are kept in their place. Basically I'm saying, "Look what happened to Marie Antoinette…"'

Opening with the bird sounds and a kitsch sample from 1970s British children's animation *Camberwick Green*, the album moved directly into 'Burundi Blues', which, as the title suggested, combines African grooves with an old blues track. Both are underpinned by a loping bassline, a repeated African nose flute sample and a muted jazzy horn solo. With the addition of vocals lifted from an old electro cut, Norman laid down his album blueprint in the one track.

'Burundi Blues' proved to be one of the album's high points, although when it was eventually released as a single in September 1990 it only managed to reach the lowly position of number 51 in the UK charts. In retrospect, this track would lay the foundations for many of his Fatboy Slim excursions while also providing the template for some of Moby's *Play* album, among others.

'Dub Be Good To Me' follows 'Burundi Blues', with Lindy Layton's naïve vocals and Norman's wide-eyed arrangement sounding just as strong in the context of an album. 'Before I Grow Too Old' was the first track to display the cracks in Norman's approach to dance. Once again, the main influences came from African sounds, embellished with electro and hip-hop frills. However, in much the same way that 'For Spacious Lies' had sounded as though it belonged to another era, the combination of the horn refrains and melody line sung by Lester Noel located 'Before I Grow Too Old' in the early to mid 1980s.

Lester Noel was introduced to the media at the time as the only other full-time member of Beats International. Born on 3 September 1962, Lester had previously been a member of the indie outfit Grab Grab The Haddock, which had been formed from ashes of Tracey 'Everything But The Girl' Thorne's first band, Marine Girls. Grab Grab The Haddock was formed by sisters Jane and Alice Fox, and Noel would join later to record the band's two EPs for Cherry Red Records.

Perhaps thanks to their ridiculous name, Grab Grab The Haddock failed to capture the imagination of the British nation and they split in 1986, when Noel went on to form the much-vaunted indie band North Of Cornwallis.

Norman Cook had actually met Lester during his Housemartins days, when he was a regular at their gigs. 'You couldn't fail to spot him at gig,' explained Norman to *NME*. 'I mean, all right we were an indie band. Lester, this nutty, seven-foot-tall black kid with a high-top haircut, was pogo-ing away at the front of the audience. It was weird.'

'I'd been into indie stuff for years,' continued Lester. 'I used to sing and play guitar with an indie band called North of Cornwallis and we even supported The Housemartins a few times. To be honest, it's only very recently that I've started to like black music, and I think that lots of indie kids are similarly switching their allegiances because of people like The Beloved, The Stone Roses and Happy Mondays making dance records. The problem with the indie scene is that it has become hopelessly stagnant and far too serious. Dance music is much less po-faced.'

Ironically, Lester Noel had also been Housemartins' Stan Cullimore's first choice of vocalist for his solo project. When he contacted Norman for Lester's number, the Brighton producer wouldn't pass on the details. He already had plans for Lester!

Despite Lester's rich and smooth delivery, his tracks would prove to be the weakest links on *Let Them Eat Bingo*, due largely to the material he was singing, which tended to sound forced. Indeed, these vocal tracks seemed to be more in line with an indie record label's concept of dance music.

'The Ragged Trouser Percussionist' continues the album's obsession with Afro-Beats, proving again that Norman's strengths lay in the more rhythmical instrumental arena – a fact once again underlined by the inclusion of 'For Spacious Lies', with its weak melody, followed immediately by the dancefloor fave 'Blame It On The Bassline'.

In a report in *Record Mirror* at the time, 'Blame It On The Bassline' was apparently given the seal of approval by Michael Jackson, who was at the time the undisputed king of pop (his album *Thriller* remains the epitome of dance pop at its best). However, given Go! Beat/Go! Discs' managing director Andy MacDonald's love of scam stories, it's possible that he had invented the story to provide Norman with kudos. After all, despite success with his remixes, singles and DJing, he was still regarded in the dance world as an indie chancer.

'Won't Talk About It' followed, proving to be the album's high point. The main reason is that Billy Bragg's vocals and melody line supplied enough of a groove for Norman to create a backing track that oozed soul. On this track, Norman came closest to transcending any accusations of appropriation of black music. Instead, he created a track which displayed a natural feel for the sensuality of soul.

A month after the album's release, Beats International put out a new version of 'Won't Talk About It' with vocal duties taken up by Lindy and Lester. Although not as good as the original, the single went to number nine in the UK top 20.

'Dance To The Drummer's Beat', a remake of Herman Kelly and Life's 1978 track of the same name, continued the DJ mix theme of raw instrumentals, lifting King Sunny Ade-style guitars, adding Italian pianos and sax hooks galore to create a Funkadelic-inspired groove. 'Babies Makin' Babies (Stoop Rap)' found Norman resurrecting some of the ideas from his Housemartins-era 'The Finest Ingredients' track, only added to the cut-and-paste DJ mix was a human beatbox, a laid-back De La Soul-style rap courtesy of Double Trouble. The track was very much in the spirit of Coldcut's groundbreaking '(Say Kids) What Time Is It?'.

On 'The Whole World's Down On Me', Cook himself delivers the vocal line. Although weak in comparison to Bragg's inclusion (Cook, by his own admission, is not a singer), on this track the vocals fuse perfectly with the Rockers reggae meets electro-style track. In one of the album's many jokes, British Radio 1 DJ Simon Bates (a household name in the 1980s) could be heard asking, 'Please would someone tell me about Norman Cook? I'd really like to know. Norman Cook, it's a wonderful song.' Perhaps unsurprisingly, the post-acid-house revolution would soon consign Bates to the Radio 1 scrapheap.

The final track came in the shape of Norman's 'Tribute To King Tubby'. Despite its portentous title, the somewhat lightweight track proved to be one of the album's most disappointing moments. King Tubby had been a leading light in 1970s reggae production, inventing many aspects of the dub mix and passing on his techniques through his own studios. Sadly, his life ended abruptly in February 1989 when Tubby was shot and killed during a robbery outside his home, although his legacy lives on in many of the techniques still employed in contemporary leftfield dance music.

Cook's tribute is one of his most pedestrian DJ mixes, using obvious samples (Ladysmith Black Mambazo, among many others) and relatively clumsy production. Overall, like much of the album, the main influence comes from the music of South African townships. Any Jamaican influence you might have expected in a track called 'Tribute To King Tubby' went by almost unnoticed.

Initial quantities of the album came with an extra eight-track album of bonus beats called *Bingo Beats*. This was a tactic employed by a number of hip-hop outfits at the time. In the UK, The Stereo MCs' 1989 album *Supernatural* had created quite a stir while Norman had been working on the Beats International album.

In many ways, *Bingo Beats* was superior to the main album (arrangements were stripped to the rhythm and bare melody for DJ use) as it was a remix work, and it was here that Norman was delivering his most interesting productions. Furthermore, thanks to its stringent DJ focus, this set was more cohesive than the original.

Beats International's debut album wasn't the runaway creative success that people might have hoped for. With it, Norman faced the dilemma that would cause problems for dance producers for years to come: the needs of the album were completely different to the needs of a single. One was for long-term home listening while the other was aimed squarely at the dancefloor. The dilemma which always faced the artist then was how to translate the ephemeral nature of the single for the timeless nature of the album.

Let Them Eat Bingo suffered enormously from sounding dated, as opposed to sounding timeless. By the time of its release, it seemed to be belligerently in opposition to the culture of the times. More than anything, *Let Them Eat Bingo* sounded like Norman's own take on Malcolm

McLaren's *Duck Rock* album from 1983. On this hugely influential but often-overlooked album, the one-time Sex Pistols boss assimilated the indigenous sounds of Africa (among those of other continents) and mixed them with hip-hop to create a world-music party album. Very much the blueprint for Norman Cook's united world vision at the end of the 1980s.

1990 was the year in which England responded to the house explosion with its own hardcore sound, where breakbeats previously associated with hip-hop were sampled, cut up and speeded up. They were then added to furious techno sounds to create hard, energetic dancefloor sounds.

1990 was also the year in which artists like Aphex Twin and Black Dog first started to deliver their own idiosyncratic takes on electronic music, in which LFO created the soundtrack to northern England's industrial landscape, and in which ambient artists like Dr Alex Paterson's The Orb project laid down the blueprint for the chill-out. The dance arena had changed almost beyond recognition from only 12 months earlier, and Norman Cook was found to be defiantly stuck in the past.

'When I was doing the album,' Norman explained to *Melody Maker* at the time, 'I thought, "This is going to flop, 'cos it's so unfashionable. But if it does flop, at least I've tried." There are people who like different kinds of dance music, and they're the people who are at the bar in clubs at the moment because the music they like isn't being played. We're not getting very good reaction from specialist people to the album, and I can fully understand that because it's not an out-and-out soul album. If you strip down the samples and all that, they are just pop songs.

'There's nothing uncool about a good tune. I can't listen to most dance albums because normally they're just regurgitated versions of the single. So, if you're doing an album, you've got to try and do something different. Make it listenable, make it interesting, make the tracks varied!

'Obviously, when Technotronic [Belgian hip house turned pop act who scored huge hits with tracks like 'Pump Up The Jam', 'This Beat Is Technotronic' and 'Get Up (Before The Night Is Over)' between 1989 and 1992] go into the studio, they're thinking sales, they're thinking hip. I just think, "I'm going to make a record and see what it turns out like." I just made a whole lot of records, put them together and it sounded like an album.

'I don't mean to ghettoise my music and say everything's got to sound really cool, hard and tough. That's why "Dub Be Good To Me" was the perfect crossover. It started with ravers, because the bassline was so heavy and nutty that they could get into it, and they knew the song. And yet that could cross over, be bought by housewives and be sung by my five-year-old next-door neighbour! But some of the tracks on the album she probably couldn't cope with because they're so heavy, and other tracks ravers couldn't cope with because they're so poppy. I suppose I'll always be floundering around the middle, not quite knowing which one is me!'

In truth, Norman saw the Beats International collective and sound to be more in keeping with developments in the UK hip-hop and soul arenas, drawing more comfort from comparisons to Soul2Soul, thanks to their eclectic sound and collective nature. 'The number of people [in Beats International] grows daily, but at the moment I guess there are 25 or 30 people all told,' he told *Melody Maker*. 'That includes the graffiti artist who opens up our gigs by paining the backdrop live [Req] and the guy who designs our T-shirts. Basically, anyone can be in Beats International. It's been described as a kind of Soul2Soul, which is flattering and I guess fairly accurate in view of the fact that it's more of a collective than a pop group, with different people appearing on different records. Mind you, I've no plans to open a clothes shop just yet.'

Let Them Eat Bingo failed to go top 10 in the UK, settling in the number 17 position and remaining in the charts for only 15 weeks. For a chart-topping act, this was disastrous. Of the many reasons why the album failed to ignite the British public in the same way that 'Dub Be Good To Me' had, perhaps the most obvious was that they faced discrimination from the record-buying public. The white indie kids had declared Norman to be a traitor; the dance cognoscenti were increasingly hung up on house and techno and subsequently didn't give a wrap about Norman's brand of the DJ mix.

Another section of the public to vent its feelings was the hip-hop scene. Despite Norman's obvious love of the techniques of breakbeat manipulation as invented by New York DJ Kool Herc, the hip-hop kids simply hated Beats International. At a Kiss FM live show in support of LL Cool J in the summer of 1990, the band were canned off stage in a volatile expression of the crowd's hatred for them.

Lindy Layton's explanation of the event was defensive to say the least: 'It was just a few people down the front who thought we consisted of one ex-Housemartin and a Heinz spaghetti girl, and that we didn't belong on the same bill as some of the acts,' she complained to *Record Mirror*. 'Even I thought, "What the hell are we doing here?". The London crowds diss just horribly. It's true. They just stand there holding their bits as if to say, "Go on, impress me." It's cool not to move, to look proud and not to be impressed by anybody.'

On more than one occasion, Beats became the targets for disgruntled punters with over-filled beer glasses. Indeed, in 1990 Norman was reported to have become so fed up with the constant rain of beer being spat and thrown at him and his band that he finally snapped and threw a can into the throng. 'Let's see how you like it!' he shouted.

When asked later if this was the responsible thing to do, Norman revealed that behind the mild-mannered exterior is someone who will only go so far before he hits back. 'I'm not into violence,' he declared to *NME*, 'but if something needs sorting out, I'll sort it out. It used to be a lot simpler with The Housemartins, though. All you had to do was swing the bass at someone and they'd back off... You can't do much with a pair of turntables.'

Despite continued gigging, more often than not to rapturous reception, Beats International's record sales started to slip dramatically. In September 1990, they reached only number 51 with the release of 'Burundi Blues'. However, it could have been argued that this was largely due to the track being yet another lift from the album.

The release of the final single from *Let Them Eat Bingo* saw the first version of Beats International drawing to a close. Although strictly a collective, there had been certain standard musicians throughout. Vocalists Lindy Layton and Lester Noel had contributed to the live shows constantly. Keyboard player Andy Boucher was another constant, as was MC Wildski. The live show had also featured live graffiti from Brighton artist Req.

The first person to move on from the Beats fold was Lindy, who finally launched her solo career in 1990 with a version of 'Silly Games', which was produced by Norman. The single went top 20, suggesting that Lindy might have more longevity as a solo artist than as a member of Beats. In January 1991, she would release the Prince-like 'Echo My Heart', which failed to follow its predecessor's success. The album which followed, *Pressure*, contained three more Norman Cook productions and a song called 'Do Me', written especially for her by the pre-symbol Prince.

'There's no point going around thinking you're something special, because you're not. I want to be approachable and there's no one standing over me with a big stick saying, "You'll do it this way,"' she told *Record Mirror*'s Johnny Dee of the album's direction. 'It was hard writing and going round the world with Beats at the same time. But the people I've worked with are very professional and very much on the same wavelength.

'Norman's started the next album and I'm going to be singing on just one track,' she continued, 'but I'm not going to be fronting anything with them any more. I don't have to tear myself between the two things any more. We still help each other. He's produced three tracks on my album.'

Lindy's album was received poorly when it finally appeared in 1991. Perhaps unsurprisingly, it also sold poorly in the UK, but it proved to be very popular in Japan, which resulted in her spending a large amount of her time over there. She also increasingly took up DJing throughout this period, gaining quite a reputation in the process.

In 1997, Lindy returned to music as one half of the big-beat duo Hardknox, signing to Brighton's Skint imprint and gaining two *NME* Single Of The Weeks with their first two singles. In 1999, they signed to US label Jive and toured with Moby before releasing their self-titled debut album, which displayed a movement towards the rockier sound of Prodigy. Again, the album failed to cross over.

The disappearance of Beats International is one of the mysteries of modern music. Despite their earlier successes, when it came to their second album you would have been forgiven for thinking that they were an unknown band, such was the lack of interest in them. And yet, the period between the band debut album and their second instalment,

Excursion On The Version, had been an insanely busy time for Norman. Primarily he had stepped up a gear with the remix work, taking on numerous high-profile projects – The Osmonds' 'One Bad Apple', James Brown's 'The Payback Mix', Fine Young Cannibals' 'Not The Man I Used To Be' and Aussie superstars INXS's 'Elegantly Wasted'. Perhaps the most interesting thing about Norman's remix work was his willingness to be more experimental. However the foundation of this work still lay in his love of old-skool hip-hop and DJ mixes.

Beyond the remix work he toured the world with Beats International and continued with his DJing outings during this time. He had also found time to do production work for Lindy on her album and for various other artists, including tracks on British soul singer David Grant's acclaimed 1990 album *Anxious Edge* and rap reggae fusionist Shinehead's less well-received *Sidewalk University* project.

The David Grant album was particularly notable as it cemented a working relationship between Norman and Island dance offshoot 4th And Broadway. Among the other projects that Norman undertook at this time was a remix for London freeform jazz funk outfit Microgroove, featuring Ashley Slater who would go onto become one of Norman's longest-standing songwriting and production partners.

Ashley Slater was born in Canada in 1962 and grew up in California before moving to England in 1977. The move coincided with the first wave of British punk rock, and his parents feared that the young music lover would be turned on to this particular brand of freakery. Luckily for them, his main musical loves lay in the no-less-freakish areas of jazz and funk, while he also had a love of artists like Frank Zappa. As a young adult, Ashley built quite a reputation as a trombonist, working with some of the jazz world's more experimental musicians (including Brass Fantasy with Lester Bowie, who would later achieve global acclaim with his Arts Ensemble Of Chicago). Bowie's brothers, Joe and Byron, also gained some notoriety in the early 1980s, working as Defunkt, a band whose influence would feature in Ashley's work with Norman.

Ashley formed Microgroove in the late 1980s and signed to Island Records. However, the band were dropped before their first single was released – which is when he started working with Norman (who had remixed the single) in Beats International. Slater's first introduction to Norman Cook came through a trombone session he did on Norman's remix work for revered UK soul pop outfit The Christians. Norman had seen Ashley with Microgroove and had become a fan of both the band and the imposing and flamboyant figure of trombonist/vocalist Slater.

Although Norman's remix of Microgroove was never to be released (Slater's band were unceremoniously dropped from Island instead), the Christians' session was a huge success and the first sparks of the duo's working relationship were to be seen. Soon afterwards, Ashley would become a regular visitor to Esselle, with the Microgroove Horns supplying brass to Norman's productions, while Microgroove themselves would become Beats International's backing band for live work.

At a time when the band had seemed to be on the skids, Beats International supplied Microgroove with regular paid work as session musicians, both live and in the studio. They were also provided with exposure for their own material when they took on the role of support band throughout the world tours. It was an arrangement that worked perfectly for both Cook and Slater, despite the fact that the two were rumoured not to have liked each other to start with.

Norman was in a workaholic state of mind, and his remixing and production work started to melt seamlessly into a Beats International session for their second album. Indeed, at times it wasn't clear which project he was working on as ideas from remixes would quickly spill over into Beats tracks, and vice versa.

Kevin Stagg recalls the atmosphere in the studio throughout this period: 'It was a really good, positive period. I had this arrangement with Norman that he could just call me on the day to see if the studio was available. When he and Simon [Thornton] were working, there would be this constant stream of people just hanging around in the courtyard. It was hard to tell who was actually in Beats International. Everyone had a part to play. My wife even did some backing vocals on a couple of tracks.'

Indeed, in an alleyway beside Esselle, there lies a testament to this period. Norman's now-rusted Vespa scooter still sits there, complete with smiley stickers and only 3,000 miles on the clock. 'Norman just arrived on this scooter one day,' recalls Stagg, 'and we all had a go on it. I crashed it straight away, but Norman just thought it was hilarious.'

In February 1991, two months shy of a year since the release of *Let Them Eat Bingo*, Beats International delivered their second album. There was no lead-in single, no hit to try to hang the album on, just a 12-track collection going under the name *Excursion On The Version*. Promotion and marketing were virtually non-existent and the British media hardly even noticed, while the only US magazine to give it even the most cursory mention was *Creem*.

It is conceivable that Norman had wanted this collection to enjoy a more organic growth, as befitting a dance artist. He had increasingly grown wary of the media and hated doing interviews, so it would have suited him for the promotion to have come via word of mouth and through promos being played in the clubs. The problem was that this album was even further removed from the contemporary dance scene than *Let Them Eat Bingo*.

Excursion On The Version arrived at a time when the indie pop-dance crossover was typified by vaguely 1960s-sounding melodies played over a Stone Roses-style shuffle groove. British hip-hop had all but disappeared, its producers and MCs defecting to either the rave arena or the nascent acid-jazz scene.

It was in the latter area that Beats International might have found the most likely musical allies, thanks to their joint love of funk, jazz, hip-hop and Afro beat, but it was a scene which was built around the cool of the right clothes, as much as the music. And if there was one thing that Norman Cook could not lay claim to, it was being 'cool'.

The heart of *Excursion On The Version* lay in the title itself. The 'version' was the name the Jamaican producers would use when creating dub, or instrumental dub plates, of tracks for soundsystem MCs to chat over. These precursors to remix and DJ culture would have a huge influence on Norman's music, most notably the sounds culled from the ska and rocksteady era between 1965 and 1971, the era that directly preceded the roots (or African cultural roots) era typified by Bob Marley.

The jump-up, half-beat rhythms and horns of ska would become regular references for Norman Cook, but it was the slower rocksteady sound that he could be found exploring on *Excursion On The Version*. In this sound, the horns, although prominent, took a back seat to the vocal melody, while the bass and drums took on a greater importance. The overall sound was subsequently smoother, and in many ways funkier.

Among the finest moments of rocksteady were cuts from the likes of Jimmy Cliff, Desmond Dekker and The Wailers. However, it was the producers behind the artists that were ringing the real changes in the sound. People like Lee 'Scratch' Perry, Lesley Kong, King Tubby and Bunny Lee came through with their innovative approach. Among these innovations was Perry's versioning technique of delivering lengthened instrumental cuts with rhythm underlined and melody all but removed.

The rocksteady sound and version technique would not only give way to the 1970s dub reggae but, much later, would also go on to influence the dancehall sounds, which would then give way to bashment, which in turn would become a huge influence on the late- and new-millennial R&B of Timabaland, Missy Elliot, NERD, Kelis etc and the UK garage sound of So Solid Crew etc.

With *Excursion On The Version*, Cook could be certainly heard wearing his rocksteady heart on his sleeve and melting the influence into the now-expected brew of the sounds of South African Soweto townships, hip-hop, electro and 1980s DJ mix-production techniques. However, despite the album's title, this excursion seemed to be anything but a holiday. Beneath the seemingly joyous, celebratory nature of the music lay a sense of sadness. Lyrically, many of the album's tracks walked a darkened path.

The album's opener was the deceptively positive 'Brand New Beat'. However, sonically it laid down the blueprint for much of what followed. Despite its title, 'Brand New Beat' features a number of old ideas, most notably the heavy use of South African rhythm, melody and guitar, rocksteady horn arrangements in three-part harmony and lyrical content based on 'me ragamuffin dumpling'. Added to this was a spoken rap reminiscent of many of the UK MCs of the time, from Galliano to Massive Attack. The overall effect was a kind of Anglicised Afro-reggae, a theme which ran throughout the album.

'Change Your Mind' is the first Cook-only composition. Featured within the Afro beats were easy-listening film-score flutes, laid-back funk bassline and a Philly-soul ambience. 'Change Your Mind' found Cook picking up the atmosphere of his debut, Bragg-penned single 'Won't Talk About It' and adding a more personal twist. In many ways, the track acted as a precursor to Cook's Freakpower output a few years later. Lyrically, however, it was far removed from Freakpower's beat, hippy leanings. Here Cook could be found in contemplative mood, looking closely at relationships gone wrong and, in a leap of apparent misogyny, blaming all women! The chorus reads, 'Now nothing in this world can change my mind I find/Now I've suffered ritual torture at the hands of womankind/And nothing in this world makes any sense except violence/Desperate and directionless, I'm trying to make amends.' However, the lyric does have duality. In his address to womankind, he also appears to be dealing with his thoughts about Prime Minister of the time Margaret Thatcher and, more pertinently, the need to act against her. 'When it comes to affairs of the state,' he sings, 'You know we'll always be violent when you dictate.'

In essence, it seemed that Cook was using 'Change Your Mind' to lament both his marriage – which by this time had gone sour – and a country in collapse. And the common link? Women! Given the state of the nation at this time (mass unemployment, houses being repossessed due to sky-high interest rates, etc) and the apparent frailty of his marriage, the lyric was not perhaps as strong as it might have been.

'Love Is Green' developed the groove of 'Change Your Mind' further, this time adding the Brit-funk bass synths of 1980s acts like Imagination and the horns of 1980s chart act Lynx. As a result, the song sounded remarkably out of date. Lyrically, the theme once again involves relationships. This time, however, it is based around music as a saviour when a relationship crumbles. Using an unnamed 'saint-like' musician as the central figure, the lyrics consider, 'Now my life's in doubt, there's always a reason to belong/And when my wife was gone, his music made me strong.'

What follows is perhaps the album's high point (and the only track which has stood the test of time), 'Echo Chamber'. Returning to the main theme of the previous album's closing track, 'Tribute To King Tubby', 'Echo Chamber' is the tribute its predecessor failed to be.

Taking a synth-fuelled rocksteady groove as its core, the track builds around a loop of Bob Marley's roots classic 'Exodus' and a pulsating acid-house-like bassline. Over the top, MC DJ Baptiste adds a flourish of ragga when David Grant delivers an understated, forlorn melody which hints at melancholy. Lyrically, it draws on the history of black music being raped at the hands of the racist white music industry (the first time that Cook attempted to justify his position in dance music, despite his previous concerns). If the track opens with a subdued ambience, the full force of the dubby middle-eight and ragga chatting fires the song into the boxing ring. Not downtrodden but fighting.

After the impact of 'Echo Chamber', the following track, 'The Sun Doesn't Shine', sounds lightweight thanks to its the ska-lite horns and keyboards and watery vocals. Although reminiscent of artists like Junior Marvin (whose 'Police And Thieves' was a favourite track of Norman's at the time), this version of the sound lacks any real depth.

The final track on the first side of the vinyl edition of the album, 'Herman', featured the vocals of UK dance-meets-hip-hop duo Definition Of Sound, whose style was inspired by the Native Tongues approach of acts like The Jungle Brothers, A Tribe Called Quest and The Dream Warriors – artists who were all enjoying a huge amount of success at this time.

Like many of the UK's MCs, Kevwon (Kevin Anthony Clark) and The Don's (Desmond Raymond Weeks) of Definition Of Sound took the American style and failed to add their own voice. As a result, accents were more New York than UK, while lyrics verged on the LSD-inspired pseudo-psychedelia of their US counterparts. They would, however, capture the imaginations of the British public soon after the release of *Excursion On The Version* thanks to their top 20 hit 'Now Is Tomorrow', which used numerous house mixes to cross over to the rave scene and employed rave diva Elaine Vassell on the chorus.

Definition Of Sound had strong links with the early days of UK house thanks to former graffiti artist Kevwon's guest spot on seminal hit 'House Arrest' by Sheffield outfit Krush (which included Mark Brydon of Moloko in a production role). In an earlier incarnation of Definition Of Sound, called Top Billin', the duo held the honour of being the last Western group to play East Berlin before the wall came down.

In many ways, Definition Of Sound walked a very similar path to Beats International. Both existed on the poppy edge of their genre. Both owed huge debts to reggae. And, perhaps most significantly, both took a stand that was at odds with even those musicians with whom they were most closely affiliated. Neither act was deep enough for the underground or poppy enough for the mainstream; both rode a middle ground which was doomed to failure. Definition Of Sound would go on to release three albums, including the debut 1991 collection *Love And Life: A Journey With The Chameleons*, which contained the band's biggest singles, 'Now Is Tomorrow' and 'Wear Your Love Like Heaven'.

'Herman' found a typical Definition Of Sound vocal laid over another rocksteady-lite arrangement which again drew heavily on the music of the South African townships. Sadly, however, the finished track was insipid, thanks partly to the MC's cute lyrics and the cod-reggae atmosphere of the musical arrangement.

On 'Three Foot Skank' Cook offered the album's definitive rocksteady sketch, owing the greatest debt to African beats. The combination of Prince Buster And The All Stars' Madness-covered 'Al Capone', rocksteady bassline, ska horns and African chants, beats, and vocal melodies presents one of Norman's first real successes in combining disparate styles. Essentially, it is here that he manages to capture an essence of each genre he's appropriating. As a result, there is a sense of respect which translates into musical depth, whereas all previous attempts at fusion had been relatively shallow, concerned with effect and artifice.

The following cut, 'No More Mr Nice Guy', presents the only Lindy contribution, and despite her claims that she was to be singing the whole of one track, her involvement actually only boiled down to a sample from 'Dub Be Good To Me' on which she sings, 'Tell me I am crazy.' The track itself is a funk-lite combination of the ubiquitous (by this stage) reggae basslines and Afro melodies. However, it represents one of the album's lowest points. Lyrically, 'No More Mr Nice Guy' opens with a couplet that could happily become Norman Cook's epitaph: 'I feel like having a great big party/that'll last until I grow old.' Sadly, this wasn't the party track to match that lyric, despite the production hinting at the kind of old-skool hip-hop cuts which appeared on the debut album.

'Eyes On The Prize', another songwriting collaboration with Lester Noel, once again found Beats looking at slower funk beats. With a bassline sound lifted from 1980s Brit-funk (as with so many moments on this album) and a melody which echoed the same era, the track seems more suited to Paul Weller's post-Jam soul outfit The Style Council. The track's only redeeming moment comes with a guitar solo which is so close to sound of The Isley Brothers' 'Summer Breeze' that it could have been the Isleys themselves playing.

On the slow skank of 'Ten Long Years', Cook lifts a direct sample from General Saint and Clint Eastwood's version of Queen's 'Another One Bites The Dust'. Again, the bassline and chugging guitars owe an enormous debt to reggae while the horn section plays a Mexican calypso version of rocksteady. Although the music itself isn't the most startling contribution to the album, with the lyrics Cook is at his most effective. As in 'Change Your Mind', he relates the state of a personal relationship to the state of the nation. The title itself refers to Margaret Thatcher's reign as Prime Minister (which would go on for more than another 10 years), but the lyrics have an obvious duality from the start: 'My baby, she insults all my friends/This lady, with islands to defend/My baby, she rules our house with force/She plagues me, I wish I could divorce.'

What follows next is the album's lowest point. A terrible cover version of the Elvis Presley classic 'In The Ghetto'. The lightweight arrangement (popping Roland 101 synth-beats and drum-machine rhythm, electro bassline and sugary synth strings) and the watery vocals courtesy of Jordan Bailey comprise a track devoid of all the original's sinister edge.

The closing gambit of 'Come Home' represented a slight return to form thanks to its sub-level bassline, duck quacks and chicken-grease guitar. The addition of a Melodica added a deeper reggae atmosphere to the already rocksteady-soaked arrangements. Even the steal from Bill Withers' 'Ain't No Sunshine' works in the context of the track's goofy take on Jamaican groove.

Despite being a lot more musically focused and far more serious than

Let Them Eat Bingo, Excursion On The Version was in actual fact very lightweight. Its arrangements were far too often merely reverential to the original source rather than an attempt to engage and go deeper. As a result, the heavy leaning towards reggae seems like a reliance on the effects and surface style of the genre rather than an attempt to relate to the musical motivation.

Similarly, Cook's employment of African sounds seemed to be devoid of nuance, focusing instead on the immediate. It was as if the entire album had been constructed from the icing, but he'd forgotten the cake itself. Indeed, perhaps the album should have been called *Let Them Eat Icing*.

The final area in which *Excursion On The Version* failed as a work in itself was in the total loss of the naïveté which marked out its predecessor's finer moments. Gone were the raw DJ cut-ups, the innocent reference points and the party atmosphere. In their place was a slickly produced collection of songs (Cook and Thornton had definitely improved their technique) which aimed at longevity but ultimately failed. Despite the few high points (many of which would hint at Cook's future with Freakpower), *Excursion On The Version* found him failing 100 per cent to discover his own voice.

It's possible that one of the biggest problems with Cook's focus on this collection lay in his continued rejection of the contemporary dance scene. Increasingly, he kept a tight grip on a vision of dance music which belonged in the past. As a result, he seemed perverse in his actions. *Excursion On The Version* was Norman Cook trying to be King Canute. In every track, he presents the image of an arrogant King commanding the seas to retreat from the shores of Brighton. (In his case, the seas were represented by the rave scene in which his career was drowning.)

Perhaps with lyrics like 'So don't tell me everything is all right/when its clear as my nose that it's not' from 'Change Your Mind' or, more pointedly, 'My baby, she walked out in the end/Basically she'd shafted all her friends/But major peace without her won't be found/Till my sweetheart's rotting underground,' from 'Ten Long Years', it comes as little surprise that the album was created during a period of relationship breakdown.

His marriage to Pippa came to an end because his demanding workload had left little time for his home life. Added to this, Norman had turned into what he has described as 'an ego-driven idiot'. 'I thought I was cock of the walk,' he told Stuart Maconie, 'thought I could do anything. But I became a workaholic. I thought I'd see how far you could push the boundaries of dance music and found out that it wasn't very far. The hits dried up and then my biggest fan goes. My wife left me, saying I'd turned into an arsehole.'

Although there is little doubt that Norman's pointed lyrical digs were not exactly autobiographical in terms of detail ('Ten Long Years' draws more on the blues tradition of analogy presented as seemingly literal storytelling), it was true that he'd immersed himself in a world where relationships can't last. This in itself was an irony considering the pressure placed upon Norman by The Housemartins, who had argued that he didn't have the time to get married. Inadvertently he had proven them right.

Excursion On The Version also mapped out the loss of other relationships. Pippa wasn't the only person to suffer at the hands of Norman's workload and ego. Success, no matter how minor, had brought with it numerous hangers-on, and many of these people had become quite close to him. At a time of emotional weakness, he embraced many of the music industry's more false characters as friends. His real friends became increasingly forgotten. 'I had turned into a dickhead,' he told *The Observer Magazine* a few years later. 'I had serious ego problems. I was an arrogant workaholic who'd forgotten what living was about.'

The Beats International star was on the wane, however. *Excursion On The Version* failed to chart at all, while the first single from it, 'Echo Chamber', released a month after the album, only managed to reach number 60, remaining in the charts for a pathetic two weeks. The follow-up, 'The Sun Doesn't Shine', reached the lowly number 66 slot the following August before disappearing altogether, its depressing tune seemingly at odds with a nation enjoying the positive aspects of dance.

The final nail in the coffin came when Go! Beat decided on the ill-advised release of 'In The Ghetto'. Although it managed to turn the tide slightly (much to Canute's relief, no doubt), reaching number 44 in the British charts, it spelled critical disaster for the Beats crew.

Long-time band ally Dave Jennings summed up the general feeling on the lacklustre record in his *Melody Maker* review: 'In the past, Norman Cook's blending of seemingly incompatible musical forms has produced minor miracles. Here it's produced a minor tragedy. "In The Ghetto" is all about violent crime, oppression and despair. Matters of life and death. It's full of drama and fury – or at least it was when Presley and Nick Cave sang it. But Cook's subdued, polite dance shuffle treatment renders the song bloodless and toothless – especially since the normally excellent Jordan Bailey's vocals carry so much burning conviction that you can almost see her glancing at her watch and yawning in the vocal booth. Even so, it looks set to succeed where far-superior BI releases have recently failed. You have been warned…'

'In The Ghetto' was released in the same week as 'Justified And Ancient' by groundbreaking sample duo KLF. The success of this and subsequent KLF tracks offered the clearest picture of why Beats International were failing to score. Quite simply, they had become so at odds with the tastes of the dance scene (and the newly converted indie-dance crossover kids) that they had painted themselves into a stylistic corner. Certainly it was a beautifully crafted corner that had been painted, but essentially it spoke only to Norman and his collection of friends.

The Beats collective also proved to be a little more open than people had at first thought. While Lester Noel had featured on only a couple of tracks on the first album but had been presented as the only other full-time member, he appeared on a good deal more on *Excursion…*, sharing songwriting credits on 'Love Is Green', 'No More Mr Nice Guy' and 'Eyes On The Prize'. However, his name wasn't even included in the list of musicians involved.

It is possible that Norman simply forgot (other musicians, like Andy Boucher, were similarly omitted from the list). However, since Noel played such a large part in the public face of Beats International this seems unlikely. The other reading would be that Norman liked the irony in the image presented by Noel and himself as a working partnership. It was a relationship of opposites and dichotomies. Cook was the dance-loving white guy who had become known for playing indie music while Noel was a black kid who loved indie, had been in indie bands, hated dance music and was now in a dance collective.

In many ways, putting Noel at the forefront made a mockery of any accusations laid at Norman's feet that Beats International was just a white guy trying to write black music. As a duo, he and Noel turned that theory on its head. With Norman's oft-verbalised fear of being seen as appropriating black music, it is highly possible that such motives, no matter how subconsciously, lay in his actions.

This is not to say that Norman invited Noel into the Beats camp for the specific purpose of turning the music-and-race issue on its head. His actions were motivated by a more naïve, and positive, instinct. It was obvious the singer had a huge talent. It is more likely that he embraced the oppositional natures of Noel with excitable humour rather than cold calculation.

In the months that followed the release of that final single, Noel would be found at Esselle still talking about his involvement in Beats International as Norman started demoing tracks for a proposed third album. Indeed, he would lay down numerous vocal tracks, including one for a 1970s funk pastiche called 'Turn On, Tune In, Drop Out'.

With Go! Beat finally withdrawing support from Norman after the failure of 'In The Ghetto', and following the divorce that followed the break-up of his marriage, Cook would descend into a deep depression that would subsequently have huge effects on him.

'[I] pissed all my friends off, pissed my nearest and dearest off,' he explained to *Deluxe*. 'They, bless them, took me to task over it, and rather than doing something about it, I went into a spiral of depression.

'My wife leaving me was only the start of it, because I just thought, "She doesn't know what she's missing. She'll come back. How can she give this up? You don't leave someone who's successful and popular." That's how arrogant I was,' he told *The Observer Magazine*.

Too ego-driven to take heed of his family's concern, and too arrogant to get help, he took to his bed, unplugged the phone and refused to answer the door to the house on Robinson Road, which he'd once shared with Pippa. At one stage, he didn't talk to any one for over three weeks, despite being aware of people's desperate attempts to contact him.

'I couldn't sleep, so I used to try and knock myself out,' he once said. 'I put my head through the kitchen cabinet. I got quite self-abusive. Not eating. Just wandering around howling quite a lot. It is just this spiral where every day's worse. Every day you don't talk to anyone, you're more scared to face them the next day.'

Norman took to drinking to try to sleep. However, the only effect was that he became a wide awake drunk. Eventually, he went to see his doctor to find out what was wrong. He seriously thought he was going insane, but the doctor diagnosed clinical depression and prescribed anti-depressant drugs.

What followed was a two-year period of near inactivity, a time that Cook has described as 'the wilderness'. For a full year he was unable to work and then, when he finally resurfaced, it was to produce the most questionable remixes – and even worse, in his eyes, to record the soundtrack to a Smurfs computer game and sell his treasured sample collection for 'a bag of silver'. The collection of samples numbered over 1,000 and would see the light of day on the Studio Master Music Creation Software, under the dubious title of 'Skip To My Loops', and on a CD called *Sampladelica*.

In retrospect, Norman has called the work he did during this period as 'whore work'. Quite simply, he needed the money. With Beat International's failure to deliver any more big hits, he wasn't earning huge amounts from them. Furthermore, the costs of employing an army which included session musicians, vocalists, MCs, graffiti artist an engineer, etc, both in the studio and on the road throughout their extensive world tours, were extortionate. As a result he had come nowhere near to recouping the advances paid to him by the record company. Beats International had turned into a financial black hole.

If this wasn't enough, the divorce had created its own money problems. Norman had remained in the couple's house, but the monthly mortgage was a crippling £800. With interest rates still at an all-time high, this situation didn't seem likely to improve.

'It got hairy. I wanted to die, basically,' he once said.

Norman's only course of action was to take on the 'whore work'.

TURN ON, TUNE IN, COP OUT

'That was my crazy drug time. Total hedonism. We were just a
bunch of friends – 12 of us – endlessly driving around Europe
doing shows, having a laugh, and getting off our nuts every night.'
– *Norman Cook, & Magazine*, 2000

Norman Cook was saved by ecstasy one night in 1993 when he went
to see a flatmate's girlfriend who worked in the cloakroom of Brighton's
Escape Club. He was offered ecstasy and decided he had nothing to
lose. The pill had the desired effect. After a lengthy period on
antidepressants and regular visits to his psychiatrist, the positive effects
of an illegal substance succeeded where the medical fraternity had
failed. The track he recalls from this evening was Robert Owens' superb
'I'll Be Your Friend'. 'In the morning, my face ached from smiling so
much. This, from a bloke who'd been clinically depressed for over a
year. Suddenly I had this whole other thing about life that makes it
worth living. Like sunshine in the morning. And love. And house
music…which I'd never got until then.'

The first thing that Norman did when he woke up in the morning
following the pill before, was 'a fat line of coke and another pill'. What
followed was a five-year period of intensely focused productivity as he
launched his music under numerous different names, almost
concurrently. He DJ'd and toured throughout the world while
continuing his onslaught of remixes. If his breakdown had been partly
due to overwork (he has said that he thought he was like Prince, taking
on a superhuman workload), this new regime was no less frantic. The
major difference was that a new attitude epitomised this new period
of activity. He seemed to have gained a sense of what was important

to him and taken control of his life. He even started a new relationship. Her name was Bella, and she would feature prominently in the next few years of his life.

The newly rejuvenated Norman became a regular face around Brighton's clubs once again, taking in a wider variety of sounds than ever before. He also took to ecstasy like a fish to water and began enjoying the effects of the drug to their fullest. Soon Norman's house became an after hours destination for his friends, turning into a shrine for the smiley logo and becoming renamed the House of Love in the process. Parties there were legendary.

Just as Norman's life had seemed to be coming together, however, another bombshell threatened to blow it apart. Thanks to his spiralling debts and losses incurred by Beats International, he was advised by his accountant to bankrupt his business so as to avoid losing his house: 'It was funny because, just as I came out of rock bottom personally, I hit rock bottom professionally – which was quite cool because it didn't hurt. Part of my therapy was to realise that it didn't hurt, not having a career, and that people still liked me.'

Norman considered giving up music completely at this point. He was booked to DJ in Africa and nearly didn't turn up. At the last minute he went for it, and while he was there had a dream about becoming a fireman. Despite the success of the gig he did seriously consider the idea, even going as far as to try to measure his chest expansion to see if he had the lung capacity to make it as a fireman. He even contemplated giving up smoking.

'It's a bit like being a musician' is how Norman explained his fire-fighting ambitions to Chris Heath. 'You hang around for ages with your mates, doing nothing, cracking jokes and playing pool, and then you go and do something really exciting – save a cat or a life – and everyone loves you. The uniform's quite nice. You get laid a lot, apparently. A desperate desire to get laid has driven my career, from DJing to being a musician to being a fireman. Ugly pop stars get laid. Ugly accountants don't!'

Any thoughts of giving up on music were soon dispelled, though. For the first time since the acid-house explosion of the late 1980s, Norman started to understand what his friends were on about. Ecstasy use unlocked the secrets to the language of house and suddenly the linear structures, the emphasis on nuance and the attention to layers came to life for him. Suddenly he saw new possibilities in his own music.

He didn't immediately start to write house tunes to soundtracks for this newer experience, however. Returning to his bedroom studio in his house on Robinson Road, he embarked on recording demos for a new project, inspired by his love of 1970s funk, 1960s psychedelia, Blaxploitation soundtracks and Jimi Hendrix. With a few tracks laid down, Norman called his old Beats International collaborator Ashley Slater to discuss the possibility of forming a songwriting partnership. Slater immediately agreed.

When Ashley first got the call from Norman to get back down to Esselle Studios, he assumed it was to be his trombone services that were wanted for the third Beats International album. However, Norman said he wanted Ashley to sing on the new tracks that he'd written. In effect, Ashley was to be to the new band what Lester Noel had been to Beats.

Among the first tracks that Ashley added vocals to was the new Cook gem 'Turn On, Tune In, Cop Out'. At this stage, the vocals had been provided by Lester Noel, so Ashley simply replaced them with his own take. The track itself was already a done deal.

As soon as he heard the track with Ashley in tow, Kevin Stagg knew it was destined to be a hit. The combination of Norman's songwriting reaching heights previously only hinted at, and a vocalist who had all of the qualities of Sly Stone, was perfect.

'Ashley could really deliver the goods,' says Stagg. 'The brains in the engine room was Norm, but Ash could deliver the goods. I think Norm brought the commercial side out of Ash, but I also think he's got one of the finest soul voices in the country. You could hear it immediately.

'Ash just turned up during the Beats days, when there was a constant stream of people coming through. He was this strange-looking bloke who hardly ever spoke. It took me a year to realise that he didn't drink tea! He wasn't very communicative in those days. But I've got so much respect for him. Like Norm, he's very quick when he's recording stuff, so they complemented each other perfectly.'

With a few tracks recorded, Norman's manager Garry Blackburn – whose company Anglo Plugging had promoted both The Housemartins and Beats International – set up meetings with various record companies. In the end they signed to Island Records offshoot 4th And Broadway, which had been set up by A&R man Julian Palmer in the wake of huge success with Tricky.

Norman and Ashley had chosen the moniker Freakpower for their new project. Freakpower came from the rallying call of Hunter S Thompson (a constant source of inspiration for Norman, who looks upon himself as the Hunter S of the dance scene – the Gonzo beatmaster) when he stood for election as mayor in Aspen, California. For a writer whose name had become synonymous with drug use and bringing the Hell's Angels into the folds of Kesey's Merry Pranksters, any chance of becoming mayor in such a right-wing part of the US was mildly ludicrous. However, it did the serve the purpose of stirring people up a bit.

Gradually, through the Freakpower recording process, Ashley started to take a more prominent position. Whereas his initial brief was to add a touch of Sly Stone to Norman's funk grooves, he increasingly collaborated on lyrics, and in the case of 'Rush' and 'What It Is' he wrote the entire tracks. It was fitting then that Freakpower were actually signed to Island as a duo.

Just as the Freakpower plot was coming together, Norman delivered a single under another name and working with a different partner. (According to the terms of the 4th And Broadway contract, both Norman and Ashley were free to produce tracks under different names for alternative labels. The only condition was that they weren't to publicise their involvement in other projects in any way.) In April 1993, he teamed up with Gareth Hansome (with whom he would develop a very close friendship) to launch The Mighty Dub Katz on the duo's own Southern Fried Records. The single 'Super Disco Breaks' was notable for the fact that it used house beats, despite Norman's long-time dislike of the genre.

As the title suggested, 'Super Disco Breaks' combined the four-to-the-floor of house with the 16ths of disco and layered the grooves with Norman's trademark hooklines. It was not the most inspired single, but it represented the first time in a number of years that Norman Cook had been in tune with the atmosphere of the times. And feeling the influence of the ecstasy.

'Return Of The Yeke Yeke', a second Mighty Dub Katz single released two months later in June 1993, found Norm once again employing African influences, but the main vibe of the track was defiantly progressive house. Although both tracks proved to be big club hits, neither touched the charts. However, the release of these singles did introduce a pattern which would be repeated continually over the next few years – that of Norman ducking and diving between aliases, often coinciding releases for maximum pressure.

During the few months that followed 'Return Of The Yeke Yeke', Norman concentrated on putting together the Freakpower band for the launch single. However, he did have one scrape with the UK charts during the summer when he secretly got involved with novelty summer hit 'Suntan' under the name of Stan. Norman provided the remixes and even appeared in the video.

Stan was actually a pseudonym for Kevin Stagg and his writing partner. Norman agreed to be involved out of friendship. Over the years, a criticism would often be levelled at Norman that he didn't know how to say no to his friends. It was one of the reasons why he needed management to handle his affairs for him. However, it is unlikely that even the intervention of Garry Blackburn would have stopped his involvement in this track. Over the course of his time recording at Esselle, Kevin had become a good friend to Norman. The remix was just a mark of respect.

In the months between signing the contract with 4th And Broadway and the final release of their debut single in October 1993, the duo of Norman and Ashley set to work putting together a live band and completing recording for the album.

Among the people who got the Freakpower call was drummer Jim Carmichael, who had already built quite a reputation for his involvement in both Talkin' Loud act K-Creative and London funk outfit Izzit. Both bands had built a reputation for taking the acid-jazz blueprint and pushing the boundaries towards contemporary dance culture. K-Creative especially fused the usual acid-jazz mélange of funk, hip-hop, soul and jazz with go-go beats and aspects of the early house sounds. However, following a relatively successful tour in support of their debut single and the subsequent failure of their album, K-Creative were dropped from their label.

Izzit faced a similar fate with their acid-house-influenced classic funk. Following their demise, the band's central duo formed the highly respected jazzy drum-and-bass label Hospital Records, recording under the alias London Elektricity.

Jim Carmichael was initially introduced to Norman and Ashley through a mutual acquaintance, Ed John, who had bagged the job as Freakpower's live engineer. Ed had previously been K-Creative's live sound engineer after he'd done the sound for them at a gig at the Lakota in Bristol. The band were so impressed by the sound that they asked him to join them, which he duly did.

Jim's inclusion in the Freakpower family wasn't, as it turned out, the first time that Jim had met Norman. Thanks to his older sister, Sarah, Jim had been introduced to the DJ when Jim was only 13. 'The first time I ever met Norman, I didn't even realise it was him,' he laughs. 'Basically, my sister Sarah lived down in Brighton years ago – she worked at the Zap club and she knew Norman from the local parties. Anyway, Norman ended up DJing at her birthday party and so I inadvertently met him. I was only 13 at the time. Later, when I mentioned to my sister that I was going to be working with Norman, she was like, "Oh my God, he DJ'd at my party." So that was the first time I'd met him.'

Even though Freakpower songs already featured programmed beats, when Jim went into the studios with Norman he was asked to play along to the existing tracks, adding an extra groove in the process. 'From a drummer's point of view, it was a dream because he didn't tell me what he wanted beyond saying, "Play along to this,"' he says. 'We laid down drum tracks for the entire album over only two days. There was stuff which didn't get used, but in the end the album featured about 80 per cent live drums. Norman was very good at making decisions about what actually worked. I think that's one of his greatest strengths as a producer.'

With a live band now completely formed, Freakpower went into rehearsals at Sunday School Studios in London. Norman played guitar while Ashley took on his customary trombone and lead vocals. Within a month Freakpower had played a few low-key gigs in London.

In October 1993, 4th And Broadway finally released the debut Freakpower single, 'Turn On, Tune In, Cop Out'. It was the perfect introduction for the band, displaying a new maturity to Norman's songwriting in the process. With a huge nod of respect in the direction of Sly And The Family Stone and War, 'Turn On...' aimed directly at the heart of the funk and acid-jazz scenes that had raged over the previous three years.

Acid jazz was less a style than an attitude, drawing as it did on a myriad of different sounds from the same period of the 1970s (1975 onwards). Ironically, the scene was actually one of the less popularised areas, in which the effects of ecstasy saw a new unity. Through the 1980s, the funk- and soul-based rare groovers (the soul boys) were in direct opposition to the jazz heads. In Home Counties towns like High Wycombe, Watford and St Albans, this friction often spilled over into violence.

With the onset of Balearic and the free-party scene, which saw a huge and speedy growth in the Home Counties, many of their old differences were quickly forgotten. Disparate scenes would subsequently merge and a period of acculturation occurred as influences spread backwards and forwards.

In London the direct roots of the acid house experience have been traced to Norman Jay's late 1980s Shake and Finger Pop parties, which offered an eclectic soundtrack of soul, jazz, funk and hip-hop. However, the notion of the people who had been drawn to these parties being in some way a part of a scene didn't actually occur until Gilles Peterson pushed the idea with his Sunday Sessions at the Belvedere.

These parties proved popular with the post-Shoom crowd who would decamp from the Balearic party to enjoy Peterson's sets. Again a meeting of influences occurred and the scene started to develop a more defined sound. This was capitalised upon by Peterson and Patrick Forge, who opened a new Sunday Session at Dingwalls. Called 'Talkin' Loud And Saying Something', it became a regular haunt for future dance stars including Leftfield, Moloko and Maxim from Prodigy. This event also saw regular performances from bands like The Brand New Heavies, The Jazz Renegades and Galliano.

The acid-jazz scene would quickly gain a popularity which would challenge the dominance of rave culture, appealing to many of the clubbers who had been turned on to the open-minded aesthetic of Balearic and acid house but turned cold by the comparatively narrow rave soundtrack. Interestingly, acid jazz also found a natural following in the US cities of Los Angeles and San Francisco. Subsequently, the scene crossed over to the US far sooner than rave.

If any problem lay in Freakpower's leaning towards this particular scene, it was in the fact that acid jazz was, by then, on the wane. Leading light Galliano had gone into a creative decline, with sales following suit, while latecomers Jamiroquai were well on the way to following The Brand New Heavies on the path to global domination through their radio-friendly version of the sound. Always a sure-fire scene killer. Indeed, by late 1993 the downtempo experimental sound of trip-hop had been firmly founded, and acid jazz was in the process of being usurped.

Among the more groundbreaking outfits in acid jazz were The Sandals, who would offer the blueprint for the downtempo trip-hop sound that was to come with their own takes on the sound. Their 1994 album *Rite To Silence* suggested that the acid-jazz cognoscenti had much more to offer than modern rehashes of 1970s funk.

Another negative aspect with this sound was the media's almost wholesale rejection of it. With the exception of specialist magazines like *Straight No Chaser* and underground magazine *Overall There Is A Smell Of Fried Onions*, acid jazz was, despite its successes, treated as a joke, thanks to its apparent obsession with style over content. Indeed many of the bands were simply offering well-dressed assemblies of the Blaxploitation era. At a time when Apex Twin, Orbital and global beat outfits like Transglobal Underground were dominating the dance pages of the UK's mainstream music press, acid jazz seemed trivial.

'Turn On, Tune In, Cop Out' was immediately victim to this. The single featured an update on the 1970s funk of Sly And The Family Stone and injected the wayward acid soul of 'Psychedelic Shack'-era Temptations. Even its title was an appropriation of another era, being a play on Dr Timothy Leary's LSD battle cry, 'Turn on, tune in, drop out.' This offers yet another glimpse into Norman Cook's ongoing obsession with the Beat Generation and its subsequent development into the hippy.

'Turn On…', gaining almost no coverage at all upon its release, had to rely on radio promotion and live gigs for any exposure. Fortunately, it did receive support from Radio 1's Mark Radcliffe. Coupled with the band's growing reputation on the gig front, this was enough to see the single go into the UK charts at number 29, hardly the auspicious start enjoyed by Beats International but a good foundation nonetheless.

The remixes of 'Turn On…' offered a full introduction to Norman's newer club vision. 'T-Empo's Club Mix' stripped the track down to a string-led soulful house groove with Ashley's vocals to the fore. The 'Play Boys' Reloaded Dub' found Brighton boys JC Reid and Tim Jeffries teaming up with Simon Thornton engineering out of Esselle Studios and pushing the tracks with an on-the-one house beat and distorted rolling bassline. Vocals are delivered in reverse over an insistent keyboard refrain before handclaps lift the track towards a simple, Parliament-esque riff. As the track builds, bongos started to filter into the mix, adding to the sense of crescendo.

As a track, this mix delivered a perfect ecstasy soundtrack. It had all of the right builds, crescendos simulating the rushing experience of the drug, and arm-raising beats. The final mix, however, came from Norman's latest guise as Pizzaman, formed in alliance with JC Reid and Tim Jeffries. This mix opened with a sample of a passage from Jack Kerouack's infamous beat novel *On The Road*, thus providing another hint as to the ideological influences of the band. The rest of the mix took many of the riffs from the 'Play Boys' Dub' but emphasised the main refrain with an organ sound lifted directly from early Chicago house records.

Rhythmically, it echoed the work of Kevin Saunderson's earlier incarnations while the build featured a skewed choral sample twisted around the main riff, building towards another rush climax. Again it was a success. Again Norman was displaying that his heart lay as much in the world of house as planet funk by this time.

Furthermore, the mix that Norman had been involved in displayed a strong understanding of the needs of the club crowd. He proved to the world that his understanding of the musical language of post-acid house dance music was well honed. He had not only a sharp ear for house music's understated hooks but also a deft touch for the subtler nuances associated with the sound as an experience. Put simply, by this stage there was no doubt that Norman was enjoying ecstasy to the maximum.

By the end of 1993, Freakpower's first album had been completed. Although the sessions at Esselle had enjoyed the usual relaxed atmosphere, the relationship between studio and label hadn't been quite so enjoyable.

Previously Esselle's Kev Stagg had had an arrangement with Norman that he could use the studio whenever he wanted, if it was available. However, the new regime wanted him to operate a system of block bookings, with time reserved well in advance. 'I remember telling this women at the label that this way of working just wouldn't happen with Norman,' recalls Stagg. 'I told her that we had a flexible arrangement in place that suited all of us, but she wasn't having any of it. She wanted us to fit into her system.'

It's safe to say that Norman Cook was the last person to fit into anyone else's system. He continued to record in his own way, to his own schedule. However, this early example of record company and artist at odds with each other would be a portentous warning.

The second instalment from Freakpower came in February of the following year. It was an Ashley Slater-penned track called 'Rush', which came in a 'Magic Eye' sleeve. Magic Eye art featured recurring images built around fractal patterns. The idea was that if you stared at them long enough, a dominant image would slowly surface through the brain's left side. Not surprisingly, the images were particularly popular with E and LSD users.

Given the anti-acid jazz vibe of the time, 'Rush' was not perhaps the obvious critics' choice for a single thanks to its overtly jazzy edge. However, its high-tempo funky beats, brass stabs and insistent hooklines were very radio-friendly, and with the growing success of The Brand New Heavies, 4th And Broadway no doubt saw this track as having maximum hit potential.

Sadly, the track proved less exciting to the record-buying public than its predecessor, stalling at number 62. In truth, despite its obvious commercial edge, the track's arrangement was perhaps too complex for the UK's pop ears. Basslines twanged like Bootsy Collins on speed, percussion chattered away like an amphetamine freak's teeth while the horns were delivered with the nervous twitch of a cokehead in rehab. 'Rush' was perhaps one of the more obvious drug songs to have hit the stands since The Eagles penned 'Hotel California' and Lou Reed delivered 'Perfect Day'. and the accompanying 'Pizzaman Mix' only added to the drug-punch of the single package.

However, 'Rush' was a live favourite, turning occasionally polite crowds into a sweating mosh pit whenever it was played. Throughout this period, Freakpower toured with a missionary's zeal. No doubt influenced by Ken Kesey's Merry Pranksters and their 1960s trips on the bus named Further, they took to the road loaded with drugs, drink and a desire to push the Freakpower party to the extreme edge.

Throughout 1993 and early 1994, they toured Europe in support of artists like Carleen Anderson (previously with The Young Disciples, whose 1990 'Apparently Nothin'' single was one of the UK urban soul scene's finest moments); Hammond-organ-fuelled outfit The James Taylor Quartet; acid-jazz-meets-psychedelia crew Mother Earth; and UK hip-hop band US3.

As a live band, Freakpower were gaining a reputation for being something of a wild show. Norman's onstage antics had already been one of the most enjoyable aspects of The Housemartins, but behind the decks for Beats International he had been somewhat restricted. Now back onstage with a guitar, he was able to get up to all sorts of hijinks, fooling around with other bandmembers, simulating Chuck Berry's duck walk and simply giving good guitar-hero poses.

Ashley similarly made quite a statement as a frontman. Whether wielding his trombone or delivering vocals, his bald head and pink fur coat helped him stand out. Indeed, both Norman and Ashley had rare charismatic presence on stage. Together they were incredible.

Ash gained a name for his onstage pimp-style clothes, while Norman was becoming known for his gold lamé shirts, but the reality was the band were becoming notorious for their need to get butt naked. It was a habit that would also surface during photo sessions and, infamously, during a Radio 1 recording for Mark Radcliffe's *Evening Session*.

'We bought loads of drink in for the session and gradually got drunk during the show,' recalls Jim Carmichael. 'We did one track and then there was a half-hour break and we just got increasingly pissed between our songs. Gradually we took our clothes off until at the end we were pretty much all stark-bollock naked. Rumours got back to Mark Radcliffe, and when we started the last song he ran from his studio to where we were playing to see if it was true. Then he announced it to his listeners.'

In today's era of webcams and total access, it's hard to imagine such shenanigans going on at Radio 1 any more. However, at the time it only served to enhance Freakpower's reputation for being very out there. Indeed, it were these kinds of antics that helped separate them from the more faddish aspects of the acid-jazz scene.

Only two months after the release of 'Rush', Norman unleashed another slice of house action under his Pizzaman guise. His involvement in the project was kept very low key as, according to his contract with Island, he was allowed to release dance records under an alias but not under his own name. Pizzaman was a collaboration between Cook and the Play Boys duo of JC Reid and Tim Jeffries, but all tracks were credited simply to Pizzaman.

The trio's debut release came in the shape of 'Baby Loop', coupled with 'Sans Bateaux' on their own Loaded imprint. 'Baby Loop' was built around a sample of a baby's heartbeat, over which they created an understated progressive house track with hooklines and vocal refrains played down until the middle section found a string-driven riff developing a dominant melodic theme. The build came through a combination of treated guitar samples and 303 sequences and the customary rush of the elongated drum roll, which was almost omnipresent at this time in house. The end result was quite dark in its mood, but the insistent off-beat handclaps and cowbells provided a hint of the trio's future output.

'Sans Bateaux' owed much of its ambience to UK techno artists such as fellow Brighton band Orbital, thanks in the main to its looped analogue pulses, systematic music structure and overuse of reverb. Rhythmically, however, it was a full-on pumping house track with an epic feel. The sampled choir introduced for the drop only adds to the larger-than-life feel.

A month later, in May 1994, Norman once again resurfaced with his Mighty Dub Katz moniker, this time around with the disappointing 'Keep On Truckin''. A hook-laden mash up of raw loops and samples, this latest variation on the house theme failed to ignite either the club underground or the mainstream. The coupling of Norman and Gareth Hansome proved too hard to swallow for the times. Ironically, though, many of the ideas tried out with this production would resurface in Norman's later productions.

With Freakpower still working the live circuit across Europe, it was surprising that Island decided not to capitalise on their increasing popularity with a single release over the summer months. However, as August 1994 drew to a close, the band's third single was promo'd to the media. Its release date was set for early September.

'Get In Touch' was pure Brand New Heavies-style acid jazz with its bossa-nova rhythm, Rhodes piano, chicken-grease wah-wah guitars, Isley Brothers guitar solo and Sly Stone vocal melodies. A remix from Ashley under his Colonel Kurtz pseudonym added a sense of lunacy to the single, but its all-too-obvious references to 1970s funk proved unpopular with the public. Despite the live success, Freakpower's third single failed even to chart, and the band looked to be stuck on the same downward trajectory that had killed off Beats International.

If the label considered dropping the band at this stage, it's possible that they were saved by a single released by Norman a few weeks before 'Get In Touch'. Called 'Trippin' On Sunshine', it settled at the number 33 position, a chart performance completely usurping that of Freakpower. This single was as Pizzaman, though.

Given the amount of hard work that Freakpower had put into their live show, it is possible that the success of Pizzaman – an act whose entire promotional work came through the white-label network – came as a source of huge disappointment for Norman's band. With their singles failing to sell, it's possible that everyone expected to get dropped from Island. However, given the amount of investment that the label had already put into Freakpower, they must have hoped that Norman's success with Pizzaman would rub off on their act. Certainly, around the time of 'Trippin' On Sunshine', the fact that Pizzaman was Norman became common knowledge among the dance media – a story happily confirmed by Island, despite the contractual limitations placed on releasing that kind of information

'Trippin' On Sunshine' found Pizzaman signing to the near-legendary Cowboy Records. Cowboy had been founded by Charlie Chester a couple of years earlier and had enjoyed success with the progressive house scene, which grew in opposition to rave's hardcore uproar. Progressive house, a term coined in 1991 by *Mixmag* journalist Dom Philips, adopted many of the ideologies of the Balearic scene, and many of its frontrunners had once been known faces in the Shoom family. The progressive sound took the rough edges of UK house and married them with the soulful edge of the Chicago originals.

The leading DJs of this era, which had its spiritual home in Nottingham's Venus Club, would go on to become among the most influential in dance music. Among them were Andy Weatherall (The Sabres Of Paradise, Two Lone Swordsmen), Justin Robertson (Lionrock), Darren Emerson (ex-Underworld), David Holmes and Billy Nasty. Among the scene's earliest successes was Leftfield's classic 'Not Forgotten'.

Cowboy Records were one of the leading imprints (along with would-be Madonna producer William Orbit's imprint Guerilla) during this era, thanks largely to hits from The Aloof and, a little later, Boomshanka. By the time Cowboy had signed Pizzaman, however, the label was in a certain amount of trouble.

When Boomshanka manager Chris Heester was brought into to try to sort out the mess that Cowboy had got into, he discovered numerous anomalies. Among them was the habit of doing exclusive track licensing deals to more than one compilation, often pre-release. Thus record sales were affected and 'exclusives' were non-existent.

Many of the questionable tactics of Cowboy were not born out of Charlie Chester being a shark, more of him being a wide boy. Cowboy, as the name suggested, epitomised an era of anything-is-possible naïveté, where previously well-meaning clubbers were suddenly thrust into the role of businessmen. Given the way most clubbers and partygoers lived their lives at this time, it was hardly surprising that many a label found itself in a financial mess.

Cowboy did, however, leave behind it numerous classic records. Among them was the offering from Pizzaman which reached number 33 in the UK charts. 'Trippin' On Sunshine' takes a salsa bassline, a piano line, an old soul vocal sample, lifts from electro classic 'Walking On Sunshine' by Rocker's Revenge and a pulsating house beat and enough drops and snare builds to keep even the most funk-free clubber happy. Despite the happy-house tag that it attracted at the time, 'Trippin' On Sunshine' actually had more depth than many of the tunes emanating from that arena. Furthermore, much of the Fatboy Slim style found its roots in this track.

In October 1994, Freakpower released their debut album *Drive Thru Booty*. A far smoother and more self-assured affair than any of the Beats International albums, benefiting immensely from the live instrumentation, *Drive Thru Booty* included enough Beats signatures to suggest that the collection may truly have started life as the third Beats album.

Perhaps the most significant track was the reworking of 'Change Your Mind' from *Excursion On The Version*. Now called 'Change My Mind', it took the original's jazzy leaning and added a tone of Blaxploitation sleaze, according to the Freakpower sonic blueprint. With the addition of Ashley's soulful baritone in favour of Lester Noel's sugary vocals, the track was given a new depth which sidestepped any sense of the naïveté (sonic and political) that dogged the last Beats album.

Lyrically, the track was changed from the immature dual attack on Norman's ex-wife and Prime Minister Margaret Thatcher, to a personal declaration on the need for self-growth. Furthermore, with Slater's own lyrical addition, 'Change My Mind' turned from a near-misogynistic diatribe into a celebration of womankind.

Drive Thru Booty opened with the Sly Stone pastiche 'Moonbeam Woman', immediately laying down the main obsessions of the 11-track set. Hammond organs play counterpoint with funk guitar while a bass walks a fine line between slap and jazz. Slater's vocals ooze sexuality (owing a huge debt to Sly Stone's smokey phrasing) while lyrics offer an obsession with the pop-culture icons of the 1970s, relocating them in contemporary club culture. On the face of it, the track might celebrate a bygone age of girls with 'moondust in her 'fro', but in the second verse the song's leading lady is reintroduced: 'Three years late she's back in her stride/Down Full Circle doing the bump.' (The bump may have been a 1970s dance fad that involved bumping ass with your dance partner, but Full Circle was in fact a hugely influential Sunday-afternoon session at a pub in Colnebrooke, near Slough, which opened in 1990. The brainchild of Phil Perry and Fiona Crawford, Full Circle proved immensely popular with the post-club crowds and became the breeding ground for the nascent progressive-house scene.)

With singles 'Turn On, Tune In, Cop Out' and 'Get In Touch' following, the album kept the psychedelic-funk atmosphere to the fore. This was amplified by the Jimi Hendrix-sampling, acid-rocking track named after the band. It was here that Freakpower stood apart from the UK acid house scene, instead walking a similar path to US bands like 1970s funk rockers Funkadelic and the subsequently influenced metal funk outfits like The Red Hot Chili Peppers and 24/7 Spyz.

The principal sound at work was the raw funk of The Meters, the psychedelia of 'Jungle Boogie'-era Kool And The Gang (from the *Wild And Peaceful* album), the psychedelic rock and soul of Funkadelic's 'Free Your Mind, Your Ass Will Follow' and 'America Eats Its Young', the disrupted blues of Jimi Hendrix's 'Electric Ladyland' and finally the sleazy acid grooves of Sly And The Family Stone's 1972 album *There's A Riot Goin' On*.

It was the last of these influences that would surface on the next track, namely a cover version of Sly Stone's 'Runnin' Away' from *There's A Riot Goin' On*. A beautifully understated groove gave ample space for Ashley Slater's brooding trombone and proved to be one of the album's non-single highlights.

It was perhaps unsurprising that the band had looked towards Sly And The Family Stone for their inspiration. Apart from their brand of acid funk, the band also shared Freakpower's love of chemically charged hedonism. However, if Norman still held any of his old fears about being seen as a white person playing black music, he couldn't have chosen to cover an artist who was more than outspoken in his expression of the black experience. And 'Runnin' Away' was an example of Sly at his most vocal in expressing that black experience.

Since his first record, Sly Stone had attempted to break every genre barrier presented to black musicians. He actively attempted to reclaim rock music from white America in order to reunite it with its black heritage. Furthermore, he took his mélange of black radical funk and fuzz guitars into the heart of mainstream pop, further pushing his ideologies and beliefs on an ever wider market. However, by the time he recorded 'Runnin' Away' (Sly actually played all of the instruments on *There's A Riot Goin' On*, a fact which would no doubt have appealed to Norman), he was speaking to an internalised aesthetic based on his identity as a black American rather than that of a 'white pop' singer. This was a track from an artist going deeper into the realms of soul, expressing an experience which white rock fans couldn't hope to share. And yet Norman felt to compelled to try.

Perhaps this was because the track explored Sly Stone's own reclusive tendencies, which were a feature of his life at the time. This must have resonated with Cook following his breakdown. Or it could simply have been the fact that 'Runnin' Away' remains one of Sly's greatest tracks, often ignored in the face of the more popular cuts like 'Family Affair' and 'Thank You (Falletinme Be Mice Elf Again)'.

Whatever the reason behind Freakpower's cover of the track, it proved to be a hugely effective cover and one that transcended any issues of race that might have dogged it. Freakpower may have been largely a white band, but from Jim Carmichael shuffling groove to Ashley's falsetto vocals, the track was played with enough soul for it not to be an issue. Quite simply, Freakpower were no Simply Red.

If 1970s acid funk had been the biggest influence on the album as a whole, 'What It Is' benefited from the inspiration of early 1980s New York new wave artists Was Not Was and, more accurately, Defunkt. The interplay between hard funk bass, brass stabs, stuttered trombone blasts and heavily punctuated vocals present on the stunning 'What It Is' could have come from either Defunkt's eponymous 1980 debut album or the *Thermonuclear Sweat* collection that followed two years later.

Defunkt was the brainchild of Joseph Bowie. Interestingly, Ashley Slater had done some session work with the Bowie Brothers in his pre-Freakpower years.

Following on from the hard New York funk of 'What It Is' was the commercial acid-funk war cry of 'Waiting For The Story To End'. With its low-slung groove and the 'boom boom, it's the freak of the week' chant, it proved to be one of the album's most insidiously catchy tunes, providing a stunning introduction to the speed induced fever of 'Rush'.

The final coupling of 'Big Time' and 'The Whip' added little to the story of *Drive Thru Booty*. The Prince-sampling, tongue-in-cheek 'Big Time' featured Ashley in smooth-operator rap, while 'The Whip' walked downtempo terrain, which again echoed Sly Stone while hinting at the psychedelic explorations of The Beatles on *Sgt Pepper's Lonely Hearts Club Band*. The result provided a gorgeous liquid rock finale to the album.

Despite ultimately being a derivative album, *Drive Thru Booty* was by no means substandard. With a sound which was dirtier, and a groove that was more sleazy than the acid-jazz bands that they were being compared to, Freakpower were presenting their own unique vision of the 1970s psychedelic dream. Sadly, it was all but ignored on its release, failing to make any impact on the chart.

One of the interesting facts about the album was that it was claimed that it was recorded at the Esselle Beat Company in Oakland, California. In reality, like every other post-Housemartins release from Norman Cook (until Fatboy) it was recorded at the Esselle Beat Company in Brighton, with Simon Thornton as usual in the engineer's seat. 'It was a little joke really,' recalls Kevin Stagg. 'I remember Norman saying they were going to do it. At first I was a bit miffed about it, to be honest, but when it came out people kept on saying, "I didn't realise you had studios in America." Our reputation actually grew.'

The first 500 copies of *Drive Thru Booty* contained the extra *Fried Funk Food* EP. Essentially a remix set, it presented a clear vision of where Norman's own productions were going. Initially, these mixes were inspired by Lynch Mob's 'SXDub 2000' reworking of Paul Weller's 'Kosmos', which appeared on 1993's *Sunflower*, and the subsequent 'Kosmos (Lynch Mob Bonus Beats)' and 'Sunflower (Lynch Mob Dub)' which appeared in 1994.

On the *Fried Funk Food* EP, Norman explored the downtempo arena of abstract beats similar to the work of Austria's Kruder and Dorfmeister,

Parisian artists The Mighty Bop and La Funk Mob and Tokyo's DJ Krush while also finding a resonance with British artists like Portishead, Howie B and Fila Brazilia.

'Turn On, Tune In, Find Joy' opened the collection with a spacious and soulful dub of Freakpower's debut single, where a slo-mo bass sample is washed by analogue synths and a gospel vocal. A masterpiece of undulating jazz-noir, it became a regular fixture in the leftfield DJ sets by Howie B, Ninja Tune's DJ Food and Pressure Drop.

'At Your Own Pace' continues in the same the chilled vein with its distant, echoing horns and dislocated keys. An Eastern flute refrain introduces a shuffling percussive break punctuated by echo drop snares. Over the top of this Cook layered a vocal performance from Alan Lomax's field recordings of early-20th-century indigenous American blues singers, thus pre-dating Moby's *Play* explorations by some five years.

On 'Sugar Lump', again the main feature is a combination of analogue synth noise, flute samples and a rolling bassline. However, this time Norman introduced an African percussion track and exotic bird sounds lifted directly from rainforest recordings. The inclusion of a 1960s BBC presenter narrating as musicians go under the influence of LSD for the purposes of documentary research only adds to the track's surreal flavour.

'Freakpower Is Beautiful, Baby', a radical reworking of the band's title track, incorporates a speech about 'Power' over a languishing jazz-noir groove until Ashley Slater delivers a Vocodered vocal. It's also one of the most upbeat moments on the EP, but still quite beautiful.

What follows is the EP's *pièce de résistance*, 'My Heart Sings', which had a huge impact on the leftfield abstract beats and trip-hop scenes. It was eventually licensed for inclusion on Mark Jones's seminal Wall Of Sound compilation *Give 'Em Enough Dope Vol 2*, and it's easy to see why this track had such an impact. There is a repeated three-note piano refrain, a loping breakbeat, dreamy analogue ambience, a ghostly voice telling the story of what makes his heart sing, a distant sax solo and an outro drum break that kicks like jazz drummer Gene Krupa. Working on various levels, the track is at once melancholic and positive, chilled and upfront.

The closing 'Where I'm Going' uses a repeated sample of a Balinese gamelan orchestra over rolling bass, pulsing synths and an easy piano motif. Again, the finished track is a sublime exercise in free-floating leftfield dub.

It's perhaps one of the strangest ironies that this album was restricted to such a limited pressing as not only does it provide an early indication of Norman Cook's future work, but it also displays him at a creative high delivering a near-timeless collection. Indeed, the *Fried Funk Food* EP still sounds contemporary in 2002 – something that has eluded every other Norman Cook release up until this point.

Despite his chart successes with Pizzaman, Norman remained resolute in his desire to push Freakpower to the top. Perhaps as a direct result of the self-imposed exile during the worst points of his breakdown, he had come to need the camaraderie of a full band. Increasingly, the House of Love became the focal point for the entire band's lives, and despite the lack of success, a solid sense of self-belief in Freakpower grew. However, Norman was still clearly aware of the band's shaky position.

'Life really revolved around Brighton, so I decided to move down,' recalls Jim Carmichael. 'Norman was quite concerned that I was changing my life and moving to Brighton just because of the band. He said, "You know, there isn't anything guaranteed for the future here, you leaving your life behind." I just said to him not to worry about it. But that was typical of him, to worry about why I was moving down. I was touched that he actually considered my situation.'

This consideration has long marked Norman as a person. With the exception of the brief period of egomania (with its disastrous results), Norman has always been regarded as one of the nicest people in the music industry. His memory for faces (if not conversations) is impeccable, while his motivations have always been genuine, if occasionally misguided. 'I will always remember Norman as a diamond of a bloke – generous, open, almost too open at times, an easygoing fella with a small dog,' recalls Freakpower's press officer Steve Philips. 'A lot of people in this business seem to forget who people are and just pretend they remember. It surprised me but he still remembers me even now. I remember the very first time I met him in a club in London. I was completely wasted and went up to him and did a complete rendition of

"The Housemartins Rap". He was chatting to Boy George at the time. Boy George told me to fuck off, but he was nice to me, which he needn't have been.'

Throughout what have become known as the House of Love years, Norman's hospitable nature took on new proportions. The house infamously sucked people in and didn't let them go for days at a time. What went on inside would have made the tabloid newspapers blush, had Norman been a celebrity at this stage.

'I probably took my first E round at Norman's house,' recalls Jim. The thing was, when you went to his parties, you just wouldn't ever need to leave the house again. A lot of vodka and orange was drunk. It was a bit of a life-changing time for a lot of us. There was one time I went round on a Friday night and woke up on Monday with no recollection of what had gone on before. There was a lot of lost time at the House of Love.'

Inevitably, the band's love of ecstasy and vodka spilled over into other aspects of their band life. Jim recalls, 'There were times when we'd be driving to the airport in a seven-seater bus, all a little bit shaky from the night before. Norman hated flying as well, which made it even worse.'

On another occasion, an all-day session would result in chaos for an interview with UK dance magazine *Mixmag*. 'This journalist, who shall remain nameless, was on his first ever press trip,' laughs Steve Philips. 'He'd never even stayed in a hotel before. We arrived at the House of Love at four o'clock and started partying. The photos ended up with Norman and Ashley in the bath together! A lot of drugs were consumed and the photographer got paranoid and burst into tears. I had to take him back to the hotel and spent the rest of the night calming him down. The House of Love was legendary, but this photographer just freaked.'

During this period of intense hedonism, Norm and his associates would systematically push each other to further extremes of drug-induced lunacy. Perhaps most famous among these exploits was the time when Norman and some friends snorted cocaine off the main London-to-Brighton train line that ran along the bottom of the Robinson

Road gardens. 'Some friends and I did it so we could tell our grandchildren,' he told UK celebrity gossip magazine *Heat* in 1999. 'We knew it was stupid, but it made a good story. We could dine out on it. It was the London-to-Brighton line. But we were quite careful. You could see whether the trains were coming or not.'

Another episode found Norman and his A&R man scaling the outside of his house in order to plant a flag on the roof. Their only climbing aid was a knackered old rope: 'We only got to my bedroom. We worked out that the peak of my house was on top of my wardrobe. So we planted a flag on it. Why? Because that's what you do when you get to the top of mountains. You have to show that you've been there. It wasn't actually a real flag because obviously we didn't have one. It was the letter off one of those belt buckles you used to have with names on them. But it was a flag to us. It was actually a very senior A&R man, who was the smallest of us, that had to go to the summit.'

It was at the House of Love parties that Norman would often try out his new tracks on people. Despite his acid-funk sounds for Freakpower and house excursions with The Mighty Dub Katz and Pizzaman, he had also started exploring more downtempo-inspired sounds, songs which were intended to be ambient but ended up being more in tune with trip-hop. Among the tracks he recorded during this period were early versions of the Fatboy Slim singles 'Sunset (Bird Of Prey)', which featured a sample of Doors frontman Jim Morrison, and 'Praise You'. When he eventually released a version of the Morrison-sampled track seven years later, it would receive a level of criticism from 'serious' music fans to rival his post-Housemartins defection to dance.

During this time, even the influence of the breakbeats so beloved of Norman made a real impact on the mainstream. Drum and bass developed from its dark rave and jungle roots into a household genre, while the trip-hop scene developed out of the nu-soul sound of Soul2Soul, the abstract hip-hop stylings of Massive Attack and the leftfield acid-jazz explorations of artists like The Sandals. Trip-hop, a term coined by *Mixmag*'s Dom Philips (who had also been responsible for the progressive-house tag) started to flourish in the mainstream thanks largely to the hype surrounding James Lavelle's MoWax imprint.

In the rapidly changing dance environment, Island realised that Norman's *Freakpower In Dub* output was perfectly placed. However, they also felt that releasing something like it under the Freakpower name might be damaging. The band had become almost irrevocably tied in with acid jazz, and given the industry's near-inability at this time to perceive that an artist could have appeal beyond the rarefied circles of a specific genre, such attachments were viewed as being negative – never mind the fact that many of the artists then emerging as the trip-hop frontline had previously been seen as acid jazz acts!

In February 1995, the second instalment of *Fried Funk Food*, called *The Real Shit*, was released. *The Real Shit* remains one of Norman and Ashley's defining moments, a six-track cut-up of hip-hop loops, weird ambience, rocksteady flourishes, house strings, analogue moods, soul, funk and electro cut-ups and a low-slung groove as cheeky as it is smokey. Fittingly, perhaps, the album appeared on the new Island offshoot (set up specifically to release trip-hop) called Blunted.

The Real Shit opened with the title track, a reworking of 'Big Time' from the debut album, which featured a series of analogue sci-fi burbling over a huge hip-hop break. In the background, a Roland TB 303 meanders while echoed keys sift in and out of the mix. A horn refrain and vocal sample brought the whole thing even deeper into the hip-hop lexicon.

The next cut, 'Freak Of Da Week', was a version of 'Waiting For The Story To End' from Freakpower's debut album. This remix became a massive tune on the breakbeat underground, finding a huge amount of support from Boy George, who played it regularly at London's Venom. It was the tune he chose to introduce US breakbeat combo Crystal Method when they played their debut London gig. The track featured a shuffling breakbeat, a tuba bassline, vibraslaps, copious amounts of scratching, funky wah-wah guitar and Ashley Slater's gumbo-sleaze trombone playing.

On the dub-soaked epic 'George', Cook and Slater combine a slow break with freeform guitars, echo-drop sound effects and the virtually omnipresent 303, while on 'Rhapsody In Loop' they take a horror-movie soundtrack and add a full-frontal funk break and snarling analogue synth line. Elsewhere, 'Rhapsody…' explores house ambience while it also features a vocal sample of Lord Finesse from his track 'Vinyl Dogs Vibe' (lifted from a bootleg called *Tracks Of The Vinyl Dogs*), declaring the words 'check it out now'. This sample would, a few years later, propel Fatboy Slim to international stardom.

'B-Boys On Acid', on the other hand, is perhaps the first inkling of the Fatboy Slim sound. On it a reverbed four-to-the-floor beat is stitched to burbling acid lines and a repeated vocal refrain. By the time the breakbeats kick in, it's already declaring all of the party-hard hallmarks that would come to epitomise his sound.

The closing cut, 'The Real Bonus Beats', is, as the name suggested, a version of the title track. In this version, the hard-EQ'd beats are pushed to the fore, the swinging bassline is dropped and the jazz/funk/dub flavourings are completely removed. It is, to all intents and purposes, a big-beat track.

Perhaps the most notable aspect of this album was the influence of The Chemical Brothers. Their 1994 single 'My Mercury Mouth' (under the original name The Dust Brothers, after the LA-based producers of The Beastie Boys' *Paul's Boutique* album) had spawned one of Norman's favourite tracks, 'Chemical Beats'. On it, he started to hear artists creating music from the dual influences of hip-hop and house. Rather than accelerate the hip-hop elements to breakneck speed, as had happened with the hardcore sound of a few years earlier, The Chemical Brothers pitched them at their original tempo.

While they were still working on 'Chemical Beats', another Brighton-based producer, DJ and Loaded Records employee, Damian Harris, was also developing sounds along the same trajectory. Harris had attempted to produce house music along the lines of the stuff that he was DJing with at the time but found it too hard. So he decided to go back to his hip-hop collection and use this as a starting point.

Harris grew up in the south-coast town of Whitstable and moved to Brighton in 1989. His given reason for the move was to study for an art degree, but he chose Brighton because it was a hotbed for his two main musical loves: hip-hop and house.

In the Skint Records biography, Damian explains how this love of music also infiltrated his degree: 'There were three parts to my degree show. One was performance – I had three turntables stuck on the same grooves, playing increasingly dramatic music that finished with the themes from *Dambusters*, *Star Wars* and *Superman*. Then there were two record players on the wall in the corridor outside my room that kept playing *Chariots Of Fire*. The final part, the *pièce de résistance*, was nine record players in a room all playing the run-out groove to *The Sound Of Music*. Really loud. I got a third.'

While at college, Damian followed in Norman's footsteps and got a job behind the counter at Rounder Records, where he would subsequently meet Norman and DJs like Carl Cox, Dave Clarke and Luke Slater. Damian quickly hit it off with Norman and he moved into the DJ's Dyke Road flat. He even went on to design some of the sleeves for Beats International. He was also involved in the design for some of the Pizzaman sleeves and would eventually also create the Fatboy Slim logo.

Following the completion of his degree, Damian was taken on as office assistant, or office dogsbody, for JC Reid and Tim Jeffries' Loaded Records label. Gradually, he started to spend more and more time in the Loaded Studio, developing his own sound. Inevitably, his office work started to be affected as all-night sessions in the studio would result in his being late for work.

Everything came to boiling point in late 1994, when he was close to being fired. In fact, it was an option that Norman himself was pushing for – despite the fact that Damian was a tenant in Norman's flat and that he owed quite a lot of back rent. Instead of losing his job, however, he struck a deal with his bosses whereby he could launch his own label. The proviso on this agreement was that he broke even by the third release!

That label would become known as Skint. The first record Damian wanted to release was *The Real Shit,* which he had heard on numerous occasions at Norman's house. Unfortunately for him, it was already signed to Island, so Damian was forced back to the drawing board.

When *Fried Funk Food Volume 2* finally came out on Island's Blunted offshoot, it failed on a commercial level, but it was quickly adopted by DJs like Justin Robertson, The Dust (Chemical) Brothers, Howie B, etc. It would go down in history as an influential moment in the growth of what the *NME* would later coin big beat.

Around this time, Levi's Jeans had created quite a stir with their new advert featuring a girl sitting in the back of a yellow cab, legs stretched out as the driver salivates in the rear-view mirror and plays with the shift stick. The advert's finale comes when the girl is revealed to be a transvestite.

The advert itself was a huge hit, thanks to its sheer irreverence towards the traditional jeans marketplace, while the spoof 1970s funk soundtrack also created a buzz. A week later, on 18 March 1995, 4th And Broadway reissued that track. It was 'Turn On, Tune In, Cop Out' by the previously ignored Freakpower. This event proved to be the salvation – and, ultimately, the undoing – of the band. 'It was a revitalisation of the band because the singles hadn't gone clear and the label were maybe reconsidering the situation with us,' explains Jim Carmichael. 'The whole band's future was looking a bit rocky. When we got the Levi's gig, it just changed everything. I remember the look of total relief on Norman's face. He knew what it could mean to us.'

'Turn On...' finally settled at the number three slot in the UK charts, but from that moment on Freakpower would be perceived by the media as an advert band, a particular type of band who were destined only ever to enjoy one hit, disappearing as quickly as they had appeared. The music landscape was littered with these bands, often connected to Levi's ads.

Carmichael on the other hand recalls the positive aspects of the single's success: 'It was great because it increased the profile of the band, which meant that we were going to be playing a lot more gigs. And we did a few TV shows in England, like *The Word*, *The White Room* and *Hotel Babylon*. And it got us a really good slot at Glastonbury, which was the biggest audience we played to. We must have played it at every gig, so we ended up messing around with it a lot, so we still enjoyed it.'

Incidentally, the track that had originally been pencilled in for the Levi's advert was by Donna Summer. However, when she saw the synopsis of the film, she decided not to give permission for the use of her music. Transvesticism was, she declared, against her religious beliefs. Throughout the process, the editor had been cutting the film to the Freakpower track, which he had bought on its initial release after he caught them playing live. When the Donna Summer track was ditched, he showed a cut of the film with Freakpower inserted to the clients. They were blown away and immediately agreed to this apparently unknown British band.

If the new-found mainstream penetration suggested that Freakpower would curtail their extra-curricular activities, their actions around this time proved otherwise. On 25 February, the band were stopped at the border between Northern Ireland and Eire and caught in possession of class-A drugs. 'We were driving across the border and the guards pulled us over and asked we had any drugs,' related Ashley to *Melody Maker*. 'We said yes! I had some acid and E, which was sandwiched between my, erm, cheeks. They asked me if I had any drugs and I said yes and gave them a damp, crumpled piece of paper with the stuff. Then we were strip-searched and given an anti-drugs campaign badge.'

Throughout their tour of Ireland they had used an Elastica tape box to hide their pills. However, when the guards boarded the bus, they forced the box open with a screwdriver and found the drugs. The band were subsequently ordered off the tour bus. Sniffer dogs were sent in and 22g of cannabis and five tabs of LSD were retrieved. Ashley was taken with two other members of the band to be charged with intent to import drugs while the rest of the band were escorted to their gig in Dublin. The strip-search that followed uncovered even more illicit substances.

'We got stopped at the checkpoint and they took Ashley and a couple of others in for questioning,' explains Carmichael. 'Basically, we had to drive to Dublin with two policeman in the bus. They were actually totally cool, saying that they were just doing their job and that they wouldn't normally pull bands over, but they were like, "You're busted now, so that's that." Ashley and the others had to go off and be cautioned while we went to the venue. It was getting really late and only half the band were there. The crowd were getting more and more noisy. And then

Ashley and Jesse and that got given a police escort from the police station to the venue. They just ran in and started playing. The crowd just went mad. Rumours had started to get around that we'd been busted.'

The following morning Jim and the rest of Freakpower went along to watch as the offending band members were fined £50 in a Dublin court where the judge asked, 'Do you take all these drugs so you don't have to listen to your music?'

'We were charged with importing drugs, but we made the point that we would be exporting them after the gig,' added Ashley to the *Melody Maker* at the time.

As 'Turn On, Tune In, Cop Out' gradually climbed the charts, the music press were increasingly full of snide remarks about Norman Cook's latest project. Derogatory comments were made in unassociated features and all mentions of the band came with the acid-jazz comparison. Acid jazz was a still a joke among the majority of the media. However, thanks to the advert, Radio 1 A-listing and apparent wall-to-wall screening of the video on MTV, Freakpower were able to reach a brand new audience.

They had moved into the notoriously fickle area of 'here today gone tomorrow', where people don't so much become fans of artists as fans of songs. As an immediate test of this, and as a direct response to the success of 'Turn On, Tune In, Cop Out' in its post-Levi's incarnation, 4th And Broadway decided to re-release the previously ignored album *Drive Thru Booty*. The release date was 15 April 1995, the same week as *Clear* by Island priority artist Bomb The Bass. Obviously, despite their need to promote *Drive Thru Booty* on the back of the advert, the album was destined to take a back seat behind Tim Simonon's long-awaited third Bomb The Bass album.

In that week's *NME*, the until-now-indifferent music weekly temporarily forgot its ongoing obsession with the recently missing Manic Street Preachers member Richey Edwards and printed a glowing 8/10 review by unlikely ally John Perry:

Right, see, this foxy chick gets into a cab. Taxi driver fondles his gear stick and gets all hot under the collar. But guess what? It's a bloke. Hah! Buy more jeans! Spend! Spend! Consume!

Confused? Hmm, yes, unfortunately shoving Freakpower in to tight trousers ads means that Joe Punter simply thinks 'Freakpower? They're just another Stiltskin, righty?' Wrong! Freakpower have moondust in their 'fro! Freakpower, they the MAAAAN!

Originally a cunning studio project dreamed up by Norman Cook to stop kids shouting 'Hey! It's Happy Hour again!' at him in the street, Norm recruited jazz funkateer-in-Big-Bird-outfit Ashley Slater, and Freakpower quickly mutated into one of the sexiest live acts in Funkville. Stabbing brass and throbbing bass all added up to one big serving of hot groove pie. Big happy grins on everyone ensured the jealous Jazz Mafia whined into their cappuccinos; Freakpower knew just where the party was.

And the debut *Drive Thru Booty* is damn near the greatest fancy dress party album…ever. It is a brilliant collection of uplifting smiley grooves: 'Freakpower' thrusts like a pimp in P-Funk platforms, 'Rush' is slick with wah-wah and slinky little flute hooks, while 'The Whip' is an epic Vegas skyscraper of a tune. And of course 'That Denim Related Track' is as mellow yellow as any transvestite in hipsters.

Drive Thru Booty is simply pure glitter pop, as smooth and shiny as Kojak in a pink turtleneck…who loves ya, baby.'

In the end the album missed the top 10 by one place: good enough for the label to underscore further tours by the band and take up the option on a second album. At the time it seemed as though the band had managed to sidestep the one-hit-wonder hex of the Levi's ad single, no doubt as a direct response to their increased live profile.

In June 1995 the band were invited to play the biggest gig of their existence, Glastonbury Festival, immediately before headliner Tricky. The gig proved to be a huge success for the band as their positive, funky vibes tuned in perfectly with the atmosphere of the festival. With Norman in his gold lamé shirt delivering those goofball guitar-hero antics he'd become known for, Ashley sporting customary psycho-pimp chic gear and the rest of the band suitably attired in a mixture of crushed velvet

Norman with The Housemartins

Freakpower and entourage backstage at the Radio 1 Evening Session. The whole band finished up naked

Backstage on one of Freakpower's endless European tours. (Left to right) Ashley Slater, Norman Cook, Jesse Graham, Jim Carmichael

Norman plays barman on tour with Freakpower in Spain

Norman seizes his favourite tipple from the Freakpower tour bus

Norman looking pensive in Cannes

Bellboy Slim – Norman considers
a new career at Brighton's
infamous Grand Hotel

Kitsch or chic? You decide

Norman dons the DJ gloves for his traditional Glasto gig in 1999. A year later, there would be twice as many people outside the tent as in, all trying to hear the Funk Soul Brother

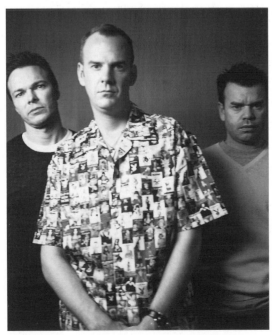

Norman is finally embraced by the DJ elite as he lines up with Pete Tong (left) and Paul Oakenfold (right) for the *Essential Millennium* mix album

With wife Zoë Ball, leaving London's Portland Hospital with their newborn son Woody

Norman delivers the finest ingredients

Fatboy Slim in the area

On the good ship HMS *House* on Millionaire's Row, Hove

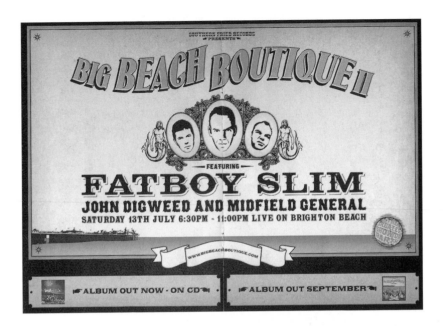

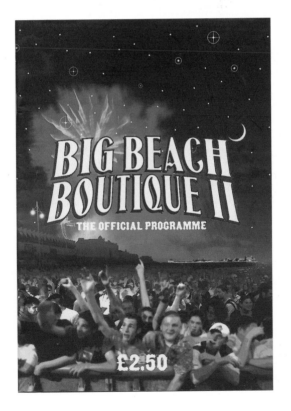

The calm before the chaos

Norman poses for the press as the beach fills up with party people

Flag Day 2002

Fatboy Slim brings Brighton to a standstill for the chemical generation's version of The Rolling Stones at Hyde Park

and silk, they lifted the spirits of the entire field. For many of the festival-goers, they ended up being the band of the weekend.

The question was whether or not that would translate into record sales. On the face of it, the answer was 'no' as the single 'Waiting For The Story To End' – released to coincide with the festival appearance – failed to chart. However, this wasn't the whole story, as the album was given a fresh shot in the arm and started selling again. Their tireless live shows had resulted in them translating into an albums band. Exactly where they wanted to be at this stage.

However, despite the levels of popularity that the band had achieved, they continued to be all but ignored by the music press. In one extraordinary live review in the *Melody Maker*, Julian Cravan took such a critical high ground that he successfully slated the band and their audience in a stroke of anally retentive arrogance. That people had enjoyed the gig at the Garage in Glasgow was irrelevant to his negative perspective:

There's a swan by the river behind my flat. Right now, I could be baptising it with breadcrumbs and admiring the easy grace with which its head snakes back to nuzzle its tail feathers. Instead, empty of wallet and yawning like a cavern, I'm watching two follicly challenged clowns and their garish friends entertain the sort of complacent, easily impressed tossers who'd applaud a tap for running.

At one point, Ashley jokingly refers to himself as a wanker. Not since Bryan Adams appeared in a video strumming away in a toilet has any band made such an inadvertently telling judgment of its own efforts. Condemning Freakpower as retro would be too obvious; for reasons we'll discuss in another dimension, dismissing bands thus is a cheap, lazy conceit, betraying a fundamental failure to grasp pop's territorial imperatives. What reduces Norman Cook and his cohorts to just another acid-jazz dribble is their inability to replicate the bacchanalian excesses of Clinton and Stone. Those bands sounded like an army of adults who thought monogamy was a board game and that inhibition had something to do with the banning of alcohol, getting together for an orgy of depravity that would shame the Borgias; Freakpower are, at best (THAT single), two accountants shagging atop a dead washing machine, at worst (anything else) a spotty kid with a lingerie catalogue.

As I leave, I hear a woman repeating the received wisdom about the stamina of bald men in the sack. Never heard of Samson, obviously.

Sadly, the review was representative of the level of coverage that the band were now receiving.

As had become an almost regular occurrence with Norman now, the last Freakpower single, 'Waiting For The Story To End', coincided with one of his club singles. Once again, it was the Pizzaman guise that was in the frame, and once again the club single scored a huge hit. Pizzaman 12 was 'Sex On The Streets' and it reached the number 24 position in the UK charts.

Once more, the Pizzaman formula found Norman's ear for a hookline coming to the fore as his funk samples were layered over a cowbell – frenzied, whistling-blowing, near-tribal beat. With its major-key strings and Italo-house pianos, 'Sex On The Streets' quickly consolidated Pizzaman's position as purveyors of the finest happy house – a genre that had been coined to describe the post-rave return to dance culture's disco roots. Not surprisingly, the 'serious' music press slammed it for its trivial, throwaway ideology.

If 'B-Boys On Acid' from *Fried Funk Food Volume 2* had offered the first true hints as to the direction in which Norman's home recordings were going, the next Pizzaman single would make the picture crystal clear while also drawing heavily on older Beats International themes. 'Happiness' uses boogie-woogie piano which opens onto a rocksteady Hammond riff before a 303 winds its way round the building breakbeat. The pay-off cp,es with a spiritual choir sample singing 'Happiness' before another soul sample declares, 'Set yourself free.' From the opening chords through to the gloriously positive, party-time finale, the track is 100 per cent Fatboy. Except this is Pizzaman.

It was November 1995 and 'Happiness' reached number 19, but Norman Cook was off with Freakpower again, this time to the exotic Compass Point Studios in Nassau in The Bahamas, where Freakpower were recording their follow-up to *Drive Thru Booty*, which had shifted a staggering 500,000 units in Europe.

'I thought we were going to Esselle again,' laughs Carmichael. 'And then there was this rumour that we might be going to Nassau. I was like, "OK, that sounds good." And once we got out there, it was like the pinnacle of our career, you know? Recording an album in the Bahamas, getting paid for a couple of hours drumming a day and spending the rest of the time bumming around on the beach.'

In actual fact, the Nassau session had come to fruition thanks to The Stereo MCs' inability to follow up their *Connected* album. Island had block-booked the time for them, and when they were forced to pull out due to creative inactivity, Freakpower were offered the time at a special rate. Not only did this prove to be an unforgettable time for the band, but it also marked the end of the Esselle Beat Company era. Not even Norman's imagination could stretch to suggesting that the Brighton studio also had a base in the Bahamas! Simon Thornton, on the other hand, was still very much involved.

With the exception of a lone female band member, Freakpower all stayed in Talking Heads bassist Tina Weymouth's complex of flats. 'There weren't enough rooms for everyone, so Lucy, the backing singer, being the only girl in the band, got an apartment in the actual resort,' says Carmichael. 'Anyone that came over, like the A&R guy, would stay in the resort. So we actually thought we were a bit hard done by, because the resort was like beach huts with fresh fruits delivered every morning and an idyllic surrounding. But we went down there and hung out.'

In fact, some of Freakpower were increasingly feeling hard done by in other areas of band activities. Although the band was only signed as the duo of Norman and Ashley, the rest of the group had started to feel like they were getting a raw deal in certain areas. Most notable was the fact that Norman and Ashley had brought their partners to the Bahamas. When Norman's girlfriend Bella later joined the band on tour, some of the band resented her presence so much that she was referred to as Yoko Ono, much to Norman's disgust.

The Nassau sessions were incredibly relaxed, with Ashley taking on a far greater production role, although this did lead to occasional sparks between the band's two main men. Both Norman and Ashley are very strong personalities with a definite vision of what they want to do. Inevitably, this would lead to occasional disagreements, but things would quickly work themselves out – with Norman invariably getting his own way.

At the end of the band's recording sessions, Freakpower and their ever-growing entourage arranged one final celebration at the resort's restaurant. It was to prove to be more dramatic than anyone had anticipated. Carmichael exclaimed:

> It was the last day for me. It was supposed to be a celebration of us finishing the band sessions for the album. Ashley and Norman were due to stay for another week to finish the programming and doing vocals and stuff. We were sitting in this restaurant and these two guys came in with guns demanding money. I remember sitting under the table with Garry [Blackburn] next to me, with a guy waving a gun at our heads saying, 'Give me all your money.'
>
> There was quite a lot of us there – the band; a German film crew making an EPK [promotional documentary film]; Garry; Jane Middlemiss, who had been interviewing us for some TV show; Julian Palmer – and we just heard these loud crashes from the kitchen and the chef came running out saying get under the tables. I just thought, 'Shit this looks like it's going to be quite bad.' I didn't have anything with me, but Garry had to give his gold Rolex. All I could give was a packet of fags!

With recording over, and lives and limbs still intact, the band returned to England while Norman and Ashley remained for another week to finish off some of the programming and start initial mixing. However, neither Norman and Ashley nor the record company were happy with the mixes and the tapes were duly dispatched to LA, with Norman in tow, where Prince's engineer Carmen Rizzo provided the final mixes in March 1996.

This final twist displayed an obvious sign of the label's intention to break the band in the US. Until this point, Freakpower, as with all of Norman's bands, had failed to have any impact at all in America.

∩EW DIRECTION

'One time I was onstage in Switzerland at a festival in front of 50,000 people. We played after The Red Hot Chili Peppers and BB King, and there's me with my four chords... I thought, "What am I doing here?"'

– Norman Cook, 1999

Back in August 1994, when Freakpower were just gearing up to release *Drive Thru Booty* and Pizzaman were playing footsy with the national charts, the Heavenly Records team including Jeff Barratt, Martin Kelly and Robin Turner opened a Sunday club event at the Albany pub in Great Portland Street, London. It was less a chill-out space than an attempt to redress the increasingly stifling sense of snobbery which had overtaken the dance world.

Acid jazz and its trip-hop offspring had turned the celebratory beats of funk and hip-hop into a joyless arena for posers and trainspotters. Techno had turned into an elitist genre which found people obsessing on the minutiae of sonic details rather than partying. Drum and bass had seen many of its founder DJs and producers ganging up to create the Committee. They intended to control the business surrounding their genre, but in reality only attempted to hijack people's careers. Musically, the once-energy-filled primal grind of jungle had turned onto another head-nodding arena for trainspotters. Even house and garage had turned into shameful versions of their former glories.

What these scenes were in danger of forgetting was the joyful essence at the roots of all dance music. The Heavenly Social's aim was a simple one then: to bring back a sense of fun to clubbing. As a result, the soundtrack was drawn from old ska and rocksteady, northern soul, rare groove, hip-hop, funk, Motown, acid house, Madchester, punk rock and even indie artists like The Manic Street Preachers – anything, in fact, which could guarantee a snobbery-free party.

Central to this music policy were the DJ duo The Chemical Brothers, whose ability to mix disparate sounds from Public Enemy to My Bloody Valentine and The Jimmy Castor Bunch to The Wolfgang Press quickly gained support from older Balearic clubbers and, perhaps more importantly, from the newly defected indie kids looking for a dance scene which didn't patronise them or leave them feeling ignorant.

By 1995, the Social was so popular that it moved to Smithfield's in London's Farringdon, while other similarly minded clubs like the Big Kahuna Burger Company were opening their doors. Once again, sweating like an idiot to great dance records that weren't only on DAT or one-off acetate was cool.

Back in the House of Love, Norman Cook had been messing around, at Damian Harris's suggestion, with sounds which fused the primal energy of hip-hop's breaks, delivered at house tempo, with the unhinged madness of the 303 in full swing. Over this time, he had played tracks to housemates and to Freakpower to gauge a reaction but had come to the conclusion that no one but him (and Damian Harris) liked the sound.

It was one of these tracks that Norman gave to Damian in the summer of 1995 to launch Skint. That track was called 'Santa Cruz' and was backed by 'The Weekend Starts Here', a Beastie Boys' guitar-sampling acid groove complete with the ramblings of seminal beat figure Neal Cassidy. For six full months, Damian played the acetate of 'Santa Cruz' at every DJ date he played. Each time, without exception, the track would get two or three people asking about it.

In Damian's experience, that level of public interest whenever a Loaded record was coming out would be sure to translate into guaranteed sales of at least 10,000 units. And so it was, with a wave of positivity in March 1996, that Skint Records launched the first Fatboy Slim record. However, despite earlier reactions, 'Santa Cruz' sold only 800 copies. Norman was therefore convinced that his earlier assumption had been correct. No one else but him and Damian liked the mix-up of acid and hip-hop he was producing.

He was completely wrong, however. In Germany, Air Liquid member Khan had been pushing at the same boundaries with his 4E project on Force Inc, '4E Speaking', creating an unholy marriage between the swing beats grooves of Janet Jackson and the 303s of acid house. America's revered Bassbin Twins had also been delivering raw breakbeat noise with a huge helping hand from Brit Miles Flanegan, aka Atom Smasher, whose 'Honka Fonka' and 'Macha B' had introduced a big beat flavour to drum and bass in 1994.

One evening, Norman received a call from Lindy Layton saying that she'd been to a club in London which was playing the kind of music he'd been making in his House of Love bedroom. Cook went to check out the Heavenly Social and the Big Kahuna Burger Company with Lindy and Damian and, to his surprise, discovered similarly minded people creating similar-sounding music. And, to add to the delight, The Chemical Brothers dropped 'Santa Cruz' in their set (Pizzaman's 'Happiness' had also been a regular favourite). Norman was elated. He jumped around all night, celebrating his new-found spiritual home, and ended up cutting his head on the ceiling in the process. 'He sent us a postcard the next day which we stuck on the wall – "Any time you're in Brighton, come and stay!"', recalled Chemical Brother Ed Simons to *Select*. 'He's a gentleman. A lovely vibe. You can't hold grudges.'

With tongue firmly in cheek, and perpetuating the favoured myth that Fatboy was never (and still isn't) Norman Cook, Damian Harris described 'Santa Cruz' on the label's website like this: 'First heard very early one Sunday morning round at Fatboy's shack, that backs onto the railroad, we sat there chewin' bacca as Slim whacked a tape on. The train lines hummed as the sublime opening chords drifted over us. When the thrashing guitars and beats kicked in we knew we were starting on a long and beautiful journey (hello?). As the guitars came out of the muffled haze and got closer and closer, so did the train, "Hey, where's that train a-headin', Fatboy?". He paused for a minute and, without taking his eyes off the sunrise, replied, "Santa Cruz." We were ready to go.'

What Damian failed to point out was that 'Santa Cruz' was a

surprisingly dark record built almost entirely around an old Lulu track yet strangely reminiscent of New Order's 'Everything's Gone Green'. The single played around with textures rather than melodies. The beats themselves were extremely muted, making the record a less-than-startling introduction to the Fatboy canon. However, it did sound unbelievably fresh for the time, evoking 'a sense of electro's otherworldliness, hip-hop's up front attitude and the madness of acid house', as I described it in *Melody Maker* upon its release.

Following 'Santa Cruz', Skint Records released singles by Arnold (including the Harris remix 'Brassic Beats', which would become the label's clarion call) and Hiphoptimist, aka Andy Barlow, who was also working on a project going under the name of Lamb. Indeed, thinking he'd signed Lamb, Damian Harris had pencilled their debut single as Skint 6. However, the drum-and-bass-meets-folk duo signed to Fontana instead, leaving Damian with an empty space in the release schedule.

In the end, Skint 6 became Fatboy Slim's big-beat war cry 'Everybody Needs A 303'. A frenzied slap- and subsonic-bass attack which featured gospel vocals lifted from Edwin Starr's 'Everybody Needs Love' and a 303 build that verged on insanity, this single immediately exploded on the Heavenly Social and Big Kahuna dancefloors. But once again it failed commercially.

The Mighty Dub Katz's 'Cangica', which was also released at this time, met with the same fate: its idiot-house approach fell flat at the first hurdle. However, it was only part of a triumvirate of Norman Cook records released in June 1997. The next two were a new, beefed-up mix of Pizzaman's 'Trippin' On Sunshine' and the first fruits of Freakpower's Nassau labours, 'New Direction'.

This time around, 'Trippin'…' reached the heady heights of number 18 in the UK charts, while 'New Direction' stalled at number 60. These results brought with them a state of confusion in the Norman Cook camp. On the one hand, 'Trippin'…' was a track that he'd knocked out with his friends in very little time. Furthermore it had become bundled in with the happy house scene, which utterly shocked him: 'Pizzaman got lumped in with this cheesy stuff like happy-clappers and such like, and I don't want to do that kind of stuff. I get sent compilations with a Pizzaman track and that kind of stuff on it and I'm horrified by the style.'

On the other hand, Freakpower's single had been recorded at enormous expense and had taken up a huge amount of his time. In fact, of all of the projects on the go at the time, it was Freakpower who had received the greatest investment from Norman.

'New Direction' found the band employing a sample from Afrika Bambaataa And The Jazzy Five's 'Jazzy Sensation', but retaining their acid funk slant and updating the sound to include 1990s tricks, which included, as anyone might have expected, copious amounts of 303 – the little box of squelches was rapidly turning into Norman's favourite toy. And the final frenzied crescendo on 'New Direction' rivalled Norman's most recent Fatboy Slim single for its unhinged attack. With the addition of Jim Carmichael's huge drums and Ashley's vocals distorted through the desk and then recorded through headphone speakers, the single was one of the band's finest moments.

Throughout the summer of 1996, Freakpower trawled around the festivals of Europe, playing to huge crowds. In places like Switzerland and Germany, they were immensely popular, regularly topping the bill at large festivals. It was while on their way to one of these dates in Norway that Freakpower had another run-in with the border authorities. Jim Carmichael explains:

> We were going from Sweden to Norway and had just received loads of merchandise which we were going through when we got pulled over. It's actually an offence to take merchandise into Norway without declaring it at the border. You have to pay 20 per cent of the value or something, which you get refunded when you leave. They impounded all of the new merchandise which we'd just got. Of course they then started wandering around the bus and some people hadn't been very careful with some of their substances and got taken off the bus. So we drove three hours to Oslo, thinking that it would be a repeat of Ireland, but word got back that they'd been deported straight away. So we had to drive all the way back to pick them up. We vowed never to go to Norway again.

★

Despite early successes, the band's popularity in the UK hadn't been sustained and the release of 'Can You Feel It?' in August of that year failed to even chart in the UK's Top 100. Despite the fact that it was an obviously commercial choice for a single, its 1960s guitars, Moog refrains and chugging breaks were reminiscent of some of Norman's Fatboy Slim material. In fact, it was a hook-laden track which walked the fine line between cool and kitsch. The UK weren't buying it, though, and history looked to be repeating itself for Norman.

Throughout the year, Norman had become immersed in the Heavenly Social scene and felt suitably inspired to push his DJing even more. He'd had a residency at Brighton's Escape Club for four years and was a regular at clubs like the Ocean Rooms and the Zap, but with the invitation to play the Sunday Social in July 1996 all the different music he'd been into over the years fell into place. His set was a meltdown of funk, ska, northern soul, hip-hop and flashes of acid, and he interspersed every track with the intro to Underworld's 'Born Slippy'.

Norman played his debut Heavenly Social set in the smaller upstairs bar while The Chemical Brothers headlined the main room. 'We wouldn't book him downstairs because he wasn't a big enough name,' says Social promoter Robin Turner.

One of Norman's favourite mixes at the time was the fusion of Josh Winx's 'Higher State Of Consciousness' (Norman had blatantly lifted its 303 and built it onto his own tracks) and Public Enemy's 'Bring Tha Noise'. When his own Fatboy tracks went down a storm, quickly turning into Social anthems, he was given the incentive he needed to explore the nascent big-beat sound further.

This had been underlined by the opening of the Big Beat Boutique in Brighton in April 1996. A blatant copy of London's Heavenly Social, the club quickly became a focal point for Brighton's disaffected B-boys, one-time ravers and clubbers who couldn't get into the happy-house sound that dominated the mainstream clubs.

In September 1996, some four months after it was actually recorded, Norman released the third Fatboy Slim single, 'Punk To Funk'. On this cut, time-stretched vocal samples are layered over a customary Schooly-

D break as a huge analogue bass pulse emphasises the groove. Then a middle-eight finds a new swinging beat introduced as a Moog line picks out an insistent melody which gives way to the final blast of 'Young Scene' by Keith Mansfield, which snakes through the mix until it takes presidence over everything else. Another big-beat anthem was born. The flipside offered the distorted and dirty 'Big Beat Soufflé', which Damian Harris has described being a track 'that kicks arse like a donkey on heat'. Norman found a fan in Prodigy mainman Liam Howlett, yet sales were still minimal. However a sea-change was occurring which was to find Norman Cook perfectly placed to ride the waves.

Rewind the clock back to June 1995. The Chemical Brothers had released their debut album *Exit Planet Dust* in the same month as Fatboy's 'Santa Cruz'. On the face of it, the two tracks were from totally different spheres. Fatboy's breaks were raw, his acid naïve, while The Chemicals produced a slick version of breakbeat indie dance. Dig deeper, however, and the album reveals itself as being inspired by all of the same sources as Norman's. In many ways, it was a mid-1990s rehash of the ideas that Norman had explored on the first album, except that, where one took its cues from 'Duck Rock', *Exit Planet Dust* was inspired by the post-acid-house anthemic rock of Oasis as much as the cut-ups of Double Dee And Steinski.

At the time, I criticised the album in my review for *Melody Maker* as having only two tricks. However, I did concede that these two tricks were better than just about any other dance or indie artist around. What The Chemical Brothers did with this album was create dance music that indie fans could understand. It was structured in the same way as standard rock music rather than taking on the textural shapes of house music, and they even used rock and folk singer Beth Orton rather than employing dance divas. Furthermore, they weren't afraid of using guitars with their beats.

In October 1996, The Chemical Brothers scored their first number one with the Noel Gallagher collaboration 'Setting Sun'. If there was one moment that the concept of a big beats scene finally found its focus, it was here. However, big beat was always a misnomer. The name may have described the breaks of Fatboy Slim, among others, but with the term the media tried to encompass every artist using breaks and guitars in unison. Furthermore, many of the leftfield experimental artists were dragged under the same umbrella.

'Lazy journalism,' cried Damian Harris and Wall Of Sound's Mark Jones at 1997's UK music-industry conference In The City. 'Lazy marketing, more like,' was my reply. They were forced to agree, because, despite the fact that no one liked the term, big beat was used by record companies to get their artists airplay, column inches and ultimately sales just as much as it was employed by journalists. The entire industry was built around genre specification.

The irony of big beat was that it attempted to turn the concept of being eclectic into a genre in itself. Subsequently, anything was OK as long as the samples came from a narrow area and the breaks were lifted from the right records. Which was the opposite to what the artists lumbered with big beat were about.

There was a world of difference between The Chemical Brothers' multilayered take on acid house and Bentley Rhythm Ace's cut-and-paste bargain-beat collages. Similarly, The Propellerheads' big-band-meets-rock-'n'-roll grooves were barely related to the Midfield General's electro-popping take on house, yet somehow they were all tarred with the same big-beat brush.

The Chemical Brothers were quick to dispel any notion of them being the figurehead for a scene. They were aware of the fact that the breakbeat had been a huge focus in all areas of dance throughout 1995 and 1996.

As the summer of 1996 drew to a close, four strands of the Norman Cook music world were about to collide as he prepared to release three albums and yet another hit single. And the reactions to each of these releases would not only paint a clear picture of Norman's future but also act as the clearest indication yet of the changes going on in the dance scene.

First was the second Freakpower album, *More Of Everything...For Everybody*, a title that came to Ashley after particularly mad night out: 'I was sitting on a bus, stoned off my nut, driving down some motorway at 5am... It's all about the way people have gotta have food which tastes better, colours that are brighter, cars which go faster, washing machines that wash better...'

More Of Everything..., much like its lead-in singles, found the band updating their original sound to embrace contemporary club culture. As a result, many of the original psychedelic flourishes are provided with a far weirder ambience – like Sly Stone on an ecstasy-and-acid cocktail, in fact.

The opening track, 'Trip Through Your Mind', is the embodiment of the 'further out there' ideology of this album. A wash of 1970s synths, low-slung beats and a vocal performance from Ashley that's as smooth as fine chocolate, along with a sample of Minnie Ripperton singing Stevie Wonder's 'Take A Little Trip'. It proved to be the perfect introduction to the album.

'New Direction' follows like an ecstasy love song. Indeed, the form of the song mimics the effects of the drug, with its formal (if a little woozy) structure suddenly taking on an almighty rush at the end. It's an effect that the band would attempt again on a later release, while Norman's Fatboy Slim output would try to capture the energy of ecstasy time and again.

Of the more soul-orientated tracks on the album, 'Husband' is a standout. With its bassline reminiscent of The Meters' 'If You Want Me To Stay', Philly strings and wah-wah guitar, the track presents Freakpower in one of its slinkiest grooves. It is very much a seduction track, taken to its logical extreme by Ashley's smooth operator vocals and lyrics.

'Can You Feel It' follows with plentiful hooks and a backing track that forms the blueprint for the second Fatboy Slim album, while 'Road Thang' continues the band's ongoing obsession with the Beat Generation, adding stories of mind travels to a Sly Stone-esque easy groove. It also features a chorus that echoes the Latin-funk sounds of War.

'Giving Up Government Drugs' continues the musical theme with its array of soul flavours, jazzy keys, slinky trombone solo and Moog refrains, which could have been lifted from Stevie Wonder's back catalogue. Lyrically, the song is an attack on the government-endorsed yet still harmful drugs like cigarettes and alcohol.

'KK Nuns' follows and is one of the weakest moments on the album, with Ashley rambling a story of gun-toting nuns over another acid-funk groove and honky-tonk piano. The track is notable only for the programming behind it, which again hints at the sounds Norman would go for on his second Fatboy album, and an outro guitar solo which echoes Funkadelic's Eddie Hazel for its lysergic ambience.

'Let It Go' comes on like the sister of 'Tune In, Turn On, Cop Out' thanks to its Sly-meets-War groove and LSD-soaked string section. 'Song #6', on the other hand, finds the band in laid-back mood with scratches, Moog washes and a synth sequence slowly echoed by a 303 and distorted guitars. The effect is typically unhinged, while also hinting at the timeless ambience that would appear on Fatboy's 'Right Here Right Now'.

'Freedom Child' is a trademark Freakpower acid-funk track with its chicken-grease wah-wah guitar, pulsing bass, wayward Moog-inflected middle-eight and chanted-cum-sung vocals, while 'One Nation One Ride' takes the chant theme even further, echoing Parliament's good-time call-and-response melodies before opening out onto a smooth funk opus.

The album is drawn to a close by the meandering 'Ghettos Of The Mind', which again echoes the rockier side of Sly Stone, complete with the Bahamian Youth Choir, whom Ashley had discovered while walking past a church during the recording in Nassau.

As with 'The Whip' from the first album, Freakpower end the album with a full-blown power-rock song. Unlike 'The Whip', however, 'Ghettos Of The Mind' is remarkably downbeat – a million miles, in fact, from Norman's other work.

Originally, *More Of Everything…For Everybody* had been pencilled in for release on 17 June, but it was put back by the record company to try to pick up on the post-festival interest in the band. Sadly, the tactic didn't work, as the album failed to make any impression on the chart. Furthermore, it was almost universally ignored by the media, with only one UK national daily newspaper, *The Guardian*, giving it a positive review. *NME* slated it in no uncertain terms.

The negative reactions to this album were unfair as it is far superior to *Drive Thru Booty*. Its production and arrangements are inventive without being obtrusive, its grooves are imbued with a deep funk and the programming takes things into the kinds of territories that The Chemical Brothers had explored on their debut album. Where all of Norman's previous albums had favoured the overuse of immediate hooklines over nuance and depth, this time around the production attempted to develop a richer sound. Furthermore, the songwriting has developed into an area far removed from the obvious surface-level hooks that had marked out all of Norman's previous work. Basically, with *More Of Everything...For Everybody*, Freakpower went some way to defining their own sound as opposed to being defined by other artists that they sounded like.

However, there was a trade-off in developing this more substantial sound: Freakpower lost the all-important fun factor to their sound. And it was this that the fans of their live show had loved so much.

Much of this change in direction can be put down to a greater involvement from Ashley on the production front. Although the first album marks him down as co-producer, he still maintains that it was only on this second album that he really got involved. Some of the sound of the album would be taken forward by Norman into his Fatboy Slim output, subsequently outlining Ashley's importance in the development of Norman's music.

More Of Everything...For Everybody remains one of Norman's great overlooked albums. Out of step with the media fads of the day, but remarkably in tune with the shape of things to come, it proved to be too individual for a media after the next big movement. 'I think it was badly handled by the record company as well,' adds Carmichael. 'They didn't know how to push it and, I think, released the wrong singles.'

Ironically, had Freakpower listened to their A&R man and released the demos of the album, they may have enjoyed more success. These recordings were like a raw fusion between Freakpower live and Fatboy Slim, underlining the fact that *More Of Everything...For Everybody* suffered from being too slickly mixed. If the object in this had been to break America, then once again they failed.

If Norman had been at all disappointed by the lack of success of the second Freakpower album, he would hardly have time to take stock. Within a month, he was back on the record shop racks with another album. This time round it was as Pizzaman with *Pizzamania*.

The contrast between Freakpower's acid funk and Pizzaman's adrenalised, positive house couldn't have been greater. However, there was a unifying factor – both were motivated by sex. Freakpower's grooves were waist-down, working directly on the true sexual meaning of the word funk, whereas Pizzaman was Saturday-night pulling music. 'I lived in a house with girls at this point,' Norman recalls, 'And I always used them as a test for my music. If I was playing something and none of them came into my room and said they liked it, then it got scrapped. I work on a very simple notion: girls dance to music they like; boys dance with girls to get laid. So getting laid is at the bottom of everything I do. If girls don't like my music, then I won't get laid.'

Pizzamania was a soundtrack to getting laid, an album of sexually charged house grooves, filled to the brim with adrenalised, positive, hands-in-the-air madness sandwiched between two mixes of the electro-disco frug of 'Trippin' On Sunshine' . Essentially, it is a singles collection, featuring the hits 'Sex On The Streets' and 'Happiness' in all of their E-charged glory. Elsewhere, both sides of the debut single are represented, while future cuts 'Gottaman' and 'Hello Honky Tonks' are introduced.

'Gottaman' features an old house riff over manic hi-hats and a repeated piano roll. The inevitable vocal hook finds a Vocodered male voice begging, 'Gottaman for a girl?' in an atonal drawl which immediately echoes Underworld. 'Hello Honky-Tonks', on the other hand, is a samba-blasting Latin-house cut flavoured by phased percussion and syncopated beats *à la* 'Krupa' by Apollo Four Forty (a track which had created a storm when anonymously promo'd on white label that summer. As soon as the dance media realised that it was by the band famed for fusing rock guitars and techno, they dropped the song like a shot.) 'Hello Honky Tonks' moves through the honky-tonk piano samples suggested by its title, suddenly bringing the ambience of a backstreet pub of the 1950s into the club arena, before closing with the repeated vocal sample of old electro track 'Rock Your Body'.

The rest of the album is made up by two tracks that would never be released as singles in their own right: 'Just Height The Ball' and 'The Feeling'. The former is a mix and match of Norman's samples over a standard house beat. String stabs, whistles, hip-hop vocal samples and funky Moog breaks jostle with each other for supremacy.

'The Feeling', on the other hand, offers the album's high point, thanks to its sample of spiritualist speech over an acidic soul-house ambience. The combination of 303 sequence, Hammond break and spiritualist vocals over the middle section is nothing short of stunning, while its multi-layered slow build and percussive collages display some of the early ideas for the track 'Song For Shelter', which would surface on the third Fatboy Slim album.

What is interesting about *Pizzamania* is that, despite being a singles album, it worked extremely well as a collection. Previous accusations about Pizzaman's happy-house crown seemed distant when presented in this multihued box of shades, tempos and atmospheres, brought together to conjure a unified theme of party music that girls can dance to.

As with Fatboy Slim and The Mighty Dub Katz, Norman's involvement with Pizzaman was still officially a secret. Indeed, the only hints as to his presence on the album sleeve came with the fact that the album was engineered by Simon Thornton and recorded at Esselle ('Babyloop' and 'Sans Bateaux'), Loaded Studios and, most tellingly, the House of Love. JC and Tim were credited by the Play Boys name and were given the credit of 'executive production and fatherly advice'.

Sadly, *Pizzamania* was poorly handled by Cowboy, and despite selling healthy amounts they were unable to translate these sales into a chart placing. However, *Pizzamania* remains an important document of Norman's transformation from King Canute figure trying to stem the tide of house to fully immersed, E-addled househead. Priceless.

As December dawned, Norman Cook brought his busiest year yet to a close with two of his most significant releases. The first was the single 'Just Another Groove' by The Mighty Dub Katz. With tongues set firmly in cheeks, Norman and Gareth Hansome (aka G Money) delivered a slice of Chicago house meets disco fusion which stripped any semblance of taste and replaced it with huge splashes of kitsch chicanery. A gloriously frivolous track, 'Just Another Groove' managed to crawl into the UK charts, settling at the heady heights of number 43, thanks largely to massive club promotion from a new label, Pete Tong's Ffrr. However, the single's significance in the Norman Cook story is that it represented the first time that he'd had any success in America!

Despite being the veteran of seven albums, numerous singles, nine different aliases (10 if you include his live outfit, Norman Cook's International Roadshow Versus the Real Sounds of Africa), a clutch of productions for other artists and close to 200 remixes, success on any level in the US had eluded him.

'Just Another Groove', however, was picked up by the San Francisco- and LA-based Breakbeat House cognoscenti. It subsequently went top 20 in the dance charts.

The second and most significant release at the tail end of 1996 came in the shape of Fatboy Slim's debut album, *Better Living Through Chemistry* on Skint Records. As a statement of intent, the combination of the album's title and cover art said it all. The title was lifted from a 1950s film condoning the use of Valium on children while also referencing one of Ken Kesey's Merry Prankster slogans, while the cover art depicts a simple two-tone image of a floppy disk. Together, title and artwork scream, 'This is DIY music made with the use of drugs, for people who take drugs.' *Better Living Through Chemistry* was a declaration of punk's otherness, sampling piracy and acid house's frontier spirit all rolled into one.

Like Pizzamania, *Better Living Through Chemistry* was a collection of the Fatboy Slim singles to date, with forthcoming 12"s and a few extras thrown in for good measure. The album opens with 'Song For Lindy', a thank-you to his long-time friend Lindy Layton. A house-tempo stomper with northern soul breaks, Italian house pianos, strings and a rolling sub-bass, the track pretty much lays out the 'what you hear is what you get' Fatboy manifesto.

'Santa Cruz' follows, with its whalesong paean to Lulu, before the next single, 'Going Out Of My Head', erupts with a flurry of rampant breaks and a cheeky sample of the opening guitar riff from The Who's 'Can't Explain'. The latter caused problems with the US release of the album on Astralwerks, as Who guitarist Pete Townshend allegedly demanded the removal of the offending sample. Norman would go on to claim that it was lifted from a different record, but he would later confirm the Townshend source following an amicable agreement between the two. In the end, Townshend received 100 per cent royalties on the track, but Norman still received his cut on sales, so he wasn't completely out of pocket.

The following tracks 'The Weekend Starts Here' and 'Everybody Needs A 303' finds the old singles being given new life, while 'Give The Po' Man A Break' highlights Cook's ongoing obsession with the old blues sounds of the Delta. With African percussion and hip-hop beats framed by analogue noise and the obligatory 303, 'Give The Po' Man A Break' is provided with extra momentum by a bassline created from a male voice.

'10th And Crenshaw' continues with the dominant theme of filtered breakbeats and squelching 303s and lysergic breakdowns, while 'First Down' is a syncopated house beat reminiscent of Pizzaman's 'Hello Honky-Tonks'. The kitsch sax sample and bouncing bassline only add to the track's feelgood vibe.

'Punk To Funk' follows before the album is brought to a close with the swamp-blues tribute 'The Sound Of Milwaukee', in which an unknown speaker urges, 'Throw your arms in the air,' before Fatboy delivers a musical sermon on rock 'n' roll, the blues and rocksteady over a huge, rolling breakbeat.

Essentially, *Better Living Through Chemistry* is the sound of Norman letting off steam and doing his own thing. As a result, this seemingly naked collection screams with honesty. The only limitation he placed on himself was the previously noted urge to make music that girls would dance to. However, whereas *Pizzamania* had its sights set on seducing the glammed-up clubbers, *Better Living Through Chemistry* was after the girls who were ripped to the gills on ecstasy, high on amyl, sweating for their country on the dancefloor of the dingiest, most unglamorous clubs in the UK. In other words, this was all about getting laid at the Heavenly Social, the Big Kahuna or the Big Beat Boutique.

Like his other two albums released in 1996, *Better Living Through Chemistry* barely made any dent on the UK charts, although it did steadily continue to sell, eventually accruing sales in the region of one million units.

Unlike Norman's previous dance material, Fatboy Slim was starting to receive almost universal critical acclaim throughout the UK media, despite the seemingly ongoing need to mention The Housemartins in every review written. *NME*'s Keith Cameron was among the most positive with his review of *Better Living Through Chemistry*, making a direct comparison between it and *Exit Planet Dust*: 'His singles have swollen the loins of all self-respecting Heavenly Socialists this year with a fervent funk-punk beat stew that begs its own definition: rip-hop. But with the advent of this LP, it is time for a wider world to acknowledge the startling truth that, under his latest *nom de groove*, the bloke who played bass in The Housemartins has made the party soundtrack of our dreams. Oh yes, Fatboy Slim is Norman Cook. And oh double-plus yes, *Better Living Thorough Chemistry* is the most consistently exhilarating assemblage of slap-happy electronica since *Exit Planet Dust*.'

Ironically, Skint had never really considered *Better Living Through Chemistry* as a proper album. To them, it was a collection of club tracks. In fact, at this time neither Damian nor Norman really considered Fatboy Slim to be an albums act.

If Norman had hoped that the US success of The Mighty Dub Katz would rub off on Fatboy Slim, he was sadly mistaken. On a short DJing trip to the US to promote the album's release on Astralwerks with the label manager John Paveley, he barely drew crowds of any significant numbers. Indeed, on a couple of dates he barely managed to attract people in their tens, let alone their hundreds.

'I'm not worried about the US at the moment,' explained Norman at the time. 'I do this for the experience. I get to travel. I get to see places I'd always wanted to see. I get to meet new people. It beats becoming a fireman.'

Throughout the latter part of 1996, Norman also toured tirelessly with Freakpower. However, following the disastrous performance of *More Of Everything...For Everybody*, they were dropped from their label. This gave rise to the suggestion that much of the debut Fatboy Slim album had originally been intended for the third Freakpower album (just as *Drive Thru Booty* had been mooted as the third Beats International long player). However, as Jim Carmichael confirms, this had never been the case, as far as he was concerned: 'There were no

FATBOY SLIM: FUNK SOUL BROTHER

promises given about our future. When we were on the road, Norman used to bring early demos with him of this other project. He would ask our opinion on what became the Fatboy Slim stuff. It's been said that this was going to be the third Freakpower album, but I didn't get that impression, to be honest. He may well have said that, but it was quite clear to me that he was wanting to work on his own more. You can take a band to the Bahamas for a month and get a good sound out of it, but at the end of the day he could do this stuff in his bedroom. And I think Norman was getting a little bit tired of having to take a band around, and the expense of it all, so I think he realised he was better off doing it on his own.'

Freakpower finally came to an end amidst squabbles about money and the continued presence of Bella on their tours. However, this was just symptomatic of the fact that the writing was on the wall for the whole band to see. 'I've been in bands where it's been obvious that things were winding down and you've just got to say, "Well, time to move on,"' says Carmichael. 'We knew Freakpower was coming to an end. It was at the end of this particularly long tour and we had about three gigs to go when we found out the band were dropped. So we said, "Let's go out with a bang." Our last gig was in Granada, in Spain, and it was brilliant. The gig was fantastic. We gave it everything, and then, of course, we did all the drugs that were left on the three-day journey home. We never saw daylight for about three days and watched as much *Ren And Stimpy* as we could! I used to call them class-A journeys – for obvious reasons.'

Freakpower would leave a lasting legacy behind them of two good albums and hundreds of notoriously riotous gigs. But they would be largely remembered for that Levi's ad.

'There's a perception that we were just a one-hit-wonder band,' confirms Carmichael. 'But I do think that we had a good group with a good fan base.'

Despite selling over two million records, they were left with a debt of over £500,000 from touring alone.

In 1998, the duo of Norman and Ashley would release one more single as Freakpower. Called 'No More' and released on the dance imprint DeConstruction, it carried the demo blueprint of the last album and took it even deeper into acid-breaks territory. Through Ashley's distorted but gloriously hazy vocal you could hear the sound of Norman furiously developing the next Fatboy gameplan. A further two Freakpower singles and an album were announced by Norman in an interview at the time, but Ashley has always maintained that this wasn't ever on the cards.

Ashley would go on to record leftfield tracks as Dr Bone (for Skint) and Colonel Kurtz (for Southern Fried) while also forming the sublime Big Lounge, whose debut album included a version of 'Husband' from the second Freakpower album. 'It was a record for people who said they loved my voice,' he once explained. Among his other ventures would be directing videos for himself (Dr Bone's 'Cop In A Coma', which featured him doing an autopsy on Flat Eric!) and another for Norman (Fatboy Slim's 'Everybody Needs A 303'), while he has also scored a film.

Of the rest of Freakpower, one notable development came for keyboard player Eddie Stevens when he went on to become a member of Moloko. Jim Carmichael went on to work with Les Rhythms Digitales (Wall Of Sound) and is now a partner in a music-production company in Brighton.

'The idea was that we'd be Simply Red on acid,' Norman explained as an epitaph to Freakpower, 'a big band you could dance to, but I'm not very good at writing songs, not interested in crafting lyrics and rehearsing for weeks. Even during the successful phases, I was unsure. One time, I was onstage in Switzerland at a festival in front of 50,000 people, we played after The Red Hot Chili Peppers and BB King and there's me with my four chords, this inept guitarist who the band are always on at to practise more, and I'm following BB King. I thought, "What am I doing here?"'

MAGIC CARPET RIDE

'I love being the centre of attention. I'm a natural born show-off, but I can only show off if I'm comfortable with what I'm doing. I've been DJing for 16 years. I know what I'm doing. I feel confident.'

– Norman Cook, Mixmag, *1999*

1997 will go down in history as the year that the British dance cognoscenti gave the breakbeats of hip-hop back to the US, dominating the charts and opening the doors for 'electronica' in the process. Two acts could be primarily thanked for this: The Chemical Brothers and Prodigy. A third was hot on their heels, however: Fatboy Slim.

The Chemical Brothers had made a certain amount of headway in the US with their debut album, *Exit Planet Dust*, and with the duo's live shows and DJ sets throughout the US. However, it was when they dropped their second album, *Dig Your Own Hole*, that the US finally embraced them. Thanks largely to the album's mix of the guitars of rock, the 303s of acid house and the breaks of old-skool hip-hop (Grandwizard Theodore, the inventor of the hip-hop scratch, featured on 'Block Rocking Beats', a track which sampled the muscle-bound funk bassline from 1980s punk outfit 23 Skidoo).

Prodigy had already enjoyed incredible success in 1996 with their MTV-dominating breakbeat punk epic 'Firestarter'. However, the full extent of their achievements wouldn't be felt until that summer when they released their third album, *Fat Of The Land*, the highest-selling British album of all time, going straight in at number one in 22 countries on its first week of release. In the US, the first week of the album's release saw it shifting 200,959 sales. In comparison, the original soundtrack to

Hollywood box-office smash *Men In Black* achieved sales of only 177,470 while The Spice Girls' *Spice* album managed only a meagre 147,922.

It's fair to say that, by the time Norman's Fatboy Slim campaign in the US was launched, the foundations were laid. Nevertheless, the initial release of *Better Living Through Chemistry* fell flat at the first hurdle. America had largely ignored both Norman's DJing dates and the album which was then withdrawn until a royalty agreement with Pete Townshend could be reached.

In February 1997, both Astralwerks and Skint issued the track that had caused the commotion, 'Going Out Of My Head'. Essentially the first single to be released in the US, it was mainly chosen at the insistence of The Chemical Brothers, who were sure that its combination of huge breakbeat, off-the-wall noises and slabs of heavy guitar would go down a storm in the US. They were right. 'Going Out Of My Head' crashed into the dance charts, went top 20 in the rock charts and even featured in the *Billboard* Top 100 – an almost unheard of achievement for a dance instrumental.

'At the moment, pretty much the whole thing has revolved around what The Chemical Brothers and Prodigy have already done,' Cook explained in *NME*, while considering his chances of being the next act to break the US. 'A lot of people are just looking to see who's going to be the next one and Tom and Ed have opened a lot of doors for people. There's that and the fact that "Going Out Of My Head" has got guitars on it and appeals to the Nirvana-with-breakbeats kind of crowd. But I'm not convinced that it isn't just that one song that they like... I've been doing interviews for Modern Rock radio, and you feel a bit like, "What am I doing here? Oh, because I used a sample of 'I Can't Explain'." So I'm not sure whether its a serious interest. But I don't actually give a fuck. If it was the one tune, that was fun. If it's more, then that'll be fun too.'

Much of the single's stateside success was put down to the fact that the liberal use of guitars attracted the country's rock and industrial fans. However, another element in the success story was the simple but effective video, which received healthy support from MTV.

Essentially, the video's narrative follows the story of the breakbeat from the block parties of New York to old-skool hip-hop's appropriation by contemporary clubland, and then the multicultural parties of big beat as the DJ returns the newly changed breaks to the US.

The video's message is executed through obvious images: the beat's taken to the streets via a boombox, the black kids are separated from their boombox (heritage) by the white authoritarian figure of a security guard, the appropriation is represented by a white girl clubber picking up the boombox and then Fatboy Slim gives it all back through his DJ sets. However, this placed a questionable spin on Norman's previous concerns at being seen as a white bloke appropriating black music. Now he was pictured as the altruistic DJ, giving it all back. The final message was quite literally, 'Without black music, there would be no Fatboy Slim.'

It's true that Norman's love of hip-hop, funk, blues and soul were at their most obvious in the Fatboy guise. Even the name was lifted from an old Louisiana bluesman. However, his skill as a producer on the Fatboy material was to turn black dance music into something to which white college kids could relate. This was more than evident on 'Going Out Of My Head'.

The subsequent reissue of *Better Living Through Chemistry* in the US in mid 1997, complete with the extra tracks 'Michael Jackson' and 'Next To Nothing' (the flipside to 'Going Out Of My Head'), would pick up on the euphoria surrounding The Chemical Brothers and Prodigy, translating into good sales performance. It would also see Fatboy's pulling power as a DJ increasing considerably.

As dance music continued to invade the US in 1997, numerous acts benefited from the increased interest. Orbital and Aphex Twin all toured extensively with Moby, while UK acts like Fluke hooked up with US breakbeats duo Crystal Method for another tour. However, in reality, the numbers attending the gigs didn't add up to the hype surrounding the so-called phenomenon. It was the dance acts that played the rock game that succeeded: people like Prodigy who presented a live show, complete with guitars and live drums.

One group that did benefit immensely from this period of interest in UK dance crews (lasting from 1996 to 1999) was Skint's Lo Fidelity Allstars. In 1999, their debut album, *How To Operate On A Blown Mind*, became the highest-selling album by a UK artist in the US, thanks to sales of over 400,000. This happened as a result of intense interest in their Pigeonhed sampling single 'Battleflag'.

With the Fatboy phenomenon finally on the move, Norman turned his focus once again to idiothouse project The Mighty Dub Katz in March 1997 and kitsch club soundtracker Pizzaman in July 1997. The Mighty Dub Katz's offering was the lacklustre 'Ghetto Girl', which again featured an unsubtle array of samples but with the Fatboy Slim nose for a party. However, it lacked the flow that marked out Norman's best work.

Pizzaman's single came in the shape of the album track 'Gottaman', featuring a stunning 'Distant Drums Mix' which fired up the track's tribal flavour. The single failed to chart (as did 'Ghetto Girl'), but it marked the end of a hugely frustrating time with Cowboy Records, which left the trio owed thousands of pounds and an intense legal wrangle with Pulse-8 Records, who now owned the Cowboy catalogue. However, Reid and Jeffries maintained that the rights to the recordings had already reverted to Loaded. The fall-out from Pizzaman subsequently proved to be very costly indeed.

As 1997 saw the popularity of the big-beat sound growing, so too the Big Beat Boutique became a magnet for like-minded souls across the south-east of England. Since its inception on 23 April 1996, when the DJs included Jon Carter, Damian Harris, Norman Cook (and Fatboy Slim!) and Sean Roley, the Big Beat Boutique had attempted to explore that area of dance music that the superclubs weren't covering. As a result, it became a meeting place for fans of labels like Wall Of Sound, Ninja Tune and, of course, Skint.

The initial idea for the club actually came from Gareth Hansome after he worked on a fashion show with Oasis DJ Sean Roley. Gareth had been working with Carl Cox, travelling around the country to attend raves (largely organised by the Centreforce Radio crew) and had become extremely bored with the sound that epitomised these raves.

He first had the idea for the Boutique almost a year before it finally opened, but he didn't have the venue. After hearing 'Santa Cruz', he went to see Damian to ask if he wanted to get involved in some way. In the meantime, he had also promised to involve Norman with the idea, following his infamous discovery of the Heavenly Sunday Social and the Big Kahuna Burger's Friday-night sessions. Eventually, Gareth worked out a deal with beachside venue the Concorde. It had exactly the right ambience for the venture: sweaty, rough around the edges, distressed from years of abuse, more rock 'n' roll than the glam surroundings of most clubs. However, they didn't initially have the name to go with the club night. After a night of throwing ideas around they came up with Kung Fu Jim Jams! Thankfully, it didn't stick.

The Big Beat Boutique was suggested as a play on the phrase that weekly papers *Melody Maker* and *NME* had been touting to describe the breakbeat music that Fatboy Slim, The Chemical Brothers and so on were making. The Boutique part of the name, however, was a direct reference and homage to The Beastie Boys' seminal second album, *Paul's Boutique*.

At the Boutique's first birthday bash in April 1997, Norman Cook and Jon Carter delivered a back-to-back duel dressed in T-shirts depicting their names and a picture of Brighton's Palace Pier. 'I'd put on a tune and say to Norman, "Right, follow that," explained Jon Carter. 'It was just insane, with the barriers down the front. It was like a fucking concert. They go nuts down there. A proper vibe.'

In July 1997, the Big Beat Boutique enjoyed its first real milestone when it promoted one of the tents at the Brighton Essential Festival. It was, according to all concerned, the first time that they had seen the extent to which the big-beat sound had become popular. From beginning to end, the Boutique tent was rammed.

Naturally Norman was the headline DJ. 'Definitely a pivotal moment,' he told *Muzik*. 'I felt like a pop star again, but doing it on my terms. I remember everyone just roaring as if to say, "Yeah! We get this!" I got there about two hours into it and there was this feeling that this was it.'

'I put on the first record and everyone went ballistic, screaming, the whole tent dancing, all 3,000 of them, with more people dancing outside,' he added in an interview in *DJ Magazine* in October 1997, having just been voted in at number 39 in their Top 100 DJs poll. 'The Boutique only holds 200 people, so different people come each time. At the festival, everyone was together, and they all knew what to expect.'

This poll showed the extent to which the leftfield clubs had started to infiltrate the mainstream culture. Usually the DJ poll was dominated by house DJs, although drum and bass had seen a few of their main players getting placed on the list.

Norman's position on the list was remarkable on two counts. Firstly, it represented Norman Cook finally being accepted by the dance scene. Secondly, and perhaps most pertinently, he achieved this accolade despite steadfastly refusing to play in the north of England. Indeed, his only residencies were at Brighton's Big Beat Boutique, the Skint monthly residency in association with Wall Of Sound at the End in London, the Heavenly Social and Kahuna Presents Freaky Dancin', again both in London.

Norman was quoted in *DJ* as saying, 'I'm honoured. Really honoured. It's a triumph of eclecticism over purism. I'm just surprised because the only people who have seen me are from London or Brighton, only about 20 per cent of the potential voting audience have seen me. I don't play anywhere north of London. I'm too lazy.'

In a *Mixmag* feature to coincide with the release of the second Fatboy Slim album, *You've Come A Long Way Baby*, he explained in greater detail why he stuck to playing in the south: 'It would take up too much of my week. I'd never get any work done. My capacity for… Well, let's just say I like a drink, so once I've played I'm not going straight to bed. I used to end up going to sleep at 11am, half an hour before I got thrown out of the hotel. I'd end up sitting in Nottingham off me nut, thinking, "How am I going to drive home?" I wouldn't get home till six or seven at night, I'd have a hairy drive so I'd need a drink when I got home… There are places I'd be flattered and excited to play – Cream or Bugged Out – but if I played Cream, everyone else would moan, so I've got to have a rule.'

In the interview, Norman went on to explain the lengths promoters were prepared to go to in order to book the DJ. 'A promoter from Wales rang up and said, "What would it take for Norman to play here? How about a stretch limo to his front door, full of champagne and cocaine, and when he plays we'll have two naked women dancing in front of him?" Tempting though it was, I have to keep my, erm, willpower strong.'

With Norman's DJing dates now piling up, the pressure was on him to release another single. However, typically, when it arrived in August 1997, it turned out not to be a Fatboy Slim record but a track by The Mighty Dub Katz. This time around, however, it was a scorcher.

'Magic Carpet Ride' melted ska on top of Latin-flavoured hip-hop beats and finished the whole thing off with a massive dubbed-up house ambience, exactly the classic party tune he'd always threatened to make – positive, adrenalised, joyful, but not cheesy.

Jumping on the record straight away, *NME*'s Kevin Braddock wrote in the paper's dance section, called Vibes, 'Cartoon breaks, speaker-poppin' hip-hoppery and the welcome return of ska to the global dancefloor. Easy now selectah!'

If this kind of support wasn't positive enough, however, a week later the same paper had John Perry awarding it the coveted Single Of The Week, writing:

Candy floss on a stick Pizzaman! This is sooo stupid, fluffy and luminous pink it'll rot your teeth. 'Magic Carpet Ride' HAS to be the dub-ska-big-beat-Latin-*It's-A-Knockout* theme tune of the summer by a mile. Obviously there was a great deal of stiff competition from a number of other dub-ska-big-beat-Latin-*It's-A-Knockout* outfits, but The Mighty Dub Katz played their joker, struggled across the slippery pole in giant foam feet and made Stuart Hall laugh like that madman he is. 'Magic Carpet Ride' is pure sunshine, the mad skanking 'Alright' for 1997, a loopy mix of cheesy spaghetti Western bass and gurgling *Blake's* 7 sound effects over a groovy moonstone beat that wouldn't sound out of place at a Bad Manners reunion. Oh, and it has a triple barbed hook that goes 'A-ring-ding-ding-ding/A ring-ding-ding!' Excellent.

Of course, this just has to be the work of baldy genius Norman Cook in about 57 cunning disguises; Norm wrote the tracks wearing his Pizzaman's daft hat, put it together wearing his Mighty Dub Katz Groucho moustache and then remixed it in his Fatboy Slim false beard. And no doubt CD2 features the Housemartins mix, the Beats International twiddle and the

Freakpower tune-up... Arrghhh! It's mad! It's ace! It's ooop and UNnnn-DER!'

As with 'Going Out Of My Head' and 'Everybody Needs A 303', this Mighty Dub Katz offering was notable because it gained heavy support from underground beats DJs like Jon Carter and Richard Fearless (of Death In Vegas) while also receiving increased attention from the mainstream people like Radio 1's Pete Tong (of course, this was inevitable considering that 'Magic Carpet Ride' was issued on his own Ffrr imprint). The song would go on to sell over 500,000 units across Europe and America.

Although it's easy to view the big-beat phenomenon as being unique to the south of England, the truth was that the beats initiative had also gained a huge stronghold in the northern cities of Manchester, Liverpool, Leeds and Newcastle while Midlands towns like Nottingham and Leicester were also rocking to the beats.

The US was also playing a major part in the development of the breakbeat generation. West Coast acts like The Bassbin Twins, Mephisto, Chris Smith, Hardkiss, Crystal Method, Uberzone and Icee were huge with the big-beat elite. Similarly the influence of Josh Winks' 'Higher State Of Consciousness' can never be overplayed. It was the acid lines and extended drum rolls of the track's infamous build that could be heard time and again on tracks by Norman *et al*. Indeed, beneath the spiritualist blues samples and hip-hop breaks, the arrangements of Fatboy Slim's records owed more to house music than anything. Where other producers and DJs looked down on the euphoric effect of the snare-roll build, he employed it to full effect.

'It works in clubs,' was Norman's response to criticisms. 'It's the rush of ecstasy in sound. And my role in the club is to play music that will help people enjoy themselves, not have a bad time because I've worked against the drugs.'

When pushed again on the subject he went as far as to define big beat: 'For me, the idea is a house tempo with all the buildups, excitement and acid stuff, but with a breakbeat instead of 4/4. In my set I play house, drum and bass, breakbeats, acid house... Everything goes, as long as the speaker blows!'

'For me,' he explained to *DJ*, 'it's big breakbeats, but not in the same way as techno or drum and bass. A lot of people think breakbeat and think of the slower rap-based stuff that Jon [Carter] plays, but I play a lot more than that. One of the magazines slagged off Jon Carter for playing house at the end. The idea was never that we didn't play house, instead we play everything.

'The whole thing for me as a DJ is going out and finding obscure records. I'm playing lots of jungle right now [1997], loads of mad house, and Brazilian stuff, along with hip-hop and ragga. Straight breakbeat records were really hard to find a couple of years ago, and now there's too many cheap shots, I won't go near those! There are brilliant records coming out every day, but you've always got to stay ahead of what people are expecting and stay away from the cheese!'

By mid 1997, the term 'big beat' was accepted almost universally almost universally. However, many of the people involved in making the music and DJing refused to accept the name. As we've seen, The Chemical Brothers rejected any suggestion that they were a part of a scene, while main players Mark Jones (Wall Of Sound) and Damian Harris suggested that it was merely lazy journalism.

Norman, however, was far more accepting of the term. Talking to *DJ*, he said that he was quite happy about it, 'on account that my flatmate Gareth, who runs the Big Beat Boutique, made it up! People were calling it hard hypo, Brit-hop, whatever, and he said one night, "Nah, it's big beats, innit?"'

However, he was less enamoured with the image that surrounded big beat. Largely thanks to the laddish culture post-*Loaded* magazine, which had become synonymous with the Heavenly Jukebox (as it had now become known), big beat had become saddled with the image of music for beer boys who can't hack it in the house clubs.

Aspects of this were true, largely due to the fact that the music (Fatboy's especially) worked the beer and fags party spirit which is unique to British culture. Indeed, in creating singalong club music (those 303 squelches were often accompanied by hundreds of drunk or E'd-up revellers singing along, acid karaoke style), it tapped into a tradition which stretched back to vaudeville – an unpretentious sound created purely for the purpose of creating the right atmosphere for having a good time.

One derogatory comment by a fellow DJ was taken as a compliment by Norman. Mancunian DJ Mr Scruff, whose sets were drawn from equally diverse sources but presented with a more laid-back, near trip-hop attitude, described big beats as 'handbag hip-hop', a reference to the pre-acid house days when girls at discos would literally dance around their handbags. Later, the term 'handbag house' would be coined to describe the happy-house sound that Pizzaman had been lumped in with.

'Well it *is*, you see – that is how I'd describe it; I used to make handbag house and I'm proud of it,' exclaimed Norman to *DJ* in November 1997, despite having previously suggested that he hated the other handbag stuff so much that he was forced to curtail his remixing. 'He [Mr Scruff] makes great hip-hop, but only spotty adolescents listen to it. The criticism I don't agree with is that whole "It's just for students and pissed up pogoing blokes" thing. There's so much more to it than that. The people who write these things have never actually been to the clubs. At the Big Beat Boutique, there are more girls dancing than there are blokes. It's girl-tastic down there at the moment!'

As 1997 drew to a close, Skint moved their operations up a gear. With an eye to the bigger game, it had become obvious that they needed the support of a major label to market their music abroad. After a healthy bidding war between major labels, Sony Records signed the label, with their SINE wing working on international releases. The deal with Sony was on the condition that Fatboy Slim was included for worldwide rights. Until this point, Norman hadn't even had the deal with Skint, preferring to act on trust and loyalty. However, with the Sony deal, he finally agreed to sign a contract with the label. His proviso was that he had complete control and power of veto over everything released in his name. He was also to be free to record under different aliases, for other labels, and also to run, record and actively promote his own label, Southern Fried.

Soon afterwards, Skint reissued 'Everybody Needs A 303'. The original release managed to shift 5,000 copies. At the time, a dance 12" which was popular in the clubs would expect to shift between 10,000 and 15,000 units, which wasn't a great figure. The reissue, however, totally blew this figure away, selling enough copies to land the single at the number 34 slot in the UK's national charts. It was accompanied by a video directed by Ashley Slater.

Norman was deeply ensconced in his most intense period in terms of workload since he first started making records and DJing. Once again, his life was taken over by work, his home life suffered and around this time his relationship with Bella broke down.

This time around, though, he hadn't turned into an egocentric megalomaniac, just a workaholic hedonist with barely enough space for a love life. And he wasn't about to let up as 1998 came into view.

With the second Fatboy Slim album now beckoning, he'd been talking of calming down his drug intake. In fact, he'd started to get the shakes quite badly after particularly heavy nights out.

However, it was the nights in that were doing the main damage. The House of Love had become the chosen stop-off place for DJs when they were passing through Brighton, clubbers who needed a place to go after the Boutique – anyone, in fact, who was like-minded and up for a party. Indeed, DJ Nicky Holloway once topped off a night DJing in Brighton by performing a 12-hour set in Norman's front room.

Such events were inevitably fuelled by Herculean drug taking. Among his bad drug experiences was one time when Norman accidentally took Ketamine: 'I took a Ketamine pill which I thought was an E... I just buried my head in my girlfriend's lap holding onto her for dear life shouting, "Save me!"'

Typically he turned the bad experience into a positive one: 'I had this thing that love saved me, so it did feel like a positive thing in the end.'

On the last time he took Ketamine, a friend of his wandered onto the railway line at the end of his garden and accidentally touched the live line. He was rushed to hospital with frazzled hair and burnt clothing. Thankfully he wasn't hurt badly, but the shock made Norman rethink his choice of chemicals. 'With Ketamine, it's all about getting the dose exactly right,' he said.

Almost inevitably, the wild nights in the House of Love created a constant supply of rumours about Norman and his friends. Nights of E-addled nudity would be reported back as mass orgies, every pill-induced embrace would be turned into a gay affair and each cocaine nosebleed would become tales of crumbling septums and impending nasal surgery.

Rumours of this nature were nothing new to Norman (and they would long continue to crop up), but among the funniest was this one that he recounted to *Mixmag*: 'When my last girlfriend [Bella] met me, she was told I was a gay smack addict. I thought that it was really nice that she gave me a chance. This rumour about me being gay always persists. When Beats International were in Africa, one of the band sent a postcard to his girlfriend saying, "Norman's bought two small boys to keep in his bedroom." Chinese whispers went round and by the time I got back to England everyone was going, "Well, now we know why your wife left you."'

Towards the end of 1997, Norman started dropping a mix into his set which would eventually take him hurtling into the mainstream. The track was 'Brimful Of Asha' by Leicester's moody indie band Cornershop, and it had just managed to creep into the lower reaches of the charts when it was released. However, Norman had taken to speeding the track up and layering it with a huge loping breakbeat.

The track was an immediate hit at the Boutique, so he worked out a definitive version and called up Cornershop's label, Wiija, a part of the Beggars Banquet Group, and offered the remix to them for free. Not wanting to look a gift horse in the mouth, the label said yes and put out a very limited white label of it. And that was that.

Except a couple of copies made their way into the offices of Radio 1. *Breezeblock* DJ Mary Anne Hobbs starting playing the record in every show, as did Annie Nightingale. Soon Steve Lamacq was onto it and before Norman or Wiija knew what was happening the station had started an on-air campaign to get the mix officially released.

It was easy to understand why Radio 1 went so ballistic about the track. Norman had taken the Velvet Underground-esque indie atmosphere of the original and added an addictive northern-soul vibe. As a result, the song's natural hooklines came to the fore while the swing in the vocals was accentuated. Essentially, the uptempo Cook version brought out all of Cornershop's understated pop sensibilities.

Ironically, part of the song's lyric was a celebration of the 45rpm single and its attendant pop ideology. Cornershop presented the celebration as a thesis while Norman Cook, on the other hand, turned it into a party.

Finally, in January 1998, Cornershop relented and agreed to the record's release. Thanks to the combination of the pre-release hype and the fact that 'Brimful Of Asha' was now a hugely funky tune, as well as a catchy one, the single went straight in at number one. 'The irony was that it's been my most successful remix ever and it's one that I probably did the least work on,' said Norman. 'All I did was speed it up, put a drum beat, a heavy breakbeat and a bassline on it and left the rest of the song completely as it was because it was brilliant.'

Famously, songwriter Tjinder Singh was less impressed by the single's success. After releasing records for the best part of a decade, he felt that he'd let himself down by allowing a remix to take the glory. Furthermore, it would inadvertently spell disaster for the band's future career. Every subsequent release was compared to Norman's remix. In 2002, following the disastrous performance of the band's next album, they would be dropped from the label.

'I met Tjinder for the first time at Creamfields [a dance festival promoted by Liverpool superclub Cream],' recalled Norman to UK tabloid *The Sun* (who had famously slated him and The Housemartins in the past) in October 1998. 'I thought I'd better say sorry for fucking up the band's career. With "Brimful Of Asha", it's like I walked into someone's life, told them to stop going out with the person they'd been seeing for the last five years and go out with me instead. Then I shagged them once and threw them away. Tjinder wasn't bothered. But it doesn't feel good, making people sound jolly if it wasn't them.'

While 'Brimful Of Asha' was sitting pretty at the top of the charts, Norman unleashed another massive remix. This time it was 'Renegade Master', undertaken as a tribute to Wildchild, who died in 1996. Southampton-born Roger McKenzie, aka Wildchild, had been a friend of Norman's and had been employed by Loaded Records. It was his shoes that Damian attempted to fill when he joined the label. McKenzie released four EPs on Loaded before launching his own Dark & Black imprint. He then released the original version of 'Renegade Master' for Hi-Life Records, which reached number 11 in the UK charts. Then, in 1996 he moved from Brighton to New York with his partner Donna Snell before tragically dying of a rare heart condition in November of that year. He would subsequently be remembered as one of the pioneering spirits of big beat, with a series of classic singles which owed much to Todd Terry's hip-house output.

Although both Cornershop and Wildchild remixes were huge hits, Norman actually didn't make a single penny from them. However, they did alter his life immensely. On the one hand, he was now able to punt his remix work for the princely fee of £15,000; on the other hand, these remixes (or more specifically 'Brimful...') were portents of the fact that big beat was about to go massive, and Fatboy Slim would be at the forefront.

'I'm certainly not the voice of the kids! I'm not the voice of anything new,' he laughed to *NME* at the time. 'All I do is just resample tons of other stuff and just put different things in context. It's going, "Well, yes you can mix that with that." Everything I do is just recycling. English dance music, all English dance music, is just becoming such a melting pot for different cultures.'

With Norman's remix work now top of every artist's Christmas list, he started receiving offers from numerous people from every musical genre. Meat Loaf approached him to produce and co-write the follow up to *Bat Out Of Hell 2*! 'That's weirdest thing,' he told *Mixmag*. 'Not remixing, but writing songs. What would it sound like? Cack out of hell, probably...'

Among the more bizarre approaches were choreographer turned 1980s pop star Paula Abdul and 1970s vocalist (and fellow Walk Of Fame and busfront legend of Brighton) Leo Sayer. He turned down all of these offers, as well as others from The Pet Shop Boys, Aerosmith and Madonna. Madonna left messages at Norman's hotel room throughout a North American tour in support of *Better Living Through Chemistry*, begging him to remix her 'Ray Of Light' single.

The mixes that he did say yes to included The Beastie Boys' 'Body Movin'', which received the Fatboy touch to startling effect, and indie dance combo Delakota, who had their single 'C'mon Cincinnati' reworked. 'I like doing tracks where you hear it and think, "That's brilliant. If only you'd done *that* to it…"'

During this period Norman also returned to his early days and rekindled a working relationship with Paul Heaton. Surprisingly, considering The Housemartins' anti-dance music stance, he was invited to work on the beats for The Beautiful South's album *Quench*: 'I got my role reduced from co-producer to executive producer to rhythm section consultant,' he explains. 'Basically, I sat in the studio for a couple of days, writing basslines, making suggestions, lending another ear.'

Following the successes of both Cornershop and Wildchild remixes, Norman suddenly found an army of new Fatboy fans clamouring for a new record. A final beat-driven single from Freakpower, 'No Way', complete with Fatboy Slim remix managed to reach the number 23 position in May 1998, but it wasn't the record people wanted. It subsequently marked the end of Freakpower.

Back in the sweaty Brighton enclave known as the Big Beat Boutique, the next Fatboy Slim single had already become a club anthem. The track was called 'The Rockafeller Skank', and from the very first time he dropped it to the baying crowd early in 1998 everyone knew it was going to be massive. In fact, before the track had even finished playing on that first airing, the whole crowd had caught the hookline, chanting it back in unison.

As the single started to filter through on promo, DJs and journalists alike went ballistic thanks to the single's mix of northern-soul classic 'Sliced Tomatoes' by The Just Brothers, a huge break and the immortal 'funk soul brother' hookline by New York rapper Lord Finesse. The last of these samples came from a bootleg Lord Finesse collection in which he namechecks the various members of his Diggin' In The Crates posse, which included rappers Diamond and Fat Joe among its numbers.

Finesse himself produced three albums in the 1990s, *Funky Technician*, *Return Of The Funky Man* and *The Awakening*. He also produced names like Biggie Smalls, SWV and Caron Wheeler. Finesse sanctioned the use of his voice on 'The Rockafeller Skank' for what Norman Cook described as a 'very modest sum'.

In the weeks that preceded the single's release the media could be found grabbing their thesauruses to find new superlatives with which to capture the Fatboy sound.

Select described it as 'a record of immense stupidity *and* genius'; *Q* described it as a 'monster breakbeat anthem'; while *i-D* said, 'Silly, catchy hooks, chunky beats and stupidly over-the-top breakdowns.' The highest accolade came from the by-now partisan *NME*, who awarded it Single Of The Week. They said:

> Here comes the accidental hero again, having rescued some folk and their sitars from obscurity...he might as well have a stab at crafting a record capable of shouting loud enough to be heard in the not altogether musically orientated week that a large sporting event commences. Well you never know, do you?
>
> The result was an unofficial World Cup anthem for all corners of the planet (it's the taking part that counts etc) of unparalleled proportions: its stupidly addictive rock 'n' rave qualities guaranteeing there'll be no escaping this record for eons. Not that you'd want to, mind. Because while much is made of records which sound effortlessly great, this – as it surges through a gearbox of neat bass tricks, resonant 1950s guitar riffs and rollicking drum effects – is the real thing.
>
> Yup, we'll be listening to it tonight, as Scotland run their socks off against Brazil, and at Glasto, as England take on Colombia. Uh-huh, and somewhere down the line we'll doubtless be indulging in mutual commiseration by getting royally drunk to it. Even big-beat-phobes can delight in this record seeing as, ironically, it could well be the zenith which can only be succeeded by the genre's decline. 'Right about now/the funk soul brother' has got triumphant on our asses again.

'I was out DJing in Bali,' recalled Norman to *Select* of the inspiration for the single. 'I was watching the surfing and thinking about the northern-soul thing that Lionrock [Justin Roberston's band] and David Holmes were coming out with, and at this stage I had a couple of ideas, which mainly came from playing the, er, original... Erm, am I allowed to say this?

'Oh, fuck it. The original record we sampled is a northern-soul record called "Sliced Tomatoes". I played that record at the Boutique one night and thought, "Hmmm, I should make something out of this," then I found the vocal, which is Lord Finesse off a bootleg album. He's not even singing, he's just introducing his mates. But when I put the northern-soul bit underneath, it suddenly sounded like he was singing. That was all I had when I was in Bali. Then I saw the surfers and got the idea for the twangy guitar. Where's that from? Er, it's just twangy guitar...'

That surf's-up, twangy guitar sound was among the central themes on 'The Rockafeller Skank'. Despite his reticence about uncovering the sample source, it did come to light that it had been lifted from John Barry's 'Beat Girl' from the album *Hit And Miss*. Ironically, this wasn't the inspirational music for the sample – that had come instead from a white label by The Easy Drum And Bass Orchestra's 'Hit And Miss' single from the previous year. Norman, who sent in a positive DJ return on the records, recognised the sample and, when he came to create the feel he was after for 'The Rockafeller Skank', dug out the original.

On Friday 15 May, Norman flew to Los Angeles with Ashley Slater (who had filmed the 'Everybody Needs A 303' video) to film the Doug Aitkin-directed video for 'The Rockafeller Skank'. The shoot lasted two days. Then they returned directly back home.

Aitkin's treatment for the video (written back in March 1998), entitled 'Rockafeller Skank – Zoom', not only revealed America's take on the DJ, but also just how much film directors had become influenced by DJs and drug culture. 'When you think of Fatboy Slim, you think of...motion...constant fast motion,' he wrote. 'This video will take Fatboy Slim's kinetic funkiness to a completely new visual level. Here, the entire video *is* pure motion. Stylistically, "zoom" will be used entirely on a single technique/concept: the camera will always be *zooming* in at a constant speed, taking us on the ultimate high-speed journey where movement never stops from start to finish of the song. We seamlessly move from place to place on a nonstop adventure. The familiar becomes mysterious: reality is turned upside-down. During the entire song, the camera is zooming, slowly revealing one environment after another, creating a sense of continuous movement, a sense of constant experience. The camera's slow, steady zooming motion takes us weightlessly from scene to scene creating constant forward energy. Here, we shatter upon the television screen and move directly into the world of Fatboy Slim's music, itself.'

Another interesting aspect of the video treatment came with the proposed look of the promo film, due again revealing how Aitken's lack of in-depth knowledge of both big beat and Norman's history gave him a fresh perspective, revealing energy in the music without resorting to current cliché.

'With "Rockafeller Skank", we are going for a very stylised look. We will use a specially designed motion control zoom device on the camera that will enable us to zoom in on every shot at exactly the same speed. The edits will always happen before the zooming stops. As in a movie, the sound design will play a major role in drawing the viewer into the complete experience of "Rockafeller Skank". For example, in certain transitions, the volume might change according to where we are. We might hear other environmental sounds, such as cars passing in the night or random noise.

'The idea with the filming is to cover fascinating locations, moving weightlessly from one to the next, giving the greatest possible diversity to the video while making it completely cohesive, unique and mind blowing.'

The finished video was a brilliant collision between chic and kitsch. The former came in the shape of the gorgeous camera work and constant sense of movement as intended by the director. The latter came in the style of the comedy Afro wigs worn by the main actors. As a result, the video not only represented the tongue-in-cheek aspect of Norman's disc but also his sheer, unstoppable energy.

'The Rockafeller Skank' was released in June 1998 and proved to be a massive radio hit throughout the US. It subsequently featured in numerous charts while also achieving his highest placing in the *Billboard* Top 100. In the UK, the single became his first top 10 hit, settling at number six. With this, he achieved a position in the *Guinness Book Of*

Records as the joint record holder for the most top 40 hits under different names. The total number was seven, and the artist he shared the honour with was Midge Ure, one-time vocalist with power punks The Rich Kids, new romantics Ultravox (post-Jon Foxx) and also half of the duo behind the Band Aid single, 'Do They Know It's Christmas' (the other half was Bob Geldof).

With the cumulative success of Norman's remixes and top 10 hits that year, big beat moved over into the mainstream, and along came the copycat tracks. Among them was major label Fatboy Slim rip-off 'Sounds Of The Wickedness' by Tzant, which was so close an assimilation of Norman's sound that it could only spell the end for the trademark big-beat effect.

However, there was another side to that big-beat effect. As a direct result of the crossover of big-beat, old-skool hip-hop started to have a renewed influence on the house scene. House increasingly adopted old-skool hooks while breaks became used exhaustively. The UK media were quick to recognise the trend.

Central to the return to the old-skool hip-hop vibe was the re-release of Run DMC's 'It's Like That' with a remix by previously unknown US house producer Jason Nevins. His mix was an international hit, complete with a video depicting a group of models breakdancing badly. Nevertheless, the mix had also excited many of the big-beat crews and it became a constant in the sets of many a self-respecting DJ. Mainstream DJs also used the track as their way in to some old-skool cool. One of the people who was most vocal in his rejection of the old-skool hype, and that Jason Nevins remix, was Prodigy man Liam Howlett. Talking to me for the book *Prodigy* (also published by Sanctuary), he explained, 'That whole old-skool thing really fucked me off, you know? People like Goldie and that, it's so obvious that they were there. He's old skool. With me, I never hung out with Bambaataa in the Bronx and shit, but I was into it at a young age. I know the music, I know the breaks. The revival is just people who don't know more than phat laces and Run DMC. To me it was just shit, all of these house DJs suddenly saying they were into hip-hop. Most of those DJs aren't fit to tie phat laces, let alone wear 'em, you know what I mean? If Pete Tong dropped an old-skool mix he'd use

Rob Base, Run DMC's "Walk This Way". You know, all of the tunes that were actually crap but people who wanted to seem like they were down would always be into them.

'Whenever people talk about old skool they always say Run DMC's "Walk This Way" or that Jason Nevin's shit,' he continued. 'They never talk about the cool tunes they did. I reckon Pete Tong would drop both "Run This Way" and "It's Like That" in his old-skool mix, you know what I mean? Actually, I really like Pete Tong, but I can't think of another DJ to say instead. Let's just say that, when I say Pete Tong, I mean every one of those commercial DJs.'

Norman's celebration of old-skool culture was nothing new, however, and as such it came as no surprise that he had also turned down the offer to remix Jason Nevins' version of 'It's Like That'. However, as he started sampling ideas, breaks and loops for his next album, the fact that both old skool and big beat had become clichés was very much on Norman's mind. 'Tzant's "Sounds Of The Wickedness" was a really important record in that respect,' he confirmed to *Mojo* 'I heard it and thought, "Time to move on, that style's been done to death."'

As if to confound those people who hadn't experienced the big beat ideology in full flow but thought they had the whole sound pegged down, on 22 June Fatboy released a mix album recording direct from the decks of the Boutique. Called *On The Floor Of The Boutique*, it featured a blistering selection of the funkiest break, hip-hop, acid and northern soul, providing a window on the true sound of the big-beat elite.

The album opens with old-skool classic break (as championed by DJ Kool Herc and used by almost everyone) 'Apache' by Michael Viner's Incredible Bongo Band before mixing into funk originator and trombonist Fred Wesley (brass arrangements for James Brown and George Clinton's Parliament and Funkadelic) and his supremely funky 'Discotown' with The Horny Horns. Norman's intentions were clear. This collection was all about partying hard, sweating torpedoes and falling over with the sheer euphoric energy of it all.

With the acidic revision of 'Because I Like It Like That' by Native Tongues hip-hop trio The Jungle Brothers segueing into west coast breakbeat party classic 'Vol 1 Side 2 Track 2' by The Bassbin Twins and

Norman's mix of Christopher Just's 'I'm A Disco Dancer' crashing into Hardknox's belligerent beat attack 'Psychopath', the beats rarely let up for a second. Naturally the highlights come in the shape of Norman's own additions. 'Michael Jackson' stands out in all of its lysergic soul-stomping glory while the closing couplet of Cut La Roc's devastatingly funky 'Post Punk Progression' and Fatboy's 'The Rockafeller Skank' conclude the set in the kind of style which demands a full rewind.

As a document of the Social at maximum overdrive, it was near perfect. As a DJ mix set, it flew in the face of the seamlessly mixed journeys that most DJs of the time were wont to do. For once, however, Norman's attempts to stem the tide were backed up by a huge and growing scene. Indeed, it was the other DJs who were now playing King Canute in the face of the eclectic mash-up crowd as represented by Fatboy Slim.

'I'm not serious about what I do,' Norman told *The Face* at the time. 'I'm well aware that when the big beat ship goes down I'll go down with it. Occasionally my music might seem like The Monkees or whatever. I never said I was clever, and I never said I was doing anything that hasn't been done before or that's better than anybody else. How can I stand there and say, "Listen without prejudice. You'll get this one day!" I can't! I'm a useless party fiend who's not a role model for anyone and who's got nothing intelligent to say apart from, "Let's 'ave it!"'

With summer season in full flow, Norman went to Ibiza for another spot of island DJing. The trip subsequently had a huge and lasting effect on him. While in an obviously chemically charged state of mind, he was interviewed on Radio 1's *Breakfast Show*. The interview had the boss of SINE reaching for his telephone and demanding to know why the artist Sony had invested in was messing around in Ibiza when he had an album to deliver. More importantly for Norman, however, it would be the first time that he met *Breakfast Show* presenter Zoë Ball. He didn't know who she was because her radio show, and the children's programme *Saturday Morning Show*, were both on too early for Norman, who would usually only wake up in the afternoon, but this didn't stop instant flirtatious sparks from flying between the two.

Famously, her opening remark to Norman was, 'Mr Cook, I presume.

His reply was, 'How do you fancy *not* going to bed with me?' Her answer: 'I'm with you, big boy.'

It might have seemed like a bit of on-air fun, but it proved to be the beginning of a blossoming romance. It was also the start of Norman's life being turned upside down with the kind of celebrity-baiting press attention he could only have previously imagined.

Norman Cook was about to become a household name.

RIGHT HERE RIGHT NOW

'I have no motivation other than to make people dance and laugh. That's pretty much all I do. I'm not a deep thinker. I'm not filled with angst. That is pretty much me. That's why I keep apologising for it.'

– Norman Cook, 1998

As the Fatboy phenomenon started to go into overdrive, Norman continued to tour the world with a DJing regime that could fell an elephant. He had, only a year earlier, been working with long time friend Carl Cox when the house DJ collapsed from exhaustion, and Norman had sworn to cut back on the workload.

However, he had always been the kind of person who got the maximum out of his life, and gave back even more. Since his breakdown, he had made a complete re-evaluation of his life and now seemed to live each moment as if it were his last.

Through 1998, he had worked furiously on everything from DJing to recording to living life – and then suddenly, one night in August, he got a huge wake-up call. After DJing until 6am for four nights in a row, he collapsed during a set in Toronto. 'My legs went and I simply couldn't move,' he told *The Observer*. 'That was a warning that the workload was getting too much.'

Another part of his life also faced collapse at this time. The venue for the Big Beat Boutique faced demolition, thus forcing the club night to move to the seafront club The Beach. Unfortunately, the new venue didn't have the same grubby energy as the original, but it did provide more space for the increasing numbers of people who were turned away from the clubs doors fortnightly. The Big Beat Boutique had become a major draw in the south of England.

Indeed, it often came as a shock to travelling visitors when they saw the Concorde. The dance scene in Britain had always prided itself on that state of the art clubs with the best sound systems and finest design, so the rustic, decrepit, enlarged beach hut that accommodated a maximum of just 400 revellers was almost unheard of.

In fact, the staging of the Boutique in this venue was an important aspect of its success. Where clubs like Ministry Of Sound, Cream *et al* had taken the lead from Manchester's Hacienda and modelled themselves on Italy's pleasure palaces in Rimini and New York's glittering shrines to hedonism, the Boutique simply went for pleasure and hedonism, with no added frills. Like the music itself, it was unpretentious and all-inclusive – the opposite to Balearic, in fact, and far more in keeping with the nutty joy of hardcore.

The move to the Beach found the club in unsure territory, presenting an almost opposing ideology to the previous incarnation. As a way to resolve this change, Gareth Hansome decided to drop the 'Big Beat' from the name. From now on it would simply be known as the Boutique, neatly sidestepping the increasingly tarnished big-beat genre (despite claiming a continuing pride in the music that they helped to define), and presenting a fresh page in the club's story. 'The Concorde was like a school hall, so people behaved accordingly. The atmosphere at the new place is a bit more stadium big beat. DJing at the Concorde was a bit like playing in the middle of a riot. At the Beach, it's like playing at Nuremberg – without the jackboots and funny armbands, of course'

'Sad about the Concorde closing,' added Norman to *NME* when asked about the last night of the Big Beat Boutique. 'But it did force us to leave, which we should have done, really. It's different at the Beach. It's not as intimate and funny, but it's bigger and more stadiumy, which is quite exciting. It's early days yet. We may move the decks out of the DJ booth because it's a bit them and us. I'm really chuffed because they asked me to play the last-ever set at the Concorde, the last two hours. I said, "I'll do it if I can take a bit of the club home with me." They said, "Bring a hammer!"'

So Norman brought a saw, a hammer and various implements.

'It was like taking a piece of turf from [Liverpool FC ground] Anfield. It was a legendary place for us. My only disappointment was that I couldn't find a copy of 'We'll Meet Again' to play as the last record, so I had to play 'Bye Bye Baby' by The Bay City Rollers. It got a laugh, mind.'

If Norman had thought, following his collapse, that life was about to calm down, he had another think coming. The ongoing hype surrounding both 'The Rockafeller Skank' and big beat, coupled with his relationship with Zoë, turned him into a personality figure, something that he'd never really wanted to be. 'Dance music isn't about the cult of personality,' he told *The Telegraph*. 'It's not about having your face sell the music. I've always loved the anonymity about it. The last few months has seen my entire life turned upside down. And then I met Zoë… This is increasingly bizarre territory for me.'

'I don't want to bang on about it,' he added in *Heat* magazine. 'It's private, it's us, and we don't want to be a celebrity couple. It's weird for me because I've never been good subject matter for tabloids before.'

Because Norman had always been so open about his drug use, an ironic twist in his relationship with the tabloids both post-Housemartins, and then post-dating Zoë, was that they were more likely to report that he was giving up drugs than report on his substance abuse.

However, it wasn't his private life that was to propel him into the spotlight next. In October 1998, he delivered both the single 'Gangster Tripping' and the second Fatboy Slim album, *You've Come A Long Way Baby*.

'Gangster Tripping' is much less dynamic than its predecessor and finds Norman returning to Beats International territory, attempting to recreate Malcolm McClaren's 'Duck Rock': old-skool hip-hop beats, rocksteady horns, calypso grooves and stuttered vocal hooks, and far removed from the 303 nosebleed of his earlier Fatboy material. Instead, Norman created a fairground fun ambience, which evoked the kiss-me-quick hats and sticks of rock sold on Brighton's Palace Pier.

'Gangster Tripping' also evoked some of the psychedelic acid-funk elements of the last Freakpower album, but with the depth taken away.

As with all of Norman's party music, he stripped away the nuance and left the hooklines, like that cake made only of icing which marked out his Beats International output.

'I always thought that Coldcut would become the iconic pop stars of the 1990s,' said serious experimental music magazine *The Wire*, 'but since they've decided to surrender themselves to their Powerbooks' randomisers, Norman Cook has stepped in to fill their shoes admirably. In the finest tradition of British pop, Cook has repackaged obscure African America music with carefree hooks for mass consumption. His latest delirious, musical Club 18–30 holiday, "Gangster Tripping", is an irresistible tea dance with Memphis Horns and Lord Kitchener. Moving back and forth between 1960s Tennessee, 1960s Trinidad and the Bronx in the 1980s, "Gangster Tripping" is the acceptable face of cultural tourism. Like the inevitable rum and malt-liquor hangover, you don't think about the politics until the morning after.'

The point *The Wire* was making was an important one that reached back to the first Beats International album. At the time, Norman joked that Paul Heaton would probably put his music down for appropriating black music and managing to make millions out of it in the process. Here he could be found employing sampled hooklines and shoehorning the result into the increasingly one-size-fits-all big-beat sound. The result was a homogenisation process with influence travelling in only one direction.

However, one of the biggest arguments against this theory was that music like Norman's subconsciously opened people's ears to the original sound sources. In the years that followed this single, all forms of reggae would enjoy a renewed interest, resulting in copious compilations, while the swamp-blues aspect of the single would find a resonance with the record-buying public in the wake of this and Moby's *Play*.

Yet Norman would argue that his records were devoid of political intention beyond the aim of 'getting twatted and jumping around'. The Fatboy Slim persona was devoutly apolitical – mirroring in the process the increasingly disinterested, or lethargic, society buying into it. Indeed, by this stage in the development of dance culture, it could no longer claim to be in opposition to anything as in many cases the culture had adopted corporate ideologies wholesale. The drugs only enhanced the consumer state of mind.

As a good-time party track which aimed to connect with the spirit of the times, though 'Gangster Tripping' hit the jugular full on. Initially mailed as a one-sided vinyl-promo the single immediately received the inevitable blanket coverage on radio and MTV and reached the number three position in the UK charts.

'The best way to make tunes is to go out, get completely caned, come home and get four hours' sleep then wake up the next day still feeling completely wired and not sure what to do with yourself. It's probably not good to operate heavy machinery, so you just sit there and make a tune. It's the day after the night before when I tend to make the best tunes,' he told *Update* of the method behind the making of 'Gangster Tripping'. However, he also extended this theory in *GQ* with reference to his own state of mind, when making records.

'When I'm happy I'm a hit maker. But I'm not always happy and I'm not always a hit maker. My angst records are shit,' Norman explained. Through his continued love of life he had increasingly developed the self-deprecating theory that his strongest material was his dumb music, because that's what was selling.

This view extended towards his portrayal of his own self-image in magazines. Despite his ongoing success he was obviously embarrassed. He increasingly joked that he was expecting to wake up and get caught out for the sham he was. He continually presented himself as a wide-eyed subservient, toiling beneath the genius of The Chemical Brothers.

While it's fair to say that Norman's motivations for these character put-downs were quite genuine, he started to echo the sentiments expressed by New York producer Moby. Indeed the proposed titles for his second album *Let's Hear It For The Little Guy*, followed by *Viva The Underachiever* would have seemed like self-pastiche on a Moby-esque level had he gone with either suggestion. It was a position that seemed to stem directly from his ego-driven times towards the end of Beats International. The combination of the bitter taste of these events and his epiphany-like first pill resulted in Norman's development of an internalised system of self checking. The oft-spoken humility was more a tool to remind himself of his ability to turn into the kind of person he hates most, a way of keeping his feet firmly planted on terra firma rather than a way of eliciting a positive response from interviewers.

'I'm determined not to get big-headed about it this time around, but it does tend to engulf your life. You don't have time for your mates or yourself. You turn into a workaholic. It is a worry that it could all be part of a familiar pattern,' he told *The Times* 'But I don't think I could get off the merry-go-round even if I wanted to, especially now that Sony's on board. I get the feeling that if I said I wasn't going to put in the work to make this album a big hit, then they'd send the boys round to set me straight.'

In an interview with *Mixmag* at the same time he expanded on this theme further, describing himself as a slacker!

'I am a slacker. Definitely!' he said. 'I win by losing and I don't have the energy to hate anybody except for Michael Jackson and Tina Turner – two people who aren't happy to be rich and famous because they'd rather be God. There's so much money in the music industry that we could all make a nice living if only we could get rid of the ego monsters.'

If the achievements of his last two singles had given him cause for apparent embarrassment, then he was about to deliver an album that would have him touching his forelock forever more. With *You've Come A Long Way Baby* he would collect together all of the influences that had featured in his music to date and throw them into the sampler to see what came out. The result was the crowning glory of the big beats movement and his finest work to date.

You've Come A Long Way Baby was light years away from *Better Living Through Chemistry*. While keeping the trademark big beats and 303s intact, Norman explored northern soul, ska, blues and hip-hop, while introducing all manner of exotica along the way. That John Barry twangy guitar on 'The Rockafeller Skank' was a good indication of the kind of musical hijinks on show – a joke perhaps, but one which didn't detract from the actual track. Similarly 'You're Not From Brighton', which featured Norman on Vocoder vocals, may have contained more than a hint of sample jokers The Art Of Noise, but it fully complemented the mid-tempo slung-back grooves.

This was the heart of Norman's genius on this album. He let the beats rule supreme, leaving the rest as simple flavour. So when 'Right Here Right Now' opened with a swathe of string fanfares before delving into soul sampling madness, or when the guitars fuzzed like Voodoo on 'Build It Up, Tear It Down', the beats remained locked in.

The album's finest moments came in the closing trilogy of the year's finest sunrise anthem 'Praise You', the big beat hard house madness of 'Love Island' and the lunatic crescendo of acid house anthem 'Acid 8000'. Each one was a testament to Norman's production skills'. Together, however, they represented the soundtrack to the best night out you'd ever had.

From acid house to hardcore, to big beat and beyond, *You've Come A Long Way Baby* represented the unmistakable sound of the 'Fatboy formula' turning the UK breakbeat sound into gold. With no added pretensions. 'Making an album is a bit more of a challenge than making a single,' he explained at the time. 'The last Fatboy Slim album was just a collection of tracks that I'd done, so you couldn't really sit down and listen to it as an album. It's a challenge to make an album a little bit more thoughtful and listenable over an hour or whatever.

'It was going to be called *Viva The Underachiever* at first,' he explained to *Mixmag* 'but since then I've had Wildchild, Cornershop and "Rockafeller Skank" and people said, "They won't get the irony because you're patently not an under-achiever. It's about how everybody is a star." So then I wanted to change the title to *Let's Hear It For The Little Guy*, but that sounded too jokey. Now it's an acknowledgment that I'm not an underachiever, even though I like to pretend I am.'

The album art featured an obese youth wearing a T-shirt with the slogan 'I'm #1, so why try harder'. It was chosen, according to Norman, as a chance to champion the underdog.

'The sleeve's about how it's all right not to be successful if you're a nice person. It wasn't actually about being number one,' he explained.

The actual title of the album had originally come from a slogan on a pair of shorts ex-girlfriend Bella had bought him on trip to Seattle years earlier. He later found out that it came from a commercial for Virginia Slim cigarettes, which he felt was rather ironic.

In *Mixmag* Norman gave track-by-track insight into the album, which *Muzik*'s Ralph Moore had already claimed had 'extended big beat's sell-by date for another few months'.

Opening track 'Right Here Right Now' he said was '…a declaration of intent – wanting to do something a bit deeper and not what everyone expects. It's kind of "Song For Lindy Part 2".' On the following 'Rockafeller Skank', the track was introduced by a kid enthusing wildly about Fatboy. 'It's 100 per cent genuine, from WBCN in Boston,' he laughed. 'This kid rung in, requesting "Rockafeller Skank", they taped him and gave me the DAT. It's just the US trying to get to grips with the Fatboy thing. He goes, "Fatboy Slim is the band of the 1990s, if you can call it a band because it's just one guy." I do a lot of interviews on modern rock radio and they're always going "Where's your band? How do you make music without a band?" These are people who like Hootie And The Blowfish. They can't grasp sampling at all.'

Of the track itself he enthused: 'It was in the top 40 for eight weeks. It's what people sing outside my window. If they stop singing fucking 'Happy Hour' [Housemartins' number one single] then anything's worth it. Mulder's done a version with Mickey Finn and Aphrodite and we'll put that out as a B-side. That's Skint's first remix. It was always quite a painful experience listening to other people's remixes of my stuff.'

'Fucking In Heaven' featured repeated samples of the phrase as delivered to Norman on a CD by US electro breaks producer Freddy Fresh.

'Freddy Fresh sent me some samples for a track and on the CD he was waffling into the mic and said: "If I could have a Fatboy Slim remix I'd be fucking in heaven." I chopped it up and he sounded like he was singing. I played it to Freddy and he said "That's great. Who's doing the vocals?"

'He asked me not to play it for anybody because he'd made it specially, which was like red rag to a bull! I also like the gratuitous use of the word "fucking". We can't have it on the Asian version.'

'The [vocals] sample from "Gangster Tripping",' he explained of the album's next track, 'is from a Dust Junkys record, but I don't think they were talking about me. When you hear a tune that namechecks you it's such a temptation to use it… It's a phase everyone goes through but I've got it out of my system now.'

The guitar frenzy cut-ups of 'Build It Up, Tear It Down' revealed yet another fact about the huge claims for royalties made by sampled artists.

'I can't tell you where the guitar sample's from because it's not been cleared,' he said. 'I can't clear everything because they all want a percentage of the royalties – I only got 20 per cent from "Rockafeller Skank". I kind of like the thrill of the chase. A lot of these samples could come back on me but you've got to live dangerously.'

On 'Kalifornea' he delivered a Vocoder vocal line, which found him singing the words 'Druggy, druggy, druggy'. However, he was criticised heavily for ripping off The Beastie Boys' 1998 single 'Intergalactic'.

'I did it back when I hadn't heard 'Intergalactic' and now everyone thinks I've copied it. At least it sounds like that and not "Mr Blue Sky" [Vocoder-based track by 1970s soft rockers ELO],' he said.

When questioned about 'Soul Surfing' and its possible drug reference with the sampled phrase 'jack it up' he replied, 'Drug references? Noooo. It's a reggae phrase. I'm not into the brown stuff.' While another Vocoder track came in the shape of the groove-bound booty track 'You're Not From Brighton' – a track that quickly became a favourite at 'the Boutique'.

'That's our personal favourite at the moment,' he explained. 'It's a bump and hustle tune. The title comes from something we misheard. I'm very proud of Brighton but, on the other hand, no one who lives in Brighton is actually from Brighton.'

For many, the album's standout 'Praise You' was intended as Norman's 'Sympathy For The Devil' epic, he exclaimed, 'Hopefully it's my anthem – 'Ferry 'Cross The Mersey'. I think I'm still ripping off Tom and Ed [Chemical Brothers] quite a lot. Them taking everything further with *Dig Your Own Hole* was the main inspiration. And also the negative inspiration of wanting to stay ahead of the cheesy big beat records that sound a bit like me, but all the wrong bits.'

'Love Island', he explained was 'a Fatboy version of a tune I did for the Manumission soundtrack. It was going to be called "Song For Manumission". I caned the house version all this summer in Ibiza,' while the closing 'Acid 2000', presented a statement for the defence of the big beat brigade.

'People get the idea we're just a load of drunk b-boys who play

Freestylers records,' he explained, 'but there's actually a whole other acidy side. I really could stay at home and listen to 303 *a cappellas*.'

It seemed ironic that even at this stage Norman was vehemently defending the big beat scene. It was something that he had been heavily involved with, however, and had helped him find his own feet within the dance world, so he had a vested interest in the common perception of big beat.

But already the tide was turning on the scene. Norman himself had noted the huge number of Fatboy Slim copyists who had surfaced. Furthermore, the dance scene depends on a constant momentum of new input. This keeps it ever-evolving, and by the time a sound reaches the mainstream it is already being superseded by a new sound.

'A lot of people say that its just lagered student music, but its not at all,' he argued. 'Big beat people have a larger knowledge of music than most. They can appreciate house music and rap records, reggae and drum and bass in the same night. That was always what big beats was about, not endless breakbeat records sounding like the *Mission Impossible* theme.'

While big beat was soundtracking adverts, film scores and mainstream daytime radio and television, the Dutch trance sound was taking a hold on the underground. Its anthemic vibes were tailor-made for a new generation of clubbers, while its drops and build ups were strongly reminiscent of those employed by Norman.

Trance was fuelled by a new form of Ecstasy pill – the Mitsubishi, which provided a greater sense of rush and a enhanced feeling of euphoria in the user. Inevitably this new pill had an effect on the music. Just as Doves had energised the early raves thanks to their loved-up vibe, and Snowballs, with their moody feel had inspired dark (which gave way to drum and bass), so Mitsubishis were inspiring this pop variation on the early 1990s hardfloor sound.

Despite *Muzik*'s claims that *You've Come A Long Way Baby* would extend the shelf life of big beat, the truth was that by the time the album arrived, the writing was well and truly on the wall for the scene. The Chemical Brothers had already started work on their next album *Surrender* which would feature a number of references to trance, while other leading figures like Jon Carter were moving towards deep house, while his own and Monkey Mafia were offering the paradigm of dub flavoured eclecticism, far removed from the big beats of the previous year. Elsewhere Death In Vegas had started to look deeper into out-rock and psychedelia while northern estate soul boys Glamorous Hooligan had discovered jazzy drum and bass.

Far from extending the life of the scene *You've Come A Long Way Baby* actually spelled the end of big beat in the form by which it had become commonly understood. As with all dance music scenes, it was like liquid. Just as soon as it bubbled to the surface, the undercurrents pulled aspects of the sound back under, while other aspects evaporated into the ether.

Not that Fatboy Slim was ready to hang up his 10-gallon hat just yet. Ironically it wasn't trance that stopped the album from reaching the number one spot in the UK. It was Norman's old mucker Paul Heaton!

'Their album kept mine off number one 'cos it came out the same day,' he told *Uncut*'s Michael Bonner. 'We figured the momentum was picking up what with "Rockafeller Skank" being such a big hit. So someone said, "Oh, you might get a number one album out of this," which was a nice thought, because I'd never had one – not even with The Housemartins. Then I was in America and they said, "Do you want the good news of the bad news? The good news is, you've gone in at Number Two, the bad news is that the record that kept you off the top is Paul's album," which I'd bloody worked on! Mates, eh?'

As the album campaign got under way, Norman was once again on the move. This time he was moving out of the House of Love on Robertson Road into a new, beachside home on the West Hove seafront. No ordinary road, his new address was located on what locals call either Showbiz Alley or Millionaires' Row.

'I will probably shed a tear. When I move, Derek Jameson and Nick Berry'll be my neighbours. I've always been loyal to Brighton and now, seemingly, that's been rewarded – they're putting me on this Walk Of Fame that's being built along Brighton Marina. There's me, Terence Rattigan, Richard Attenborough, Chris Eubank, Norman Wisdom, Desmond Lynam and The Levellers.'

Just as Norman's local standing was going through the ceiling, so too was his reputation in the US. The album had performed exceptionally well in the Top 100, bringing with it a wave of new fans. Suddenly Fatboy Slim was the chosen dance artist as his saturation of the media had become almost impossible to ignore. His music was now being used on adverts, idents and soundtracks.

Journalist Nick Duerden summed up the growing Fatboy fever in a feature at the time: 'In America, Fatboy Slim is asserting a stranglehold on the nation's youth… Right now it's everywhere. Flick through the channels on the hotel television and there it is. Click: "Going Out Of My Head" and "Fucking In Heaven" on the trailer for the film *Ten Things I Hate About You*. Click: "Gangster Tripping" is an MTV station ident. Click: "Praise You" on a Nike Jordan ad. Click: "Praise You" and "Right Here Right Now" are background music on the *Entertainment Tonight* show. Click: "Right Here Right Now" on an Oldsmobile ad. Click: "The Rockafeller Skank" on movie trailers for new Mike "*King Of The Hill*" Judge movie, *Office Space*, and a mad ad for kiddy-enticing soft drink Surge.'

Clearly Fatboy Slim had grown well beyond the confines of any big beat scene in Britain. As if to underline his global status, Norman Cook saw out 1998, his most successful year yet, playing in Melbourne, Australia. His New Year's honours top 10 went to the following records:

1   Stardust – 'Music Sounds Better With You'
2   Loop Da Loop – 'Bomb Da Loop'
3   Mr X & Mr Y – '1956
4   Wiseguys – 'Ooh La La'
5   Alan Braxe – 'Vertigo'
6   Gold Steel – 'Real Rap Superstar (Loop Da Loop Mix)'
7   Grand Larceny – 'Stomp'
8   Scott Grooves – 'Mothership Reconnection'
9   Kenickie Versus Mint Royale – 'Gun (Club Version)'
10 Ceasefire Vs Deadly Avenger – 'Evel Knievel'

If 1998 had closed on a high then 1999 opened with an even-greater high as the single 'Praise You' was released. As Norman had already said, 'Praise You' was his anthem. A near-perfect slice of sunrise funk, contemplative, soulful yet fused with a funky underbelly and spiritual atmosphere, it seemed like the last word on positivity.

The main vocal on the track was lifted from an old recording by 1970s funk singer Camille Yarbrough. Unusually for Norman he left the vocal to run uncut for a few bars so as to underline the natural melody before cutting it into newer melodies. As a result he managed to retain the flavour and spirit of the original. 'I think, for a lot of people, it really helps their career [to be sampled]. Stetsasonic said "Tell the truth, James Brown was old/'Til Eric And Rakim did 'I Know You Got Soul.'" I mean, Camille Yarbrough, who sang "Praise You", has had her album re-released, has been on chat shows, and it's turned people onto her. I'm not saying that's why I do it, to revive the careers of old 1970s soul singers, but it can do a lot of good. Camille still sends me cards saying, "Thank you."'

Perhaps more than on any other track 'Praise You' displayed the extent to which Norman would go to find obscure, unused samples for his tracks. Camille's original version had long since disappeared into the mists of time, receiving any kind of reverence from collectors only. The original vocal came from Camille's track from 1975 called 'Take Yo Praise' from the little-known album *The Iron Pot' Cooker*. If ever Norman showed his funk trainspotter tendencies it was here.

In an interview with *Update*'s Robert Heller at this time he revealed just how avid a collector of obscure records he was, and the bizarre methods he uses when looking through the racks.

'I go to these shops in America and buy up loads and loads of weird-looking records for 49 cents each,' he said. 'I buy anything from the early 1970s as long as the artists have afros or long hair and big moustaches. Anyone pictured with long hair between 1968 and 1975 means they probably took drugs, which means that they probably make more interesting music.

'There should be drug testing for musicians. If you haven't taken drugs you shouldn't be allowed to make records because they'll end up sounding like Cliff Richard.'

Norman's obsessive record-shopping habits are by no means unusual in the beats scene. Indeed, he represents the tip of a so often ignored culture.

Many DJs will go to extreme lengths to find that obscure, never previously used break. For example Simon Dine, of Paul Weller, championed Noonday Underground whose northern soul meets Velvet Underground sound was created following copious plundering of rubbish skips in Eastern Europe!

'I've yet to have one person who has recognised a sample,' he exclaims. 'The thing is the samples all come from a time when I lived in Leipzig in Germany. It's a great trade city, a cultural centre. After Communism fell everyone bought CD players and just chucked out their vinyl. I was walking past this skip one day and it was just full of this discarded vinyl so I took it. In Eastern Europe in the 1960s they weren't allowed Western music so they just copied it. So you'd have the best musicians recording these 1960s pop tracks with a bizarre Eastern twist, in the most fantastic studios, using the best microphones – because this is where microphones were invented. For me it was like I was recycling by sampling it and getting reviewed again as modern music.'

Another vinyl pilgrim is Brighton's DJ Format. 'My speciality, if you want to call it that,' he says, 'is more my willingness to go all over the place looking for the most obscure records that hopefully haven't already been sampled. I go to places like Warsaw, and find the most amazing records. Warsaw was a bleak, bleak place. We'd eventually track a record shop down and find out that it would only be open on certain weird hours on certain days. Eventually you'd go back and get told about another place that sold records. In the end we found three shops in the whole of Warsaw.'

If record hunting in non-English-speaking places doesn't present enough problems, DJ Format's language barrier is compounded by the fact that he takes a portable record player with him on all of his excursions.

'That's a strange thing to try and get over,' he laughs. 'I'd literally be going into these shops and I'd pull out my record player in front of all of these startled people who'd never seen anything like it before. I'd be motioning to them saying, "Please can I listen to this?" and then having to show that it had batteries so it didn't need to be plugged in, that I had my headphones so it wouldn't bother anyone and that it wouldn't damage the records.' So Norman Cook is not alone in his behaviour!

'Praise You' was a huge success both in the US and in Britain. In the UK charts it went to number one, rejuvenating sales of *You've Come A Long Way Baby*, and pushing that to the number one position as well.

Part of the song's success however was down to the bizarre video shot by Spike Jonze. Already famed for his work with The Beastie Boys, Björk, The Chemical Brothers and Daft Punk, Jonze had supplied a treatment for 'The Rockafeller Skank' and had been the first choice. However, owing to other commitments he was unable to take the job.

When Norman and Ashley arrived at their LA hotel to begin the shoot with second choice director, Doug Aitkin, a package was waiting at the desk. In it was a video which contained scenes of a scruffy guy with hair growing into a mullet, dirty sweatpants constantly slipping down to reveal his butt, while he breakdanced badly to a ghetto blaster playing 'The Rockafeller Skank' at full volume in front of a Chinese restaurant. As he dances, passersby throw looks of utter disgust and pure bewilderment in the direction of the hapless dancer.

In with the video was a hastily scribbled note. It read: 'Sorry I wasn't available to do your video, but I love your song a lot and thought you might like this.' Signed Spike Jonze.

Luckily Spike was available to make the video for 'Praise You' and, with a revised version of his original treatment, he started about looking for extras. What they were looking for were dancers who represented every part of the community. In particular society's underdogs.

'Imagine trying to explain to Sony Worldwide that I wanted to make this deliberately crap-looking video,' Norman told *Spin*. 'The only thing that swayed them was Spike doing it. They trusted that it would be genius, not complete rubbish. But when I first saw it, I actually thought, 'Oh no, we've gone too far. This is actually rubbish, and not genius!"

On 27 October radio station Edge 102 held a competition with Norman and Spike as judges. One of the dancers who made it was Michael Gier. Writing on his website, www.michaelgier.com, the dancer reveals:

This was one of the most unusual jobs I ever had but it was also one of the most fun. There were over 100 men at the audition and about 150 women. They hired six of us.

It's kind of funny, at the audition they taught us this great dance routine. But when we started rehearsals for the video we were pretty much doing anything except dancing. You didn't really need to be a dancer to do what we ended up doing.

Once hired, we met at a dance studio for rehearsal and all we did the first day was create unusual-looking moves. Spike Jonze, the director, had himself video taped dancing very unique moves to the song. We broke down each of his moves, named them and then started learning them. We rehearsed two days and then filmed on the third.

We met at a dance studio down in Venice, CA, the film day. The wardrobe guy gave us our outfits and we rehearsed our routine a few times and then all met at a hotel in Santa Monica, CA. The whole production crew was there, the director, producer, cameramen and many others. We talked through what would be happening once we got out on the street where we were to perform.

They wanted us to look like we were this very serious amateur dance troupe performing for the first time our routine to Fatboy Slim's song. We supposedly had been rehearsing for months for this big performance. We were dressed to look like dancers from the 1980s. It was very funny because we were dressed to look out of place for the 1990s. They didn't want anyone to know that we were filming a music video. So all the cameramen were dressed like tourists, using small digital cameras that looked like tourist camcorders. The cameramen just mixed into the crowd.

We walked over to the 3rd Street Promenade there in Santa Monica. We got a crowd, started the music and did our dance routine. It went really good but there on the Promenade there are lots of acts and entertainers performing and so we kind of fit in. They didn't want that. They wanted us to stick out. So we moved over to Westwood. A lot goes on in Westwood on Friday nights but there weren't any street entertainers and so we did stick out.

The area was packed. They decided to do the routine in front of this big movie theatre on the corner. People were everywhere, standing in line to buy tickets for a movie, standing in line to get in the theatre to see the movie, and just walking by. They decided they wanted us to get in the middle of all this and do our thing. So we walked up, made a space, turned on the music and did our dance routine. They expected that we would be asked to stop so they told us to keep on going no matter what. So we did.

It was crazy. We had this huge crowd watching us and everyone thought we were very serious about our performance and the dancing we were doing. They'd also laugh because we looked so out of place and looked so bad with this weird choreography.

During our routine, the theatre security asked us to stop a number of times. As we were told, we just kept going. The theatre manager came out and also tried to get us to stop. When we didn't, security walked over and turned off the music.

I think the manager felt pressure from the audience to leave us alone because after they turned our music off, the crowd booed them and started yelling, 'Let them dance.' So after a disagreement with the manager and his disapproval, we started again. I think he realised he should just leave us alone because the crowd was on our side.

They filmed everything – the management turning off our music, the crowd booing the management and then us starting up again and they used it all in the final edit of the video.

The artist Fatboy Slim wasn't in the video but he did make a little cameo appearance at the end. We have this little scene at the end of the video and while we're talking, Fatboy Slim slowly walks by, looks over our shoulders, and into the camera. The video aired in Europe first. They were playing it like crazy once every hour. Then they started playing it on MTV here in the States.'

In 2001 'Praise You' would be named the number one video of all time by the MTV viewers.

After achieving a double with 'Praise You and *You've Come A Long Way Baby*, Norman's year would get even better in February when, on Valentine's Day, he proposed to Zoë.

Talking on air during her Radio 1 *Breakfast Show* the next day she exclaimed: 'I was moaning to my boyfriend on Valentine's Day that he hadn't got me a present. I went to sleep, woke up and…I'm getting married! 'It's so exciting I feel completely sick and my stomach's turning over.'

Talking to *Sky* magazine, Norman added, 'All day I wanted to tell her, but I was waiting for the right time. I gave her the box with the ring in. Then she looked at me and said, "Don't say it, don't say it." She screamed, "Yes, yes," and ran around the house shouting.'

Within minutes of the announcement Norman's house was plagued with photographers and he suddenly realised what it was to be truly newsworthy to the tabloid media. At that night's Brit Awards in London it sunk in even further as the organisers gave Norman and Zoë a table at the front of the venue. This meant that everyone had to walk past their table to get their awards. As a result musicians and celebrities from all corners of the entertainment industry were stopping to congratulate the happy couple. Despite his delight at being engaged, he couldn't help but feel bemused by the extra attention. What was certain was the fact that Norman had come a long way from the faceless DJ he had hoped to be. Suddenly he was the best-known DJ in the world. In an edition of *The Guardian* researchers found that '93 per cent of young British adults don't know who William Caxton was. 93 per cent of young British adults do know who Fatboy Slim is.'

'Over the last 18 months I've been hit very hard in the face by the bemusement stick,' Norman exclaimed at the time. 'It's snowballed out of all proportion, ideally far more than I'd like. But I'm not going to start complaining about being too successful. That'd be like asking for a smack in the face.'

Inevitably, this new-found celebrity, along with his high level of success, brought with it detractors in the dance world who had started to resent the number of column inches and the amount of airtime being given over to Fatboy. Typically Norman understood, and felt for their situation, agreeing with the sentiment into the bargain.

'I'd probably resent me if I wasn't me,' he said. 'I can totally understand that they'd feel like that, if it seems I'm getting all the exposure and they're not getting a decent chance.'

In May 1999 Norman headlined the UK's Homelands dance festival. In an about-turn he actually came on after The Chemical Brothers, who he had regularly supported before then. It was all a bit strange, considering his well-documented love of the duo.

'It was weird following them,' he told *Select*. 'Normally they'll go on after me because they're the Dons and I'm like the apprentice. Going on after them it was like, "Does this mean there's been a role reversal here? Does it mean I'm bigger than you now? I don't feel that I am." But they were really cool about it.'

In support of the Homelands date Skint decided to pull a fourth track off the album as a single. 'Right Here Right Now' didn't at first seem to be the most obvious track as it featured none of the hooklines that marked out previous releases. Instead the track was imbued with an anthemic feel reminiscent of Orbital.

'[Throughout 1999] I had a reaction against knees-up breakbeat records, and went a bit mutated funky disco. Halfway back to house. I think that 'Right Here Right Now' was a pivotal point for me. The blueprint for it was [Massive Attack single] "Unfinished Sympathy" – I just thought about the strings and how evocative it was…and I thought I'd really like to make a record that's remembered in 10 years' time. Because most of mine aren't remembered 10 minutes later.

'When it became the fourth single of the album, and everybody already had the album and it still went to number two, I thought maybe I could do more adult stuff that's not Disney-breakbeat. So now I've got more confidence to do something with a little more depth,' he told *Mixmag*.

'Right Here Right Now' went to number two in the UK charts, while also offering a hint as to where his next album would go. The video that accompanied it was a regular feature on MTV, thanks to its depiction of the evolution of man, finishing with the guy on the album cover. It was a brilliant video, which continued the theme of the 'little man' being the true star, and it no doubt helped cross Norman over to an even wider market.

Behind the singles samples there was another story unfolding, however. Joe Walsh, a one time member of James Gang and The Eagles (he co-wrote their seminal hymn to cocaine abuse 'Hotel California') demanded 100 per cent publishing on the song thanks to a sample from the James Gang song 'Ashes, The Rain And I'.

'Yeah I didn't get any of the publishing on that one but I did get some of the sales so I'm still up on the deal. Nowadays, they don't tell me how much each sample costs. Because some are really easy and some are a bit shitty about it, and if I feel someone's being bit greedy or arsey about it I go off the song. The thing with Joe Walsh was that he asked for 100 per cent and we had to give someone else 20 per cent. We said, "We can't do both so you'll have to take 80 per cent". But bless him, Joe Walsh is probably struggling nowadays.'

In the months that followed the release of 'Praise You' Norman would find himself lined up to play numerous festivals. Among these, of course, was the by-now obligatory Glastonbury appearance, at which he would be such a massive draw that the crowd outside his tent was three times as big as the crowd inside.

In April he presented a series of media-baiting events where Fatboy Slim took on Arman Van Helden in a heavyweight soundclash. Presented as a cross between an old style reggae soundsystem show down and a boxing match, the two DJs quite literally took to the ring in venues which included Trentham Gardens in Stoke on Trent.

Over the summer he also played at two legendary festivals in the US. The first one was at the Red Rocks stadium in Colorado, a location famous for breaking U2 into the US, following their *Live At The Red Rocks* album and video. This time Fatboy Slim propped up a bill, which was headlined by The Chemical Brothers.

The second US festival was the near institution, Woodstock III. For this date Norman insisted on DJing inside, so they set up a stage for him in a cattle shed. 'They wanted me to play on one of the main stages, but I said I couldn't DJ on a big stage. I had to play indoors,' he told *Seven* magazine. 'So I ended up in a huge disused aircraft hangar. I was playing from two till five and I was the only thing on. All the bands ended, then there was this rave, so anyone looking for action had to come there. It all started late anyway, because it was in the contract that I couldn't start until Aerosmith had finished, in case everyone left them and came to see me.

'There were 35,000 kids dancing and then someone drove a van into the middle of the crowd. I thought it was a podium. There were 30 people dancing on it and the suspension went. And they thought it was going to tip over, so this bloke was shouting "Turn the music off!" And I said, "It's the biggest gig of my fucking life – I'm not going to turn the fucking music off!" He said, "People are going to die!" And I was going, "I don't care!" At first it was just American high spirits, but they all kind of lost it. I left at 5am, went to the airport and looked on the news, and my dressing room was on fire!'

Between US dates Norman also played alongside The Chemical Brothers at Japan's Mount Fuji Festival. When recalling his gig memories to *Seven* magazine's David Peter, it was another event in Japan that came to mind, one that dated back a year to 1998.

'I played three nights in a row in Tokyo,' he said. 'Wall Of Sound were doing one of the nights. The Japanese are so enthusiastic: it was 3am and they announced 'Special guest: Fatboy Slim!'. The noise was incredible, everyone went ballistic. There was a girl down the front with a smiley glove puppet and she was waving it around. Little did she know that I had a smiley glove puppet that someone had given me that night. So I waited until halfway through the set, then I caught her eye, winked and got out my puppet, and the two puppets started dancing!'

As 1999 drew to a close Norman could be found reflecting on what had been an incredible year for him. Understandably he was, in his own words, 'chuffed to bits'. In the last 12 months alone he had enjoyed worldwide success with his album, singles and DJing dates, and got engaged. In the last six months of the previous year he had delivered two genre-defining singles, a universally acclaimed album, more DJ dates than you could shake a pair of headphones at, a legendary season in Ibiza, a move to Millionaires' Row, inclusion on the Brighton Walk of Fame, not to mention the Boutique's continued growth, and you could quite rightly say that Norman Cook was walking on Cloud Nine – this being a Temptations album that he had no doubt sampled on numerous occasions over the years!

'It's been a blast,' he told *Mixmag*. 'It would be really miserable of me to say anything other than this year's been tops. Someone said the other day, "D'you realise that for little kids, bedroom DJs, you're living their dream?" And I thought, "It used to be my dream too and now it's come true," so I'm determined to enjoy it. To tell you the truth, I'm chuffed.'

'I'm enjoying this immensely,' he added for the benefit of *Heat*. 'I like feeling I'm doing something well. Feeling I'm doing a good job, making people dance, making people smile and…getting away with it. Indulging all my fantasies – faffing about and making music, and going out and getting drunk all the time. And getting paid for it. It's the best job in the whole world.'

Typically this new-found peace of mind came with the inevitable self effacing get out clause. In *Mixmag* he reiterated the claim that he had made throughout the last two years that he was only good when he was making dumb records – although it could be argued that some of his classic records over the years had come from the more serious side of Norman Cook (the second Freakpower album, *Freakpower In Dub*, etc).

'I've realised now that what I do is dumb arse, repetitive sample and breakbeat based dance music,' he told *Mixmag*. 'I'm not an actor, I'm not a dancer, I'm not attractive to look at, so I don't play live and I don't appear in videos. Anyway, if you start appearing on the telly people recognise you in the street and come up and tell you how crap you are.'

Norman had already well and truly crossed that line into celebrity territory. And suddenly everyone recognised him.

HALFWAY BETWEEN THE GUTTER AND THE STARS

Norman may have had achievements which far outstripped many of his dreams throughout 1999, but there was one event which stood way above everything else. On 20 August he and Zoë were married in secret at Bath registry office. A day later hundreds of guests joined them for a blessing.

The wedding was notable for the complete lack of media hype. Indeed, in an era of celebrity magazines bidding for rights to exclusive wedding-ceremony coverage, it was refreshing that neither Norman nor Zoë had wanted this.

It was, of course, in complete keeping with their characters. Since they first met they had made a point of letting everyone know that they were just normal people, and didn't want to be treated like stars.

However, for quite a time it was hard for the couple to lead an ordinary life. They divided their time between Zoë's house in London and Norman's seafront home (now christened 'HMS House' by the couple), with the tabloids continually camped outside on their doorstep. Indeed, within minutes of the announcement of their engagement, the paparazzi could be found along the private road outside Norman's. Added to this, tabloids started phoning many of the DJ's long-time friends in search of dirt. Among them was his ex-wife.

'When Zoë and I got engaged all my old friends were ringing me up saying, "I've just had a phone call offering money to say nasty things about you." Even my ex-wife rang up and said a newspaper had offered £30,000 to be horrible,' he told *Launch*.

Increased media attention was one of the more bizarre aspects of life that Norman had been forced to face up to in the wake of both his relationship with Zoë, and the huge impact of *You've Come A Long Way Baby*. The leap from the relative obscurity of his previous releases (despite the occasional number one record) to the television and radio saturation of his last opus had been a huge one, and despite being 10 years in the making, it still had its effect on Norman. But, thanks to the steadying media savvy influence of Zoë, he was able to deal with even the most persistent journalist.

'If I had the success of the last album with my first album I would be on crack by now,' he told *GQ*. 'Zoë taught me not to get into bed with the tabloids but also not to punch them every time that you see them. I go out and say, "Slow day today, isn't it?" and they say, "Well, we were outside the Gallaghers' all day and it was boring, so we thought we'd do you on the way home."'

Perhaps the couple's most effective weapon against the tabloid media was their refusal to play the media game. They continued to get on with their lives in relative normality. As a result, at any given time the paparazzi may have been able to catch the couple shopping in the local supermarket, wandering along the beaches of Hove with their dog Pickles Chickenwing, shopping in secondhand markets in Brighton and even eating out in restaurants. Or, had they really a wanted to be sure of catching them in public, the media could have wandered along to any one of the local clubs that Norman played at (including the Boutique) in the months that followed the couple's first meeting. Not celebrity gossip, that's for sure.

'I don't think I'm really equipped for celebrity,' Norman told *BBM*. 'It's not that I feel like a square peg in a round hole, but I kind of don't fill the hole…yeah, a square peg that's smaller than the round hole so it goes in but it's not actually flush with everything.'

'There's this danger that you become a *Hello!* magazine celebrity and all you do is wander around saying hello to other celebrities. I went to one première and thought "Never again!" It was at the Beach. I was going to do some music for them and it didn't fit, so I felt I should turn up and say thanks for asking me. I went to the party afterwards for about 20 minutes and just thought, "I don't belong here." I'm not very good at being a celebrity, frankly. I'm much better at being a DJ.'

Despite their reticence about being seen as anything other than normal, the media still obsessed about them – even calling them the anti-Posh and Becks after the ultimate UK celebrity couple, ex-Spice Girl Victoria and footballer David Beckham. Surprisingly it was something that tickled Norman's sense of humour: 'I like fact that everyone calls us the Posh and Becks of the chemical generation or the anti-Posh and Becks. I like that we, on the whole, probably have a bit more respect than them. We're not into stardom but we've been thrust into that, and we grudgingly accept it. We accept that we are going to have our photo taken so we smile and grin, but we don't go looking for it.'

One story that did make the headlines concerned Norman and an unlikely stalker. A 73-year old woman had taken to sunbathing on their private beach, while penning letters to Norman in which she claimed he owed her royalties for his music.

'My stalker's a 73-year-old woman, who alternately wants me to produce her new album or wants the keys to the house because she invented Fatboy Slim music in 1956 in the Lake District. And she sunbathes topless all summer outside the house while writing 40-page letters to me. So that's the class of stalker I get.

'I'd always thought of her as a comedy stalker, mad as box of frogs but not at all threatening, but when she got into my bedroom, I thought, "I don't like this any more." So my manager told her if she came near the house again we'd have to call the police – and bless her, she hasn't. But I don't want to name her or make things worse for her. Or aggravate her!'

This wasn't the first time that Norman had been the victim of an old woman's attention. In Ibiza in the summer of 1999 the DJ woke up to find a local woman in his bedroom. It was the middle of the night when the slightly worse for wear hotel guest realised that he had an intruder in his room, washing her hair in the toilet!

'This mad old woman broke into my room in this hotel in the Old Town,' he told *Seven* magazine. 'It was the middle of the night and [she] started washing her hair in the toilet. I woke up, I wasn't at my best, and I thought it was the chambermaid. I got up and said, "Not now." And then I saw that she'd dropped all the sachets of shampoo into the bowl and had put her head in it. I tried to stop her, but she just started shouting at me in Spanish. In the end I frog-marched her down to reception, and the woman in reception wouldn't go near her in case she had AIDS. We had to throw her out and then stand there with our feet on the glass door so she wouldn't come back in!'

Towards the end of 1999 another event would have a profound effect on Norman's outlook. Until now he had been DJing in bigger and bigger venues with more and more lavish set ups. In the US he went as far as performing on a revolving stage for the tour in support of *You've Come A Long Way Baby*. However, as the venues got bigger, so his DJing style was forced to change. He was having to deliver the big, epic hits in favour of the more underground cuts, so as to try to reach a lowest common denominator among the audience.

The audiences too had changed enormously during this time. Suddenly he was a huge pull for jocks and frat boys (hence the nickname 'Fratboy Slim'), while the girls in the front rows all felt the need to lift their tops to reveal their breasts – something that was all a little surreal for Cook.

'In America they just show their tits all the time,' he said at the time. 'It's quite bizarre sometimes when I'm DJing and I look up and all I see are pairs of tits! And they say, "That's for you!" I just go, "Er, thanks!"'

On Sunday 19 December Norman Cook was to have a sudden realisation, which was to encourage him to reject all the show of the big gig. At a time when he could have taken the Fatboy Slim name on to an even greater level commercially, he decided that enough was enough. He was giving up the huge events in rock auditoriums.

'It all ended that night at the Hammerstein Ballroom,' Norman told Launch.com. 'We did two nights at Christmas. Saturday night was great, but the Sunday night didn't really work. That was the night for the floating voters, the undecided, the people who thought it might be a band. It was just awful. There was some girl giving a bloke a blow job in one of the boxes. The cameramen started showing it on the big screen. All the dancing stopped and people were cheering. There were these girls showing their tits. Howard Stern was waving at everyone. I was thinking, "Oh my God, this is what I didn't want to happen." That was the last big show I did.

'In that kind of [big rock] setting, I have to try and find the biggest records. I used to turn up in the afternoon to check the stage and the decks, and that's like doing a soundcheck, that's what I vowed I'd never do,' he continued. 'Once I'd given up bands, I was relieved that I didn't have to do a soundcheck. I'd put a lot of thought into it, and then I'd turn up with a bottle of vodka and start playing.'

With his return to the closer environment of the club circuit Norman was able to start exploring more underground sounds than before. Increasingly he dropped the big beat style altogether and started employing far more house and techno sounds. Furthermore, he started to lean more heavily on filtered disco sounds as typified by Stardust and many of France's so-called 'French touch' producers.

This movement in style for his DJing dates opened up a lot of ideas for him when it came to recording the follow up to *You've Come A Long Way Baby*, while also closing down some of the trademark samples which outlined his big beat sets. Sadly, in this new, musically more serious style, Fatboy Slim had little room for those Jimi Hendrix or B52s loops that had offered some of the most enjoyable moments.

In their place came full throttle, adrenalised club sets, which were just as creative, if not as eclectic.

'I didn't want the album to be big beat, [so] I stopped playing a big beat set. I'm playing more house-y, techno-y. There aren't all those fireworks and Jimi Hendrix samples that work in a crossover environment. When we took it out of clubs and into the rock venues, it watered down the clubby side of it; it got a bit pantomime-y, showbiz, and rock. I'm happy getting back to basics, and just remembering what I loved about club music,' he told Launch.com.

Coinciding with Norman's own rejection of the larger venues came the Boutique's decision to move from its residency at the Beach into the smaller Concorde 2, on the beachfront. It was a far more dingy venue, in many ways like a scout hut once again (despite attempts to brighten up the ambience with fluorescent lighting), but the new venue was far more conducive to the Boutique's up-close-and-personal approach to clubbing.

As 2000 dawned Norman continued on his exhaustive DJ schedule, crossing the Atlantic as regularly as an airline cabin crew, but, despite the level of work load, he also started on a new album. By April the

DJing began to cut back and the recording took on a greater precedence. It became more important than ever for him to be at home, as Zoë was, by now, pregnant with their first child.

Towards the end of the summer promos of the first fruits of the recording process were doing the rounds. Called 'Sunset (Bird Of Prey)' the promo was a far more laid back affair than on previous Fatboy Slim outings. An undulating, filtered keyboard fill slowly fused with a rolling acid bass sequence before opening out onto a trance hookline, which built towards a syncopated break thanks to a huge 303 crescendo. From here on the track went through various versions of these opening bars, increasingly subverting them while constantly pushing the sense of momentum, subsequently underlining the feeling of being continually on the verge of erupting, but never actually losing control. In terms of production, the song represented a huge leap forward from Norman and his sidekick Simon Thornton.

The vocal line, however, told another story, threatening to obliterate the track itself. It was a sample of Doors frontman Jim Morrison. The reaction to this apparent complete lack of respect to an artist many see as a God, was voluble. Not since Norman Cook was depicted as traitor to indie in his embracing of all things dance had the public reacted so angrily to one of his records.

The sample itself actually came from a bootleg version of Morrison's *An American Prayer* album which featured the vocalist delivering preposterous adolescent poetry over pompous light classical music. The album was actually compiled (with music added) after the singer's death.

'He did this LP called *An American Prayer,* which is just him doing absurd poetry. There was this bootleg of the raw stuff he did without the music. Most of it is just him waffling on about Red Indians and then at one point he stops and sings these four lines. It just reminded me of every sunset I'd ever watched.

'I actually lost the original record because it was a bootleg, so we got in contact with the president of the Jim Morrison fan club who very kindly sent me a CD of the sample, so I have got some accreditation. And obviously Jim Morrison's estate agreed so his family will get lots of money,' he told *NME*.

This wasn't the first time that Norman had actually used the sample. He had originally used it as far back as 1994 for his ambient project called 'Yum Yum Head Food'. It was on these same sessions that he also first used Camille Yarbrough's 'Take Yo Praise' vocals for the Fatboy track 'Praise You'.

'I did it years ago pre-Fatboy Slim when I was doing loads of acid. It was totally self indulgent and not for release – just for me and my mates,' he told *NME* on the track's origins.

What he didn't mention, though, was that the ambient version of the track had actually appeared in 1995 on a collection called *Southern Fried House*. Ostensibly just a compilation album celebrating the acts on his own label, closer inspection revealed this to actually be a Norman Cook collection!

With the selection moving between the breakbeat house hijinks of The Mighty Dub Katz (including their paean to masturbation 'Let's Get Chinese Eyes'), Pizzaman's joyous house and the hard house extravaganza of 'Manna' by Sunny Side Up, the collection actually represents Norman fully embracing house culture.

'Yum Yum Head Food's 'Bird Of Prey' showed how Norman's new love of club culture had extended into the more contemplative ambient arena. A closer comparison between this original version and the new single revealed the only significant changes to be the addition of the rhythm.

Ironically, perhaps, Morrison was once asked in an interview what he thought the future of music would be. He replied 'I think it'll just be one guy on a stage surrounded by a load of electronics.'

Despite protestations that sampling the so-called Lizard King was sacrilege, it is probable that he would have responded positively to Norman's creative use of his voice. Morrison held beliefs that artistic integrity was paramount and, as a result, the artists owed it to the greater culture to always push the envelope. Arguably this is exactly what Norman was doing.

The fact that Morrison's estate agreed to Norman using the sample backs up the possibility that Morrison himself might have approved. The one thing he was most adamant about, however, was that his music should never be used for adverts. It's something that the surviving band members have stuck to, despite potentially lucrative offers from corporate giants like Apple.

If the Morrison sample hadn't caused enough of a stir, when the single finally received a full release in November 2000, its accompanying video, shot by Blue Source, was similarly the object of huge controversy.

It featured vintage political campaign advertising footage of the 'Daisy Girl' television advert aired only once by President Lyndon B Johnson to counter claims that he was soft on war. That TV ad featured a plane taking off while an innocent girl picked daisies. It ended with a mushroom cloud. The implication was that Johnson's adversary, presidential candidate Barry Goldwater, was a proponent of nuclear war.

Inadvertently, however, Norman walked straight into the middle of a political debate in the US as the self-same imagery had recently been used when the Texas-based company Aretino Industries created and aired a similar film to attack the Clinton-Gore national security record. George W Bush subsequently asked for the advert to be withdrawn.

Although the filming of the video for 'Sunset (Bird Of Prey)' actually predated this political broadcast, it did have added irony in the fact that Al Gore had been using Fatboy Slim's 'Praise You' as his campaign theme music throughout the year. Norman's response? 'At least it's not the Republicans!'

He further added that he was agreeing to let them use the track so that his mother would be able to hear his music when she was watching the news.

That his music had managed to penetrate the lives of everyday people in the US to such an extent offered an indication of just how high Norman's Fatboy Slim profile in the US had become during this time. Increasingly he was invited to A-list celebrity parties. His name was top of everyone's list for remix duties. Brad Pitt and Jennifer Aniston were on his guest list. Fatboy Slim had become the chosen, token weirdo for the Hollywood in-crowd.

It was a bizarre situation that he would address with the title of his third album, which would appear at the tail end of 2001, *Halfway Between The Gutter And The Stars*.

'It's about being propelled towards stardom and then slipping away

– I was always drunk somewhere or not taking it seriously. I don't just hang out with Posh and Becks all the time!' he told *Select*. 'I heard someone say it. I was in LA and staying at the Château Marmont. I had played the LA Palladium; Brad and Jennifer were there, and Bill Murray was at the bar, and I was just thinking this really wasn't meant to be. I was sweating and shaking from the partying I had been doing and I was kinda thinking, "You can take the boy out of the gutter, but you can never take the gutter out of the boy." No matter how posh a hotel you put me in, I am still going to be this drunken slob at the end of it.'

The actual recording process for the album had been fraught with problems due to Norman losing self confidence, haunted by the success of the last album. He knew that he wanted to take the project in a different direction, but the fact still remained that everyone, including himself to an extent, had a preconceived idea of what a Fatboy track sounded like. It was something he had to literally run away from every time the problem reared its head.

'Every time I thought about that I just left the studio and went to watch telly rather than face up to it,' he told *Select*. 'But everyone at Skint said, "Don't worry about anyone else – make a record for yourself." They knew that my self-indulgence has got a pop edge to it and I wasn't going to turn up with the second Terence Trent D'Arby album. It's kind of a no-lose situation. If this album isn't as successful as the last one then I get some of my life back. I've got no ambition to be any bigger than I was over the last couple of years. I'm quite happy just pootling along.

'It is hard and everybody puts so much pressure on me to work harder and harder,' he continued. 'What with a child on the way, I want to work less, not more, so if the stakes aren't quite so high and not quite so much money for people, people won't put so much pressure on me at the end of the day. You're in a no-lose situation.'

Talking to *NME* he explained in more depth the problems that faced him when he was trying to establish what the album would sound like.

'After the success of the last album, I got the feeling that something wasn't right, it wasn't what I wanted to do. It's a bit like the *Kid A* syndrome [a reference to Radiohead's uncompromising change-of-direction album], although it wasn't as extreme as that. But I didn't want to try and make "Rockafeller Skank" over and again.'

'The first six weeks I just sat there thinking, "Oh my God, I've got writer's block," but I didn't want to repeat [myself]. There's so much music around sounding like [*You've Come A Long Way Baby*],' he added to Launch.com. 'It took a while to work out what the new thing would sound like. It was quite daunting, but what I said to myself was, "You can't lose. If it's more successful than the last album, then that's great. And if it isn't, then you get your life back." It kind of takes all the pressure off me.'

Among the many pressures which faced Norman at the time was also the age dilemma. He has often said that he doesn't want to end up like an old rock star going on the road for ever more. However, with this album he needed to show a musical maturity that would dispel any suggestions that his dance stuff was disposable, and demonstrate that he had longevity as an artist. Most electronic music artists had managed to overcome this dilemma by moving into coffee table, or dinner party music territory. Artists like Moby whose *Play* served a post-acid house generation, now tied to home life with kids and bills to pay.

Norman was vociferous in his rejection of any suggestions that the Moby-route was in his mind while recording the album.

'Fuck, no! One of the main motivations of the album was not to sound like Moby,' he told *Select*.

There was another pressure on Norman at the time – one which was hardly ever picked up on by journalists. *Halfway Between The Gutter And The Stars* represented the first time he'd managed to get past album number two with any of his pseudonyms. In terms of marriage, it finally looked like he'd met someone he could settle down with!

'After four divorces, I think I may have married the right woman this time,' he joked to *Rolling Stone*. 'I think this one might last. It's going to be quite difficult for me to split up. I had kind of forgotten about it until maybe a week ago, and then I remembered this is the first difficult third album I could never do with any of the other acts. After two years, I was getting bored or no one liked us any more. Something always went wrong and we split up.'

Halfway Between The Gutter And The Stars proved to be a far more complex album than its predecessor. With a larger stylistic palette on display and a more experimental approach to production, it was a harder album to get into and, despite claims that it came from the heart of a happy, contented person, many of the tracks displayed a darkness and density never before seen in his music. And yet, throughout the album there is an almost overpowering sense of the artist in a more contemplative, positive mood.

'Yeah, I'm a more thoughtful bloke nowadays,' he joked to Launch.com. 'The person who made the last album was a bit lost and just wandering around the world and partying for the sake of it. I was halfway through moving house, and I physically didn't have anything to go home to. The studio was still at the old house, so I was working at an empty house and living in an unpacked one. Normally, when you've been away on tour for three weeks, you just want to get back. But at the end of the tour, I just wanted to stay in Australia. I didn't want to go home because I had nothing to go back to. But now I have a lovely house, a lovely wife, a kid on the way, a lot more stable home life. That kind of helps.'

This mood was partly due to the mellow 'Talking 'Bout My Baby', which opened and finished the album. It opens with a piano riff from 'Macon Hambone Blues', which sounds like a cut-up version of Eric Satie's *Trois Gymnopedies*, as a blues vocalist describes the joy of watching his girlfriend undress under 'the big bright yellow sun'. The track then surges into a monster distorted bass drone before shuddering into the opening vocal of 'Star 69' declaring 'what the fuck'. Suddenly any thoughts of this album being a Fatboy Slim compromise collection were instantly thrown out of the window.

'The gag is I want everyone to think it's that classic thing when you write a song for your child – horrifically self indulgent and apart from "Hey Jude", normally not very good. Of course it's not about that at all. It's about tits bouncing up and down,' he told *Select*.

'Star 69' featured a distorted meltdown of acid house and Detroit bass with a beat that pulsates and twists around hard b-lines and ever-growing 303 noises. The vocal sample of Roland Clarke's 'I Get Deep' declaring 'they know what's what, but they don't know what is what, they just strut – what the fuck' is repeated over and over, thus exaggerating the sense of hypnotic growth. Here was a track with its heart so deeply entrenched in club culture that it sounded like nothing off the pop friendly previous album.

'Sunset (Bird of Prey)' followed, sounding almost more complete as an album track, before opening up onto the first of two collaborations with Macy Gray – 'Love Life' (originally called 'Where There's A Way'). The other track was called 'Demons'.

'They [The Chemical Brothers] said, "You always claim you ripped us off. If you really did you'd use guest vocalists,"' explained Norman to *Select* of his decision to use vocalists instead of samples on the album. 'So when I mentioned Macy, they said, "Just phone her up." And I'm like, "Is that all you do?"'

'I was in London at the Brit Awards and he came up to my table and he just said that he wanted to work together,' Macy told *Rolling Stone*. 'People say that all that time, so you never know. He came to one of my shows and he gave me a tape to write the lyrics to, and we went in, and he's really funny. That's a weird guy, but we had a lot of fun, and we got it done. The track is hot. "Where There's A Way" is like a mid-tempo dance tune, the chorus is like gospel, and then there's like a Hare Krishna sample in it,' she said. 'It's wild. It's a trip.'

'Love Life', as it became known, was the weakest of the Macy Gray collaborations due mainly to the singer's syrupy delivery. The track itself was a lithe downtempo electro-funk tune with heavily gated, swelling P-Funk bass and a swing-meets-acid groove. Where the vocals could have accentuated what was in fact Norman's funkiest composition yet, they only managed to muddy the sound, holding back the groove in the process.

'Demons', on the other hand, was a far more successful collaboration with its easy Bill Withers sample from 'I Can't Write Left Handed' (Withers was a constant sample source for Norman) and low-slung groove. This time around Macy's vocals bring out the track's natural melody and accentuate the rhythm, while her own trademark delivery added to the track's dirty funk feel.

'I had the rhythm track lying around for ages,' said Norman at the time. 'The piano sample is actually from a Bill Withers album that I love. The song's over that riff, but luckily Macy hadn't heard that song, so she just wrote her own over it. That was a great thing. It was a pivotal moment on the album.

'I had just been working on a few sketches for a few tracks, and then I went to do the stuff with Macy. When she walked in, I suddenly thought to myself, "Oh my God, what if I hate what she's written? Do I just sit here for three days and pretend to like it, and then go home and quietly throw it away? Or do I just say, "Macy this isn't going to work," and fly back to England? I got into a real sweat about it. And she walked in and sung the first line and the hairs on the back of my neck stood up. I said, "Thank God, this is going to work." I did two tracks with her and I put them on a tape with four other tracks that I had been working on and it really started to sound like an album. That was a great relief. All of a sudden I knew I was on the way.'

'Ya Mama', which followed 'Love Life', couldn't have been further removed from the Macy collaboration. It's a full throttle breakbeat attack with thrash funk guitars reminiscent of the Red Hot Chili Peppers, mad 303s and a constant vocal sample stating 'Push the tempo'. If ever a track was created with a US audience in mind, this was it – despite featuring samples of jazz rock outfit Colosseum!

'Mad Flava' on the other hand could have come from the previous album with its distressed Bollywood hook over chunky break and old-skool vocal samples and Shinehead's ragga licks. Only the intricacy of the programming separated it from the music on display on *You've Come A Long Way Baby*. It acted as a testament to the high level to which Norman and Simon had taken the production. On the following track, 'Retox', Norman could be found once again teamed up with old mucker Ashley Slater. The track title itself came from a holiday Norman had with a few friends in which they all attempted to cut out drink and drugs. Towards the end of the week one of the girls on the holiday said she couldn't wait to get back to retox. The idea of doing the opposite to the detox appealed to both Norman and Ashley's sense of humour and they immediately set about working on the track on their return.

'Retox' features a cavalcade of funk, soul and soundtrack samples over mad acid, frequency snatches and a hard hard trance beat while Ashley delivers a vocal in his best baritone. 'Retox the freak in me', he sang, and it could have been a declaration of intent for Norman's post success attitude.

What followed was perhaps the album's weakest cut despite featuring P-Funkateer Bootsy Collins on vocals. With its standard hip-hop samples, good time groove and up beat funky bassline, 'Weapon Of Choice' could have come directly from the previous album. Not even the production values could separate it from the earlier material. Even Bootsy's addition to the track proved to be somewhat uninspiring, as Norman drew out of him a near pastiche performance. Almost a *Stars In Their Eyes* version of himself.

'I wrote the lyrics and that's me doing the vocals,' Bootsy explained in an interview with Launch.com. 'It's really good for me 'cos I got a chance to see how the new world is responding to, you know, the new technology. And it gives me a chance to get in there and check that out, how they do things.'

Ironically, 'Weapon Of Choice' worked beautifully as a stand-alone track. When it came to be released as a single in its own right, the song shone. On the album, however, it just seemed to push against the mood of the other tracks.

If anything, this fact was further emphasised by the track 'Drop The Hate', which followed. On it, a brooding Suicide-like layered drone played host to a speech by the Reverend W Leo Daniels from his 'Answer To Watergate'. As the speech built towards a gospel melody, the track erupted into a blitzkrieg of fuzzed basses, hard beats, distorted drones and acid squelches. Dark, hard and most definitely very funky, this track again represented an artist at the peak of his production powers.

The closing of 'Demons' and 'Song For Shelter' were even stronger. 'Demons' was the true funk soul brother of the second Freakpower album (it can't be underestimated just how much the presence of *More Of Everything...For Everybody* could be felt on *Halfway Between The Gutter And The Stars*). 'Song For Shelter', on the other hand, took its cues directly from The Chemical Brothers' *Surrender* album.

Featuring Roland Clarke's 'I Get Deep' in close to its entirety ('Star 69's vocal was just a snippet), and benefiting from the services of Roger Sanchez, 'Song For Shelter' harked back to the gradual builds and undulation layers of Pizzaman at its best. However, where that project revelled in its own disposability, 'Song For Shelter' has a rare timeless element to it. A hard trick to achieve in club music.

It opens like a sermon, gospel chords swelling beneath the cut-up vocals until Roland Clarke's frenetic delivery builds up its own rhythm. A clock factory, ticking like a time bomb; rigid beats grew, building on the sense of tension. A drop provided Clarke with the space to deliver his fevered sermon at a greater pace before the music returned, again pushing the tension, but never quite releasing with the expected crescendo.

In many ways this track was the extension of 'Sunset (Bird Of Prey)'. It just keeps on building, growing through more and more layers, changing moods, drawing on an ever-greater palette of colours until it climaxes as a multi-hued trance epic before melting back into a Bill Withers piano motif from the opening track 'Talking 'Bout My Baby'.

Despite its continued reliance on samples (most of the songs were still just collages of sampled material; that the vast majority were unrecognisable said much about Thornton and Cook's engineering and production skills), Norman only faced one total knockback from another artist. This came from Steppenwolf.

'We had one [sample] completely knocked back, which was "Magic Carpet Ride" by Steppenwolf, just the guitar riff at the beginning,' he told *Select*. 'I thought it was a good little guitar riff to use but they just weren't into it at all. The band's still going and they licensed it to some commercial and just weren't into it. So we went, "Oh look, there's £100,000 there!" and they said it wasn't about the money. In the end they said "Look, we're not going to reply to your faxes any more, please leave us alone. Which part of 'no' do you not understand?!" I respect them for that. It wasn't the money, they just didn't want to be sampled.'

That Steppenwolf had close connections with both Ken Kesey's travelling crew The Merry Pranksters and Hunter S Thompson must have upset Norman to some extent. His love of the track had, after all, already been immortalised by The Mighty Dub Katz.

Overall *Halfway Between The Gutter And The Stars* was stylistically a less focused album than the previous Fatboy Slim collections, but in those areas where it did shine it was a far more assured work – suggesting that the best Fatboy Slim album is yet to come.

However critics and public alike didn't want a grown-up Fatboy Slim. they wanted the cheeky sample thief with a fine line in stupid, party music. As a result the album was largely panned by the music media. Despite being dismissive in their print edition of *NME*, the online version carried a review by long-standing journalist Steven Wells, which summed up the general feeling about the album, but concluded with a positive, rather than the usual knee-jerk negative. He wrote:

Norman Cook is Joe Pesci! Think about it. For a start, he's every bit as tapped as one of Joe's pitbull-puppy-with-a-gob-full-of-wasps-type characters. What with his mad theory that Jews, Armenians and Bosnian Muslims have a better sense of rhythm than the rest of us because of the oppression they've suffered. I mean – jeez, what a friggin' LOONY! But the proof is the way that this record starts off is really, really boring. 'Talking 'Bout My Baby' is a lo-fi piano dink-donk riff with some Mick Jagger soundalike ranting on about Zoë Ball's tits resembling 'two big ole balloons in a hurricane'. 'Star 69' is some bloke swearing over a drum machine and some drain noises. 'Love Life' is watery funk-by-numbers, not helped by Macy Gray, and 'Sunset (Bird Of Prey)' is Jim Morrison babbling over some incredibly lame elevator muzak…

By now you're thinking, 'Oh no, Normo's done a *Kid A*!' But be careful. Cooky's leaning over and smiling and saying, 'Hey! We're all friends here, right?' (just like Joe Pesci in *Raging Bull*) and then 'Ya Mama' comes blasting out over the speakers and – WHAM! – he's whomped you up the side of the head with a whisky tumbler and – BAM! BAM! BAM! – he's pounding your fizzog into the glass with berserker gusto! The dirty motherf***er! It's ace! True Fatboy concrete handbag-style disco-metal! Yeah! And then it's the skull-krushing, sledgehammer fuck-funk of 'Mad

Flava' and Normo's jabbing a pen into your neck and screaming, 'Where's the big man now, huh?! Ya fuck!' And then, right, on comes 'Retox' which is ultra-malevolent ghost music recorded in an abattoir and the Cookster is slamming your head with a car door and going 'UH! UH! UH! UH!'

And then it's the totally amazing 'Weapon Of Choice', which is 1960s TV theme music recorded on drugs that won't actually be invented until the 2060s and Norm's pumping slugs at your feet and screeching, 'Dance! Dance, ya fuckin' gimp!' And you do – you fucking dance!

Fuck it! Face facts, you punks! Norman Cook is God. He is the King Of Pop. He makes 98.7 per cent of all rock utterly redundant. Now excuse me 'cos I'm going to stick 'Ya Mama' on again and again and bounce around the room 'til my fuckin' eyes bleed. Ya mooks!

Sadly the hit-single-hungry public didn't find the same redeeming features in the album as Wells. As a result the album has only shifted two million units (one million in its first year) as opposed to the six million scored by *You've Come A Long Way Baby* to 2002. Indeed the album faired particularly badly in America. This new sound Fatboy apparently wasn't Fratboy enough.

'In a way I almost wanted that [bad sales], because it got so mad before that my life wasn't my own,' Norman said of the album's relatively poor showing. 'I've never been so ambitious that I wanted to be Michael Jackson or Madonna, I'm quite happy just being me. If you had told me a year ago that I'd make an album that sold even a million copies, I would have gone, "Fuckin' hell." So this album was kind of like me taking my foot off the accelerator a bit, trying to calm things down. I'm approaching 40 now and I don't want to be prancing around on stage like The Rolling Stones when I'm old and craggy, I want to work out a way of growing old gracefully."

There was another, often overlooked aspect to the poor performance of *Halfway Between The Gutter And The Stars*; the album coincided with a general downturn in album sales, and in particular album sales by dance artists. With the electronica hype over in the US and DJ culture increasingly representing the older generation, the culture tourists who had embraced the music and the lifestyle, quickly turned to nu metal and hip-hop for a fresh injection of this week's latest thing.

The fact that Fatboy Slim managed to achieve sales of this level while all around him high profile producers were suffering, should perhaps have been celebrated.

Norman promoted the release of the album in the US with a free show in Virgin Megastore in New York, before heading out on a four-date tour, which took in Denver, Seattle, San Francisco and Los Angeles.

LIVE ON BRIGHTON BEACH

The year 2001 opened with the release of the strongest of the Macy Gray collaborations, 'Demons'. Thanks largely to its radio-friendly melody it gained huge support from all the stations and reached number 10 in the UK charts.

In between the album's release and the arrival of the single, however, Norman had been quoted as describing Macy as a nutter – something she was allegedly none too pleased with. Talking to *Select*, he was quick to sing her praises and try to put to rest any speculation of a rift between them.

'The actual collaboration was so easy we didn't really get to know each other. The minute we finished it we went outside and started shooting hoops. She's lovely. I did call her a nutter in print but I meant it affectionately. She says she thinks "Demons" is the best thing she's ever made, which is cool. It's kind of gospel trip-hop. It's the "Praise You" of this LP.'

A mere two months later saw the release of the next single from *Halfway...* For the first time Skint released a double A-side, and in a shrewd move, which displayed a full understanding of the differences between the US and UK markets, they pushed different tracks to each country. The more club-sussed UK got 'Star 69' with its hard beats and multiple swearing, while the US got the Bootsy-vocalled 'Weapon Of Choice'.

'The Americans can't cope with having the word "fuck" quite so many times in it, so they had to pick another single. Simple as that. Too many fucks,' joked Norman to *Mixmag* at the time.

Originally intended as the B-side to 'Sunset (Bird Of Prey)', 'Star 69' represented one of the album's deepest moments and as a single it seemed to make little sense beyond being a club record. However, if the aim was to remove Fatboy from his pop associations it couldn't have been a better choice.

'I'd been going on to Norman to make a booty record; he couldn't and he got very pissed off with me,' explained Damian Harris to *Select* of the song's birth. 'One night he phoned me at two in the morning and said, "What about something like this?" And it was just what we wanted, although it's nothing like a booty record. Still, that's my A&R for you!'

'Star 69' may not have been an exact replica of a booty record, but it presented the loose bass end and bouncing beats of booty bass, but with a very British twist. Just as earlier tracks had recycled US old-skool hip-hop as British big beat.

'We're not that bothered about getting it on Radio 1 [because of the swearing],' continued Harris when pushed about the single's unsuitability to airplay. 'In the past we've worried too much about what Radio 1 thinks about stuff. It's a good club track and that's much, much more important to us.'

Of course it would have been a possibility for Norman to re-edit the track with noises to mask the offending words. This trick had often been employed by hip-hop artists in order to get past the station censors.

In the case of Radio 1, however, they had long stated that they didn't ban records, they simply chose not to play them. This stance was adopted in the wake of The Sex Pistols' 'God Save The Queen' getting to number one in the week of the Queen's Silver Jubilee, despite receiving no airplay at all. In the furore that surrounded the single, some of the pro-Pistols media declared that it was wrong that the radio station, which was subsidised by the public license fee money, had banned the number one single – as bought by the very same public. In their embarrassment Radio 1 declared that they hadn't actually banned the record but hadn't deemed it suitable.

In the summer of 2002, a similar event took place with a single by electronic punks Prodigy: 'Baby's Got A Temper'. However, this time around, the station's actions displayed just how inconsistent their censorship guidelines had become.

'Baby's Got a Temper' contained a lyric which extolled the virtues of Rohypnol. Despite its connotations as a date-rape drug, the rest of the lyrics were obviously not about rape, or abuse of any kind, beyond the self-abuse of taking tranquillisers. When Prodigy main man Liam Howlett presented a version of the track with the offending word masked, Radio 1 agreed to play it. However, Liam later decided that he preferred the original version and, just as Norman had refused to mask 'Star 69', Liam decided to remain true to the definitive version of his single.

Rather than remove the track from their programming Radio 1 decided to edit the track themselves. The offending word was masked by an instrumental sample from another part of the track. Keith's words now reduced to: 'We love…she got…we take…' and so on, leaving the listener the space to insert the drug of his or her choice. And Chemical Karaoke was duly born.

Yet on the same programme 'Baby's Got A Temper' was first aired, Missy Elliot could be heard doing her thing 'for her ecstasy' people. While in recent weeks R&B and hip-hop stars from Nelly to Eminem had had songs clearly celebrating the joys of 'E' aired by the same station. Even Macy Gray had played the ecstasy card on her lyrics for 'Demons', despite claiming that the song was in no way about the drug. The words 'All of your demons will wither away, ecstasy comes and they cannot stay', proving just how easy it is to read a song either way. Especially in view of the part E played in saving Norman from his demons.

Such inconsistency was, of course, nothing new. A couple of years back the BBC plugged itself with a song about heroin use (Lou Reed's 'Perfect Day'), while at the same time girl band All Saints scored a number one and round-the-clock air play with the Red Hot Chili Peppers' 'Under The Bridge' – another song about heroin use.

'Star 69' was coupled with the far more pop-orientated 'Weapon Of Choice' – the lead single in the US. For fans of the previous Fatboy Slim album (especially from the more rock-orientated press) not only was it the better track, but it was also came with his finest video yet. The feeling of being cheated obviously rankled with *NME*.

'Britain, for reasons known only to sinister marketing spooks with giant foreheads who use phrases like "out of the loop", gets 'Star 69' as the Fatboy's latest A-side,' they ranted. 'And frankly this is one of the duffer tracks on Normski's underwhelming third opus, an aimless hard trance inflected stomp with a sampled semi-rap vocal looped to say "what the fuck" every 30 seconds. Which is about as punk rock as a struggling teen band making sure they get caught smoking a joint in public.'

With Spike Jonze once again at the helm, the video for 'Weapon Of Choice' was indeed superb. Featuring Christopher Walken in full Fred Astaire mode, dancing in a hotel lobby to the track, it not only seemed surreal but also verged on the ludicrous, playing on our preconceived ideas of what the actor, star of such films as *Pulp Fiction, Batman Returns* and *The Prophecy*, was about.

'Fred Astaire once saw him dance and told him he was a natural mover, but then his career moved into psychopathic acting,' Norman told *Hot Press*. 'He told Spike that he would love to get his dancing down on film while he was still young enough to do it.'

Certainly the video showed Walken to be a master of the smooth moves – a fact borne out by Jonze's own comments on the actor's performance.

'He's the best dancer, and I don't know, I love him. He was born a dancer,' Jonze told *Rolling Stone*. 'He danced when he was a kid, so I think he has the rhythm and you can't take that [away from him]. We shot it at the Marriott in downtown Los Angeles right before Christmas. We got to own the lobby for two nights.'

'One day we just turned the TV on, and Norman, you know, he's, he's a maniac,' added Bootsy Collins. 'He didn't let us know exactly what he was doing in the video or who he was going to get in the video, you know. Actually, we didn't even realise it was coming out that quick. So, next thing we know, we just turned it on and seen him in there and heard the song, and I was like, "Wow man." You know, we had no idea, you know, and it was like, man this is, this is great.'

If the inclusion of a Hollywood star in his video hadn't confirmed Norman's celebrity DJ position, then events at the Oscars certainly did.

'I'm DJing at the *Vanity Fair* pre-Oscars party,' he told *Mixmag*. 'These things are always a bit funny: you can end up with people asking for Bruce Springsteen and Madonna. I DJ-ed at a party for the Grammies this year with Thomas Bangalter [Daft Punk] and it was just like a wedding reception.'

Despite Damian Harris's continuous pleas for Norman to play his renowned Wedding Set (a good time collection of party records) he insisted on playing a full-on techno, house and filtered disco set, belligerently declaring that he wanted to discover if Hollywood had a sense of humour (and possibly trying to shun the DJ spotlight the Hollywood celebs had placed on him).

In the end, however, he gained quite a few fans, including Heather Hunter and star of *The X-Files* Gillian Anderson, who could be seen dancing throughout.

There was one person who wasn't impressed by Norman's taste in music though. After almost an hour of continuous beats, a disgruntled John Cleese wandered up to Norman just as he dropped Luke Slater's 'All Exhale' and demanded he 'turn the bloody noise off'.

Standing at the bar later in the evening Damian Harris would find himself next to Oscar winner Julia Roberts. Naturally he asked if he could stroke her award. She agreed – with a smile, of course.

Despite any negative feeling Norman may have held about the celebrity parties, his next step could depend on the reaction he received at this one. His aim was to get into film soundtracks and in 2001 he partly achieved this ambition by scoring short sequences for both *Tomb Raider* and Baz Luhrmann's much-hyped *Moulin Rouge*.

He did drop numerous hints to Spike Jonze about the movie he was working on at the time. 'There's a new film that [Spike Jonze] is just in pre-production with at the moment and I've been dropping all the hints. I would drop my whole career and spend six months doing the soundtrack,' he told *NME*.

'A lot of my music has been used in not very good films. Normally, someone like [the people doing] *Charlie's Angels* phone you up for a track and you say, "You're allowed to use it, but I don't want to get involved." But it's time. I'm thoroughly enjoying working with a quality director [on *Moulin Rouge*].'

'Yeah, [I'm dying to] score a film, like a really good film, a classic film with a classic score, like *Bladerunner* or *Paris, Texas* where the director works with the producer and you score the whole film,' he added to *BBM*. 'It takes about 10 months and it's really hard work,' he added to *Hot Press*.

It would no doubt have come as a shock that long-time writing partner and friend Ashley Slater would be commissioned to write a film score immediately after releasing his Big Lounge collection. However, here lay the biggest difference between Norman's and Ashley's work. Where Norman's was based on immediate response and drawn from surface-level hook lines, Ashley's sound was far more visual, exploring far greater textural depths.

At this point only very few Fatboy Slim tracks could claim the same approach, although some of his earlier tracks may have impressed directors far more (*Freakpower In Dub*, Yum Yum Head Food, etc). With the invitation to add a techno score to a can-can scene in Baz Luhrman's film *Moulin Rouge,* however, Norman threw himself into the project body and soul.

'They filmed it dancing to the can-can, but to a strict 140bpm beat,' he told *Hot Press*. 'How Baz described it is that Moulin Rouge at that time was basically what Manumission is now – hedonism – so that was what he wanted me to get across. To be honest, it kind of got a bit butchered by the time it got into the film, and you don't really hear a lot of what I did with it, but working with Baz was great. He is an absolute fucking lunatic and one of the funniest people I've ever met. I went and stayed with him in Sydney and he came and spent a weekend with me in Brighton and we sat in the hot tub, throwing out these mad ideas. He's a very inspirational person.

'If you have a quality director, I think film is an art form that goes far past music,' he continued. 'A record lasts five minutes and it's only aural, to do a two-hour film where the audience is gobsmacked, that is amazing.'

Ironically the desire to score a film encapsulated the dichotomy that faces Norman Cook at this stage in his career. As a producer and DJ who has made a point of presenting himself as an artist who only does his best work when he's writing stupid dance music, his aim is to dive directly into the heart of one of the most serious music forms around, and one that has to find the right balance between ego-driven melody and ego-less ambience – thus far, two disparate needs that Norman has found difficult to explore at the same time.

In order to achieve these ambitions he would have to learn to merge the serious side of his work, which he dismissed years ago, with the more frivolous aspects of his pop music. Indeed, in many ways it was this balance that he was attempting to achieve on *Halfway Between The Gutter And The Stars*.

In September 2001 Norman would receive six awards for the 'Weapon Of Choice' video from MTV's VMA ceremony. At a ceremony held at the New York Metropolitan Opera House, he was rewarded in the Breakthrough Video, Best Direction In A Video, Best Choreography In A Video, Best Art Direction In A Video, Best Editing In A Video and Best Cinematography In A Video awards. These would be added to the two existing awards for 'Praise You'.

In July 2001, however, his mind was set on the biggest gig of his career to date. He was to DJ at a free party on the beach of his home town of Brighton.

'Last year I was offered the chance to DJ on the oil rig anchored off Brighton beach for the performance of *The Tempest*,' he told Jakki Phillips of local paper *The Argus* at the time. 'But I was already booked at a festival. I've kicked myself ever since so this sort of makes up for things.'

The Big Beach Boutique was being organised by Channel 4 in partnership with Brighton and Hove Council. Somewhat bizarrely the event was being used as a way for the TV station to advertise their cricket coverage.

In the weeks preceding the gig, which was being called Normstock locally, Norman admitted to Jakki Phillips that he was apprehensive about it. Part of the worry came from the safety problems inherent in a gig of this scale. Only a year earlier nine people had been killed at Denmark's Roskilde Festival during a Pearl Jam show. Naturally the possibility of similar scenes caused Norman major anxiety.

'I had this nightmare the other night about that Pearl Jam gig,' he told Phillips. 'It started me thinking about how important it is for people to look after themselves and each other. I don't want anyone falling in the sea and drowning or getting hurt, so I want to give this message to everyone – have a good time, drink as much as you like but try not to hurt anyone or get hurt.

'If everyone is cool things will be fine,' he added. 'Obviously I expect people to be a little bit the worse for wear by the end, including myself, but there are tons of ways to party which don't involve harming anybody else or yourself.'

One of the main problems lay in the fact that there was no way of gauging how many people would be going to the free party. Estimates ranged between 20,000 to 40,000.

'The biggest issue has been how to light the whole thing,' Norman added. 'We couldn't afford thousands of disco lights, so we decided to go for the *Apocalypse Now* approach, with spotlights and smoke.

'We wanted to let off enormous military smoke bombs but the police were worried the smoke might blow straight across the road and blind all the motorists, so we had to scrap that idea.'

In the end, the Big Beach Boutique drew 40,000 people for a night that Brighton will never forget. An evening of good humoured, laid-back and inclusive enjoyment.

The Big Beach Boutique, which would soon after be turned into a film complete with fake documentary for Channel 4, was also host to the world première of the video for the fourth Fatboy Slim single from *Halfway Between The Gutter And The Stars*.

Directed by renowned team Tractor, the film featured people being pulled involuntarily by hidden ropes. Every time the music played the actors would react erratically, and eventually the whole scene turned into a fight.

'Its absolutely bonkers,' said Norman to *Hot Press*. 'They have got a really twisted sense of humour. They sent me this treatment, which was about a load of people who start beating each other up as soon as they put the tune on, and I thought that sounded really funny. But by the time they made it, the script completely changed – it is absolutely insane. I've met some eccentrics in my time, but they are as mad as you like.'

Although the video was undoubtedly funny, it failed to capture the essence of the album's message in the same way that Spike Jonze had. Tractor had merely honed in on the slapstick elements of Norman's music and delivered a punchline without a story. Ironically, it was a film which would have suited the previous album better.

Immediately following the Big Beach Boutique Norman headed off to Ibiza for DJ spots throughout August. September found him relaxing on holiday with Zoë before once again heading off on a promotional tour, which was to last three months. His intention was to fit in six months of promotional work before the new baby's due date in December.

On the eve of a tour which would take in Argentina, Brazil, Mexico, Japan, China, Singapore and Hong Kong, before he'd even reached Europe, London's *Evening Standard* newspaper announced that the DJ was hanging up his headphones for good.

'Some people are going to look very stupid. I have no plans to retire. You're going to have to kill me first,' was his reply.

On 5 December he played for the first time in China, at Shanghai's Pegasus club. It was to prove to be a date that would remain with him for some time to come, as police broke up the party.

Norman worked the crowd into such a frenzy that the floor started to vibrate so much that the gig had to be stopped. The police hustled him off the decks and then ordered promoters to play slow romantic music to calm the crowd down!

The final dates of this frantic tour took him to the Boutique, followed by an Air and Style Snowboard Festival in Seefield, Austria. As a final date to the tour it proved to be something of an anti-climax. Snowboarding festivals are rarely good for DJs or bands. The punters are there for the boarding, not the music. Norman's show was no different, and the attendant crowd was more interested in comparing notes on their on piste action than 'giving it the large one' with Fatboy Slim!

Seven days later on Friday 15 December Zoë gave birth to a baby boy, who would be named Woody Fred Cook.

'Norman is over the moon and so are the rest of the family,' Zoë was reported as saying, while her father, former children's television presenter Johnny Ball joked, 'Sadly he's got Zoë's and my ears and our noses. Apart from that, he's very healthy. We are absolutely overjoyed, all of us.'

A few days later the proud parents were snapped leaving the hospital with Woody. The baby was wearing a blue and white hat. 'He's a Brighton fan,' exclaimed Norman!

Over the coming months Norman would talk a lot about how being a father changed his approach to his career. Increasingly he stopped going out during the week, keeping his DJ dates to the weekend, while he would also drastically cut back on working abroad.

'I used to spend a lot of time in America, Japan and Australia but after about six or seven days I get double homesick. Now I've got a son and a wife to miss.

'I also get paranoid that I'll come back home and Woody will be walking or talking and I'll have missed it. So at the moment it is great. I DJ on Friday and Saturday night and I get the rest of the week off, which means I've been doing more remixes.'

Talking to *Hot Press* he added: 'Before it was six days a week going mad and one day a week of sleep. I was travelling all over the place. Now I don't travel so much. At the moment I play every Friday and Saturday, and the rest of the week I'm Dad, during which time I'm a lot more sensible than before. But at the weekends, I'm madder than I used to be – it's that Friday feeling!

'Most people do a boring job all week and Friday night they just want to go fucking mad. For a couple of years, I was going mad every night and it just became a job. Now I get really excited every Friday round about lunchtime.'

Despite his new stay-at-home attitude during the week, Norman was far from idle. Among the many projects he started work on was a still-to-be-released Mighty Dub Katz album, while he also started work producing the new album by one time Brit Pop act Blur.

'[It] is really nice because it's working with people who do something completely different to me, the meeting of minds can be great and when we've finished it, they have to go off and promote it for a year and I get to stay at home. That's the best thing about producing, when the record's finished you're free,' he told Launch.com.

Despite Norman's happiness at taking on such a challenging production role it was to be short lived. The sessions revealed a tempestuous relationship brewing between Norman and lead singer Damon Alburn. And when Damon's cartoon side project 'Gorillaz' started to take off he had less time to devote to the project and so it was temporarily put on hold. Eventually Norman would be dropped from production duties altogether – thanks to an argument about dance music...of all things!

'I kept bumping into Damon when he was on tour with Gorillaz, and we did have a couple of drunken late-night arguments about dance music,' Cook told NME.com. 'He said, "Dance music's shit," and I said, "Well, a) you're making it and b) what are you doing working with me then?" He said "Gorillaz isn't dance music and what you do isn't dance music." We did have a few arguments. You know what it's like, four o'clock in a hotel room when you're pissed. Maybe that's why I got gonged off!'

Throughout 2001 another of Norman's great loves was rarely out of the papers, namely Brighton and Hove Football Club. In a move strangely reminiscent of The Housemartins' sponsorship of Fulchester United in the *Viz* comic, Skint had become the Albion's sponsors in 1999–2000. In the seasons that followed the team would end up champions of the third and second divisions respectively.

By 2001, however, Norman's involvement had deepened to the extent that not only did he become a highly vocal supporter of the club's move to a new, purpose-built stadium, but he also became a part of a consortium that bought out the club chairman.

This latter event followed months of speculation, in which it was reported Norman was actually buying the club outright for an estimated £70,000.

A spokesperson for the football club would go on record as saying: 'This story is a long way from the truth. Skint [Fatboy Slim's label] sponsor the first team and the club has a great relationship with them.'

In February 2002 it was revealed that club chairman Dick Knight had launched a bid to buy out his predecessor's shareholding, backed by current investors in the club including DJ Norman Cook. The club confirmed that Mr Archer was prepared to accept a one-off payment of £700,000 for his shares.

By May 2002 it was announced that the deal had gone through, with another local businessman, Chris Kidger, stumping up the balance of funds needed. Norman was not elected onto the board of directors, but does own a minority share in the football club he supports.

In yet another twist on Norman's Boys' Own tale he announced that his love of the beautiful game would take him to South Korea and Japan in May and June 2002, as the self-appointed 'Official World Cup DJ'!

After a warm-up date at Singapore's Zouk Club he ventured to Korea on Friday 31 May, before embarking on a date in Tokyo the following night. What followed was a tour of DJ dates corresponding with England's matches. He also took in dates in Thailand and Malaysia.

'If you can have an official burger and an official beer, why not an official DJ?' he stated. 'This will be a perfect mix of party pleasure and football pleasure. This will be my first World Cup and Japan's one of my favourite countries in the world. It's going to be an amazing few weeks. Unlike some, I will be match fit.'

Joining him on the tour were Damian Harris and Jon Carter.

Prior to Norman's fantasy football tour he released a document of the previous summer's Big Beach Boutique on Southern Fried. Called *Live On Brighton Beach* it was a faithful representation of the evening, complete with safety warnings.

The US launch of the album (on Ministry Of Sound) featured a spectacular array of celebrity guests at a Hollywood event, which featured magicians, a fondue room, tarot reading and a massage parlour.

Stars who turned out to celebrate with the recent Grammy winner included actor James Woods, Rose McGowan, Lukas Haas, Alyssa Milano and Cher, who would tell Norman that she was a fan of his!

Live On Brighton Beach came as a timely reminder of a great night as, soon after its release, it was again announced that Norman would be playing a free party on the beach. This time, however, he was paying for the party and the line up would be an all Brighton affair with the Boutique promoting and Fatboy Slim, Midfield General and John Digweed DJing. He told *Ministry* magazine:

It was so much fun last time. In fact, it was one of my favourite gigs ever, so that seemed like a good enough reason [to do it again]. It seemed stupid not to ask to do it again and the council gave it the go-ahead. I like to think that this will be a regular event now – I believe there will be more people there this summer. No one was sure if it would work last year, then afterwards so many of my friends said, 'Shit! I wish I'd come along!' It was crazy.

[I remember] The roar of the crowd when I went on. I had been so nervous for two whole days – about the weather and how many people would turn up – but as soon as I walked on stage, the roar of the crowd just stopped my nerves dead. I knew I was among friends and that everyone there wanted me to do well. The other moment was when I finally looked up after concentrating really hard for half an hour or so. I looked out and didn't see one face that wasn't beaming! Then all the boats had come from the marina to watch the party – that was amazing. I held up this sign telling every one to wave at the boats and 40,000 people did. All the boats honked their horns, it was fantastic.

However, nothing he experienced at the party in 2001 would prepare him for what was to happen next!

THE BIG BEACH BOUTIQUE 2

'We have always been Brighton bonkers. We do things differently here. We are virtually an island, with the sea in front and the Downs behind. It gives this place a unique atmosphere you won't find anywhere else.'

– Gareth Hansome, *The Argus*

So here we are again. Back where we started on the pebbled beach of Brighton, on the hottest Saturday of the year so far, enjoying the party, with 250,000 of Fatboy Slim's closest friends.

250,000 people. The equivalent of the entire population of Brighton crammed into a mile-long stretch of beach! The atmosphere is insane as people dance on each others' feet, shoulders or whatever gets in the way. Others force their way to a better vantage point, squeezing their way through the crowd, arms held aloft and eyes wide with chemically charged excitement. Lines of men create a wall along the shoreline as they piss into the sea. Champagne rains from the adjacent Grand Hotel as balconies full of people bounce to the beats.

It's like nothing anyone had witnessed before. Last year's celebration of local life has its inclusive ideologies ripped inside out as crowds force families beyond the West Pier – kids to the outside and the older crowds from last year back to their homes. In its place is a scene of unadulterated, chaotic energy. A crowd of people all in one place, for one thing – to party. You can almost touch the energy. It's electric. And it threatens to spill over into pure anarchy.

As each DJ has his set interrupted by security announcements, and the noise of an overhead lifeguard helicopter drowns out the sound, people make their own entertainment, sharing jokes and laughter with new-found friends, dancing to bongo driven beats (this is Brighton after all).

The whole thing comes to a close half an hour early, with Norman shortening his specially prepared set. The finale, as with the previous year, arrives in the form of a spectacular fireworks display, and then, as 10,000 people head to the last train to London, the proverbial sparks really start to fly! The whole of Brighton descends into chaos.

In the hours and days that followed the biggest beach party ever, the national media went into a tabloid frenzy not seen since the heyday of illegal raves. At Normstock 2, according to the red tops, two people had died in what had either been a scene of carnage on the scale of the Hillsborough disaster, or a mass orgy of drugs and alcohol induced anarchy!

It was neither of course. In reality the Big Beach Boutique 2 was a celebration of all that is great about both British dance music and our national obsession with hedonistic weekenders by the seaside. It was a victim of the combined popularity of Brighton, the trendiest city in the UK, Fatboy Slim, the people's DJ, and the Boutique, purveyors of the greatest parties on Earth.

Contrary to reports, there were no fatalities at the Big Beach Boutique. One man who died of a heart attack was not at the party. Australian nurse Karen Manders' tragic fall from the esplanade occurred some four hours after the event. Skint Records subsequently received a letter from Miss Manders' cousin expressing the family's dismay that Norman, Skint and the Boutique had been held responsible for her death.

Norman and Zoë would send a wreath to her funeral with the words 'Shine on Karen' written on it.

Official statistics confirmed that 160 people were injured, with only 11 being taken to hospital. Of those, two suffered broken legs, one a broken back and the others lacerations from broken glass. However the hospital confirmed that a further 80 people not covered by the official statement made their own way to casualty to have minor injuries treated.

Based on the previous year's figures of 35,000, the crowd offically expected was estimated to be in the region of 60,000. However, both the Boutique and the local council failed to take into account the knock-on effect of the repeat screenings of 2001's legendary party on Channel 4 and the release of Fatboy Slim's *Live On Brighton Beach* album. Also unaccounted for was the effect of a rigorous media campaign, including news stories in every paper and magazine known to mankind, TV advertising and radio advertising, and of course those Radio 1 DJs not going to the Berlin Love Parade, who continually declared their intentions to decamp to Brighton for their mate Fatboy's beach party. The Big Beach Boutique 2, then, was the worst-kept secret since the Queen had her Jubilee bash.

'To be honest I thought we'd get a lot more than 60,000,' explained Damian Harris to me for *Muzik* magazine. 'From the minute it was announced we had people e-mailing us to find out about hotels so we had a fair idea that it would be massive.'

Although the numbers reached twice the capacity of Glastonbury Festival, there were only six arrests – a figure that the organisers were justifiably happy with. However, Chief Superintendent Doug Rattray, the officer in charge of policing, confirmed that with only one police officer per 10,000 people, arrests were near impossible to make. As a result they witnessed drug offences and even couples having sex (although its hard to see how they would have had the space) but were powerless to act!

Perhaps more worrying was the debris left behind after the party. With rubbish still strewn across the beach and esplanade on the following Monday evening, and broken glass crushed into the shingle, Norman paid for the clean-up operation himself to the tune of £10,000. However, ecological reports have suggested that it could take 10 years for the glass to be removed from the beach. Local television news reported six children being taken to hospital with cut feet the next week. In truth, this isn't an unusual problem with Brighton's often under-cleaned beaches.

'To be honest, I wouldn't walk barefoot across that stretch of beach at the best of times,' argued Harris. 'It's a popular area for beach parties and there's always loads of glass smashed there.'

Of the many letters to the local and national press in the weeks that followed, there was one that had a particularly pertinent message. A

Brighton raver who was actively involved in the free-party scene, regularly closed down by the police, took offence at such an open-minded attitude towards Fatboy Slim. His own parties usually only attracted 200 people, no litter was ever left and, in terms of dance culture, they were truer to the underground spirit that so many of the people involved in the Big Beach Boutique 2 had long since embraced.

'Afterwards the local paper was full of letters from locals,' confirmed Damian Harris. 'Some were really supportive, but loads condemned the party. Most of these were about noise, litter or chaos, or it had nothing to do with Brighton. But the one that got to me was from this guy who does local free parties. He was saying, "How can the council support a free party of this size, when they regularly close down raves in the South Downs with maybe only 200 people dancing?" I thought, "Yeah, he's got a point there."'

Among the more bizarre comments from local tradespeople was the one from a company that hired out deck chairs. On the night of the party they lost 200 of their stock of chairs to revellers needing firewood, while seafront shopkeepers complained of shop hoardings being removed for the fires, and an overpowering smell of urine which lasted for days.

What was forgotten in the rush to condemn the party was the fact that this need to burn anything that is not tied down and urinate into every shop doorway is a regular occurrence for Brighton on a Saturday night in the summer. 'I think it's too easy to look at the negative with something like this,' added Hove resident John Digweed. 'The fact was that it gave the local economy a huge boost after a poor summer so far. And, in terms of dance, at a time when everyone is saying that this music is dying, this proved them wrong. The party was incredible, it was this generation's Spike Island.'

You could also add this generation's version of The Who at Hyde Park, or equally this generation's Castle Morten. Indeed it was an event that will go down in history for the sheer number of people who were prepared to travel the length and breath of the country for a party. A million miles away from Norman's early warehouse parties in disused warehouses in Brighton, or those legendary raves at Shoreham Power Station.

There was a hugely positive side to the event – and one that went largely unreported. Despite the fact that many people had endured a

10-mile tail back on the A23, making a one-hour journey last five hours; despite the helicopter hovering overhead drowning out much of the sound, and the DJs' sets being constantly interrupted by safety announcements; and despite the fact that Norman was forced, at the request of the police, to cut his set short, this was a momentous and hugely positive occasion – one that may have left Brighton with the hangover from hell, but also provided the 250,000 revellers with a night they'll never forget.

'The thing I'll never forget,' concludes Digweed, 'Was the roar of the crowd when Norman came to the decks. He knows exactly how to get people going. He is a brilliant party DJ.'

Some would say the best.

POSTSCRIPT: YOU'RE NOT FROM BRIGHTON

Deep in the heart of Brighton there lies another town. It's called Normsville. It's not a sinister town, or a closed community in which one person can reign supreme over their minions, but a close but extended group which revolves around the business of Fatboy Slim. A business whose heart beats in London.

Until I started writing this book I was unaware of the close workings of Normsville. I live in the same city as many of this book's characters, I've known some of them for a long time. I wrote many of the first features and reviews on the nascent big beat scene – even giving the first Fatboy single a thumbs up – and am still in regular contact with many of the main players.

Over the years I've met Norman quite a few times. In supermarkets, on the beach, in clubs, at Glastonbury – the usual places really. I've never interviewed him, but I have interviewed Zoë a couple of times!

When I started this project I emailed Norman's management to let them know my intentions and to request an interview. Seven months later I was told that Norman wasn't up for the project at this time. The note added 'good luck and be sure to send us some copies when it's out'.

So I set about doing third-party interviews. Among the Brighton people most were immediately willing to be interviewed. They wanted to get their side of the story straight. Norman's story had involved a great number of people along the way. One of the people I approached was Norman's PA who, naturally, told his boss.

The next day, nine months after my initial communication, I was sent another e-mail from his management exclaiming that 'he really isn't interested in you writing a book about him'. Furthermore, the management weren't prepared even to send me a discography! From here on in I was inundated with requests from interviewees not to quote them directly, or even to drop certain stories.

There wasn't any conspiracy, contrary to how it might seem. People weren't ordered to withdraw from this unofficial book – they did it off their own backs, largely following conversations with each other. Brighton is, after all, a small town, Normsville even smaller. The reason people withdrew was simply because they didn't want to offend someone they had total respect for.

In the time it took me to research this book I never once heard a bad word about Norman Cook, although I did stumble on rather a lot of gossip and innuendo, as you might expect from a small town.

Norman is that rare thing, a genuinely nice bloke, with nothing but best intentions at heart. He genuinely believes in the positive, loving aspects of both his religion and the ecstasy experience.

Normsville, then, is a community of people who have been a part of Norman's life over the years. A community built upon loyalty and friendship and a community that would hate to offend or betray a friend, or each other. Something that is extremely rare in the world of music. And something which itself demands respect.

So, far from being the Hunter S Thompson-esque 'Fear and Loathing in Brighton and Hove' journey I'd hoped for, *Fatboy Slim: Funk Soul Brother* is a summary of Norman Cook's life in music. As told by over 50 different people, most of whom wished to remain anonymous! A position I have complete respect for.

And besides, I'm not from Normsville.

DI SC OG RAPHY

THE HOUSE MARTI NS

SINGLES
'Flag Day' (Go! Discs)
Flag Day / You / Stand At Ease / Coal Train To Hatfield Main

'Sheep' (Go! Discs)
Sheep / I'll Be Your Shelter / Anxious / Drop Down Dead / People Get Ready

'Happy Hour' (Go! Discs)
Happy Hour / The Mighty Ship / Sitting On A Fence / He Ain't Heavy

'Think For A Minute' (Go! Discs)
Think For A Minute / I Smell Winter / Who Needs The Limelight / Joy
Joy Joy / Rap Around The Clock

'Caravan Of Love' (Go! Discs)
Caravan Of Love / We Shall Not Be Moved / When I First Met Jesus /
So Much In Love / Heaven Help Us All (Sermonette)

'Five Get Over-Excited' (Go! Discs)
Five Get Over-Excited / So Glad / Hopelessly Devoted To Them / Rebel
Without The Airplay

'Me And The Farmer' (Go! Discs)
Me And The Farmer / He Will Find You Out / Step Outside / I Bit My Lip

'There Is Always Something There To Remind Me' (Go! Discs)
There Is Always Something There To Remind Me / Get Up Off Our
Knees (Live) (in concert 30 September 1987) / Five Get Over Excited
(Live) (in concert 30 September 1987) / Johannesburg (Live) (in concert
30 September 1987)

ALBUMS
London o Hull 4 (Go! Discs)
Happy Hour / Get Up Off Our Knees / Flag Day / Anxious / Reverend's
Revenge / Sitting On A Fence / Sheep / Over There / Think For A Minute
/ We're Not Deep / Lean On Me / Freedom / I'll Be Your Shelter (Just
Like A Shelter) / People Get Ready / The Mighty Ship / He Ain't Heavy,
He's My Brother

The People Who Grinned Themselves To Death (Go! Discs)
The People Who Grinned Themselves To Death / I Can't Put My Finger
On It / The Light Is Always Green / The World's On Fire / Pirate Aggro
/ We're Not Going Back / Me And The Farmer / Five Get Over Excited
/ Johannesburg / Bow Down / You Better Be Doubtful / Build

Live At Glastonbury (Bootleg)
Over There / Bow Down / The World's On Fire / The Light Is Always
Green / I Bit My Lip / The People Who Grinned Themselves To Death /
Build / So Glad / Happy Hour / Get Up Off Our Knees / You've Got A
Friend / Caravan Of Love

Now That's What I Call Quite Good (Go! Discs)
I Smell Winter / Bow Down / Think For A Minute / There Is Always
Something There To Remind Me / The Mighty Ship / Sheep / I'll Be Your
Shelter / Five Get Over-Excited / Every Day's The Same / Build / Step
Outside / Flag Day / Happy Hour / You've Got A Friend / He Ain't Heavy,
He's My Brother / Freedom / The People Who Grinned Themselves To
Death / Caravan Of Love / The Light Is Always Green / We're Not Deep
/ Me And The Farmer / Lean On Me / Drop Down Dead / Hopelessly
Devoted To Them

NORMAN COOK
SINGLES
'Won't Talk About It' (Go! Beat)
Won't Talk About It (featuring Billy Bragg) / Blame It On The Bonus
Beats / Blame It On The Bassline (Remix) (featuring Wildski) / Blame It
On The Bassline (Dub Mix)

'For Spacious Lies' (Go! Beat)
For Spacious Lies / For Spacious Beats / The Invasion Of The Estate
Agents / For Spacious Lies (7" mix)

SAMPLES ALBUMS
All-Star Breakbeats
Planet Rhythm / Prince Of The Beats / Leisure Boys / Two Years Ago
/ Lesson Four / Norman's War / Shriek / Station II Station / Disco
Dubwise / Lock It In The Socket / Tour De Force / Say Aaah / Big
Scratching / Check The Beat Out / Give Me A Break / Crank This
Mother / Oh No / Spanking Piano / Everybody's Dancin' / Finest
Ingredients / First Cut / I'll Get Busy / Get Busy Time / Give Yourself
To Me / Good / Bad / Good Vibration / Hallelujah / Here Comes A
Brother / Sax Begun / It Began In Africa / Children Of Afrika / Tank
Fly / Keep Bustin' / Kick Some Ass / Men Beat On Their Drums / MUSIC
/ Deep Inside Of Me / Music / Music Makes You Lose Control / Oh
Oh / Oh My God / Oh My God2 / Right On Time / Rockin' Music /
Music / Transform Scream / Your Time Is Up / Spinning On The
Turntables / Stupid Synth / Sweet Sensation / This Cut2 / This Will
Self... / Turn This Mother Out / Who's On The Turntables / Women
Beat Their Men / Work That Sucks / Work That Body Marlett / You
Get Down / Zulu / Music For The People / Get My Rhymes Together
/ Parental Guidance Advised

Skip To My Loops (Studio Master)
Music-creation software
No track listing

BEATS INTERNATIONAL

SINGLES

'Dub Be Good To Me' (Go! Beat)
Dub Be Good To Me / Dub Be Good To Me (A Cappella) / The Invasion
Of The Freestyle – Discuss / The Invasion Of The Estate Agents

'Dub Be Good To Me' (Go! Beat)
Dub Be Good To Me (Smith And Mighty Mix) / Before I Go Too Dub /
Dub Be Good To Me (Norman Cook's Excursion On The Version) / Dub
Be Good To Me (Smith And Mighty Mellow Mix)

'Won't Talk About It' (Go! Beat)
Won't Talk About It (Remix) (7" version) / Won't Talk About It (Remix)
(7" version) / Won't Talk About It (Remix) (The One Big Bad World
mix) / Beats International Theme

'Burundi Blues' (Go! Beat)
Burundi Blues / Burundi Dub / Theme From The Deerstalker

'Echo Chamber' (Go! Beat)
Echo Chamber / Echo Chamber (Boilerhouse Mix) / Echo Chamber
(Boilerhouse Junk Dub) / Daddy Freddy's Echo Chamber / Echo Chamber
(Instrumental) / Inch By Inch

'The Sun Doesn't Shine' (Go! Beat)
The Sun Doesn't Shine / Crazy For You / Wake The Dead / The Sun
Doesn't Shine (Extended Version)

'Change Your Mind' (Go! Beat)
Change Your Mind (Giant Club Mix) / Change Your Mind (Ragga
Reprise Continuous Play) / Change Your Mind (Ragga Dub) / Change
Your Mind (Cook's Mix) / Change Your Mind (Prento Mix) / Change
Your Mind (Daou Piano Dub)

'In The Ghetto' (Go! Beat)

In The Ghetto (Version One) / In The Ghetto (Version Two) / In The
Ghetto (Version Three) / Oh, That's Deep

ALBUMS
Let Them Eat Bingo (Go! Beat)
Burundi Blues / Dub Be Good To Me / Before I Grow Too Old / The
Ragged Trousered Percussionists / For Spacious Lies / Blame It On The
Bassline / Won't Talk About It / Dance To The Drummer's Beat / Babies
Makin' Babies (Stoop Rap) / The Whole World's Down On Me / Tribute
To King Tubby
(Initial quantities of vinyl included eight-track bonus album, *Bonus Beats*)

Excursion On The Version (Go! Beat)
Brand New Beat / Change Your Mind / Love Is Green / Echo Chamber /
The Sun Doesn't Shine / Herman / Three Foot Skank / No More Mr Nice
Guy / Eyes On The Prize / Ten Long Years / In The Ghetto / Come Home

Let Them Eat Remixes (Go! Beat)
Burundi Blues (Boilerhouse) / Theme From Deerstalker / Dub Be Good
To Me (Smith And Mighty Remix) / Won't Beat About It / Blame It On
The Loop / Blame It On The Bassline Remix featuring MC Wildski /
Won't Talk About It / For Spacious Lies Extended / Burundi Blues
Traditional / Tribute To King 45 / Beats International Theme

F Re AKPOWe R
SINGLES
'Turn On, Tune In, Cop Out' (4th And Broadway)
Turn On, Tune In, Cop Out (Radio Mix) / Turn On, Tune In, Cop Out
(Pizzaman Mix) / Getting Over The Hump / Turn On, Tune In, Cop Out
(Play Boys Fully Loaded Vocal)

'Rush' (4th And Broadway)
Rush (radio version) / Rush – Theme For Freakpower (X-Pressive
Superdub) / Rush (Pizzaman Mix) / Party Till We Part

'Get In Touch' (4th And Broadway)
Get In Touch (7" edit) / Get In Touch (Colonel Kurtz Remix) / Chew
The Bone / Get In Touch (Uptight Vocal Mix)

'Waiting For The Story To End' (4th And Broadway)
Waiting For The Story To End / Spike-A-Delic (Freak-U-Like) / Get In
Touch (Uptight Mix) / Chew The Bone

'New Direction' (4th And Broadway)
New Direction / New Direction (Way Out West Vocal) / New Direction
(Fila Brazilia Dub) / New Direction (Album Mix)

'Can U Feel It' (4th And Broadway)
Can U Feel It (Album Mix) / Can You Feel It (Todd's Rubber Room Mix)
/ Can You Feel It (Matty's Mix) / Can You Feel It (Bassbin Twins) / Can
You Feel It (Small World Mix)

'No Way' (DeConstruction)
No Way (Radio Edit) / No Way (Full Mix) / No Way (Norman's Club
Mix) / No Way (Dee Jay Delite Mix)

Albums
Drive Thru Booty (4th And Broadway)
Moonbeam Woman / Turn On, Tune In, Cop Out / Get In Touch /
Freakpower / Running Away / Change My Mind / What It Is / Waiting
For The Story To End / Rush / Big Time / The Whip

Freakpower In Dub – The Fried Funk Food EP (4th And Broadway)
Turn On, Tune In, Find Joy / At Your Own Pace / Sugar Lump /
Freakpower Is Beautiful, Baby / My Heart Sings / Where I'm Going
(Free with initial quantities of *Drive Thru Booty*)

More Of Everything...For Everybody (4th And Broadway)
Trip Through Your Mind / New Direction / Husband / Can You Feel
It? / Road Thang / Giving Up Government Drugs / KK Nuns / Let It

Go / Song #6 / Freedom Child / One Nation One Ride / Ghettos Of
The Mind

THE MIGHTY DUB KATZ
SINGLES
'Super Disco Brakes' (Southern Fried)
Super Disco Brakes Vol 1 / The Electronic Drum Track / Super Disco
Trance Vol 1 / Super Disco Bass Vol 1

'Return To The Valley Of The Yeke Yeke' (Southern Fried)
Return To The Valley Of The Yeke Yeke (Part One) / Return To The
Valley Of The Yeke Yeke (Part Two) / Only When I'm Dancing Do I Feel
This Disco / Only When I'm Dancing Do I Feel This Dub

'Son Of Wilmot' (Southern Fried)
Son Of Wilmot / Son Of Wilmot (Compost Mix) / Son Of Wilmot (Houze
Remix) / Son Of Wilmot (Latin Houze Remix)

'Keep On Trucking' (Southern Fried)
Keep On Trucking / Delight Vol 4 / Let's Get Chinese Eyes Man / Delight
Vol 5

'Cangica' (Southern Fried)
Cangica (radio edit) / Cangica (club mix) / Cangica (Del Breakbeat Mix)
/ Cangica (full-length mix)

'It's Just Another Groove' (Ffrr)
It's Just Another Groove (radio edit) / It's Just Another Groove (original
version) / Lisa Marie Experience Remix / Lisa Marie Experience
Instrumental Remix / It's Just A Groove

Ghetto Girl (Southern Fried)
Ghetto Girl / Work It Work It

'Magic Carpet Ride' (Ffrr)
Magic Carpet Ride (Ulti Edit) / Magic Carpet Ride (Vocoder Edit) / Magic
Carpet Ride (No Comprende Edit) / Magic Carpet Ride (Ulti-Mix) / Magic
Carpet Ride (Son Of Wilmot Mix) / Magic Carpet Ride (original version)

'Magic Carpet Ride' (Ffrr)
Magic Carpet Ride (Fatboy Slim 7" edit) / Magic Carpet Ride (Fatboy
Slim Latin Ska Acid Breakbeat Mix) / Magic Carpet Ride (Rip Grooves)
/ Magic Carpet Ride (Andy Mowat Mix)

PIZZAMAN

SINGLES
'Babyloop' (Loaded)
Babyloop / DJ's Delight #2 / Sans Bateaux / DJ's Delight #3

'Trippin' On Sunshine' (Cowboy)
Trippin' On Sunshine (radio edit) / Trippin' On Sunshine (Biff And
Amp Memphis Mix) / Trippin' On Sunshine (Pizzaman Club Mix) /
Trippin' On Sunshine (California Sunshine Mix) / Trippin' On Sunshine
(Play Boys Dub)

'Sex On The Streets' (Cowboy)
Sex On The Streets (Radio Edit) / Sex On The Streets (Pizzaman Club Mix)
/ Sex On The Streets (Pizzaman Dub) / Sex On The Streets (Red Jerry Mix)
/ Sex On The Streets (Tall Paul And Amp, Tin Tin Out–Goodfellas Mix)

'Happiness' (Cowboy)
Happiness (Eat Me Edit) / Happiness (Club Mix) / Happiness (Play Boys
Fully Loaded Dub) / Happiness (Original Mix) / Happiness (Euro Mix)
/ Happiness (Play Boys Fully Loaded Dub)

'Trippin' On Sunshine' (Cowboy reissue)
Trippin' On Sunshine (radio edit) / Trippin' On Sunshine (Impulsion Big
Pizza Mix) / Trippin' On Sunshine (Biff And Memphis Mix) / Trippin'

On Sunshine (Play Boys Mixing Thing) / Trippin' On Sunshine (Pizzaman Mix) / Trippin' On Sunshine (Californea Sunshine Mix) / Trippin' On Sunshine (Play Boy's Dub)

'Hello Honky Tonks'
Hello Honky Tonks (Rock Your Body) (Radio Edit) / Hello Honky Tonks (Cotton Club Dub) / Hello Honky Tonks (Cotton Club Brewery Dub) / The Feeling (Pizzaman Mix)

'Gottaman' (Cowboy)
Gottaman (Eat Me Edit) / Gottaman (Distant Drum Mix) / Gottaman (Pizzaman Mix) / Gottaman (Gregario Mix)

ALBUMS
Pizzamania (Cowboy)
Sex On The Streets (7" radio mix) / Trippin' On Sunshine (radio edit) / Happiness (Eat Me 7" edit) / Hello Honky Tonks / Gottaman / Just Height The Ball / The Feeling / Babyloop / Sans Bateaux / Sex On The Streets (Pizzaman Dub)

Pizzamania (Loaded)
Trippin' On Sunshine (radio edit) / Sex On The Streets / Happiness / Babyloop / Gottaman / Just Height The Ball / Hello Honky Tonks / Sans Bateaux / The Feeling / Happiness (club mix) / Sex On The Streets (Play Boys Fully Loaded Dub)

The Very Best Of Pizzaman (Eagle)
Trippin On Sunshine / Sex On The Streets / Happiness / Babyloop / Gottaman / Just Height The Ball / Hello Honky Tonks / Sans Bateaux / Feeling / Happiness (Club Mix) / Trippin On Sunshine (Play Boys Fully Loaded Dub)

FEELGOOD FACTOR
SINGLES
'The Fonktrain' (Southern Fried)

The Fonktrain (Disco Mix [long version]) / The Fonktrain (Electro Mix)
The Fonktrain (Disco Mix [short version])

'The Whole Church Should Get Drunk' (white label)
The Whole Church Should Get Drunk / Son Of A Cheeky Boy

'Coma, Drop It' (Southern Fried promo)
Coma

'Hope Your Body' (white label)
Hope Your Body

ALBUMS
Southern Fried House (Southern Fried) (all acts featured are Norman Cook psuedonyms)
The Mighty Dub Katz – Magic Carpet Ride (Son Of Wilmot Mix) / Sunny Side Up – Manna / Pizzaman – Baby Loop / The Mighty Dub Katz – Keep On Truckin' / The Mighty Dub Katz – Only When I'm Dancing Do I Feel This Disco / Pizzaman – Trippin' On Sunshine / The Mighty Dub Katz – Let's Get Chinese Eyes / Yum Yum Head Food – Bird Of Prey / Mighty Dub Katz – Magic Carpet Ride (Ulti-Mix)

Yum Yum Head Food (white label)
Bird Of Prey / Praise You (original)
No other track known. Norman claims that this ambient album will be available as a download via his website.

FATBOY SLIM
SINGLES
'Santa Cruz' (Skint)
Santa Cruz / Weekend Bonus Beats / The Weekend Starts Here / Neal Cassidy Starts Here

'Everybody Needs A 303' (Skint)

Everybody Needs A 303 / Lincoln Memorial / We Really Want To See Those Fingers

'Punk To Funk' (Skint)
Punk To Funk / Knuf Ot Knup / Big Beat Soufflé

'Going Out Of My Head' (Skint)
Going Out Of My Head / Michael Jackson / Next To Nothing

'Everybody Needs A 303' (Remixes) (CD1)
Everybody Needs A 303 Remixes (original radio edit) / Everybody Needs A 303 (original 12" mix) / Everybody Loves A Carnival / Neal Cassidy Starts Here

'Everybody Needs A 303' (Remixes) (CD2)
Everybody Loves A Carnival (radio edit) / Everybody Loves A Filter / Es Paradis / Where You're At

'The Rockafeller Skank' (Skint)
The Rockafeller Skank (short edit) / The Rockafeller Skank / Always Read The Label / Tweakers Delight

'Ganster Tripping' (Skint)
Gangster Tripping / The World Went Down / Jack It Up (Delite)

'How Can They Hear Us' (Astralwerks)
How Can They Hear Us (vinyl only)

'Praise You' (Skint)
Praise You / Sho Nuff / The Rockafeller Skank (Mulder's Urban Takeover Remix)

'Right Here Right Now' (Skint)
Right Here Right Now / Don't Forget Your Teeth / Praise You (original version)

'Build It Up, Tear It Down' (Skint)
Build It Up, Tear It Down / Going Out Of My Head / Big Beat Soufflé /
Last Night At The Concorde (AVI video)

'Sunset (Bird Of Prey)' (Skint)
Sunset (Bird Of Prey) / My Game / Sunset (Bird Of Prey) (Darren Emerson
Remix)

'Demons' (Skint)
Demons (shorter radio version) / The Pimp (vocal) / Camber Sands (edit)
/ Demons (single version)

'Demons (Stanton Warriors remixes)' (Skint)
Demons (Stanton Warriors vocal remix / Demons (Stanton Warriors dub
vocal) / Demons (Stanton Warriors *a cappella*)

'Ya Mama' / 'Weapon Of Choice' (Astralwerks)
Ya Mama (radio edit) / Weapon Of Choice (Liquid Todd edit 1) / Weapon
Of Choice (Liquid Todd edit 2) / Weapon Of Choice (album version) /
Call Out Hook 1 / Call Out Hook 2

'Weapon Of Choice' (Astralwerks)
Weapon Of Choice (Attack Hamster edit) / Weapon Of Choice (Liquid
Todd edit) / Weapon Of Choice (Spike Jonze video edit) / Weapon Of
Choice (album version) / Call Out Hook 1 / Call Out Hook 2

'Star 69' / 'Weapon Of Choice' (Skint)
Star 69 (original) / Star 69 (radio edit) / Weapon Of Choice / Weapon
Of Choice (enhanced video)

'Star 69 (Remixes)' (Skint)
Star 69 (Timo Maas Remix) / Star 69 (X-Press 2 Remix) / Star 69
(Godfather Remix)

'Ya Mama' / 'Song For Shelter' (Skint) CD1

Ya Mama / Song For Shelter (original) / Illuminati (featuring Bootsy Collins) / Ya Mama (enhanced video)

'Ya Mama' / 'Song For Shelter' (Skint) CD2
Song For Shelter (Chemical Brothers Remix) / Song For Shelter (The 20:20 Vision Rolling Mix) / Ya Mama (edit)

'Drop The Hate (Remixes)' (Skint)
Drop The Hate (Santos Napalm Reprise) / Drop The Hate (Laid Remix)

'Retox (Remixes)'
Retox (Dave Clarke Mix) / Retox (Gettin' Freqy With Fatboy)

'Rotten Criminals' (Skint, promo-only vinyl)
Rotten Criminals

ALBUMS
Better Living Through Chemistry (Skint)
Song For Lindy / Santa Cruz / Going Out Of My Head / The Weekend Starts Here / Everybody Needs A 303 / Give The Po' Man A Break / 10th And Crenshaw / First Down / Punk To Funk / The Sound Of Milwaukee

Better Living Through Chemistry (Astralwerks)
Song For Lindy / Santa Cruz / Going Out Of My Head / The Weekend Starts Here / Everybody Needs A 303 / Give The Po' Man A Break / 10th And Crenshaw / First Down / Punk To Funk / The Sound Of Milwaukee / Michael Jackson / Next To Nothing

On The Floor Of The Boutique (Skint)
Michael Viner's Incredible Bongo Band – Apache / Fred Wesley And The Horny Horns – Discositdown / Clockwork Voodoo Freaks – Deaf Mick's Throwdown / The Jungle Brothers – Because I Got It Like That (Ultimatum Mix) / The Bassbin Twins – Vol 1 Side 2 Track 2 / Mr Natural – That Green Jesus / Deeds Plus Thoughts – World's Made Up Of This And That / Fatboy Slim – Michael Jackson / Tonka – Phun-Ky / Cut And

Paste – Forget It / Buzzthrill – Everybody In The House / CLS – Can You Feel It / Aldo Bender – Acid Enlightenment / Christopher Just – I'm A Disco Dancer / Hardknox – Psychopath / Cirrus – Break In / Psychedeliasmith – Give Me My Anger Back / Cut La Roc – Post Punk Progression / Fatboy Slim – The Rockafeller Skank

You've Come A Long Way Baby (Skint)
Right Here Right Now / The Rockafeller Skank / Fucking In Heaven / Gangster Tripping / Build It Up – Tear It Down / Kalifornia / Soul Surfing / You're Not From Brighton / Praise You / Love Island / Acid 8000

Halfway Between The Gutter And The Stars (Skint)
Talking 'Bout My Baby / Star 69 / Sunset (Bird Of Prey) / Love Life / Ya Mama / Mad Flava / Retox / Weapon Of Choice / Drop The Hate / Demons / Song For Shelter

Live On Brighton Beach (Southern Fried)
Underworld – Born Slippy (Nuxx) / Fatboy Slim – Right Here Right Now / Kid Creme – Austin's Groove / Scanty – Southern Thing / Minimal Funk – The Groovy Thang / Santos – Pray / The Clumps – The Talk / Basement Jaxx – Where's Your Head At? / Jark Prongo – Rocket Bass / Love Tattoo – Drop Some Drums / The Black And White Brothers – Put Your Hands Up / Santos – 3-2-1 Fire! / Fatboy Slim – Star 69 / Raven Maize – The Real Life (Fatboy Slim Mix) / Fatboy Slim – Sunset (Bird Of Prey) / Leftfield – Phat Planet / Roland Clark – Speak Lord (I Get Deep)

RARITIES
Fatboy Slim Beat Up The NME (1997, free tape with *NME*)
Pierre Henry – Psyché Rock (Fatboy Slim Malpaso Mix) / Death In Vegas – GBH / The Bassbin Twins – Volume One Side Two Track Two / Psychedeliasmith – Fixy Jointy / Basement Jaxx – Fly Life / Elite Force – Saturnalia / Monkey Mafia – Lion In The Hall / Double 99 – Rip Groove / Old Skool Flavas Vol III – Booty Beats / CJ Bolland Vs Hardknox

– The Prophet / EPS And 2vibe – Big Time / EPS And 2vibe Hype The Funk / 175 – Volume One / Latryx – Say That / Kaleef – Trials Of Life / Mr Dan – One Man Banned / Bassbin Twins – Out Of Hand / Overseer – Hit The Tarmac / Cut La Roc – Post Punk Progression / Sensateria – Give Me My Anger Back

Halfway Between The Gutter And The Guardian
Free enhanced CD with *The Guardian*, 2001
Audio – Mad Flava / Build It Up – Tear It Down / Right Here, Right Now / Give The Po' Man A Break / First Down / Michael Jackson (exclusive) / Love Island (rare Manumission remix)
Media – Right Here, Right Now (video) / Build It Up – Tear It Down (video exclusive) / Remix Game

ODDITIES
A Break From The Norm (Gut)
Camille Yarborough – Take Yo' Praise (used in 'Praise You') / Lulu – Love Loves To Love Love (used in 'Santa Cruz') / Ellen McIlwaine – Higher Ground (used in 'Song For Lindy') / Stik E And The Hoodz – Shake Whatcha Mama Gave Ya (used in 'Ya Mama') / Bill Withers – I Can't Write Left Handed (used in 'Demons') / Yvonne Elliman – I Can't Explain (used in 'Going Out Of My Head') / Doug Lazy – Let The Rhythm Pump (used in 'Ya Mama') / Dust Junkys – Beatbox Wash (Rinse It Remix) (used in 'Gangster Trippin') // Just Brothers – Sliced Tomatoes (used in 'The Rockafeller Skank') / Keith Mansfield – Young Scene (used in 'Punk To Funk') / Andre Williams – Humpin', Bumpin' And Thumpin' (used in 'Sho Nuff') / The Olympics – I'll Do A Little Bit More (used in 'Soul Surfing') / Leo Muller – The Acid Test (used in 'Build It Up, Tear It Down') / The John Barry Seven – Beat Girl (used in 'The Rockafeller Skank') / Colloseum – The Kettle (used in 'Ya Mama') / The James Gang – Ashes, The Rain And I (used in 'Right Here Right Now')

Fatboy Slim's Greatest Remixes
Wildchild – Renegade Master (Fatboy Slim Old Skool Mix) / Stretch 'n' Vern – Get Up! Go Insane! (Fatboy Really Lost It Mix) / Deeds Plus

Thoughts – The World's Made Up Of This And That (Fatboy Slim Remix) / FC Kahuna – What Is Kahuna? (Fatboy Slim's Smell The Kahuna Mix) / Psychedeliasmith – Dubby Jointy (Fatboy Slim Remix) / The Might Dub Katz – Magic Carpet Ride (Fatboy Slim Latin Ska Acid Breakbeat Mix) / Christopher Just – I'm A Disco Dancer (And A Sweet Romancer) (Fatboy Slim Remix) / Lunatic Calm – Roll The Dice (Fatboy Slim Vocal Mix) / Underworld – King Of Snake (Fatboy Slim Remix) / Jean-Jacques Perrey – EVA (Fatboy Slim Remix)

Fatboy Slim / Norman Cook Collection
Beats International – Won't Talk About It / Pierre Henry – Psyché Rock (Fatboy Slim Malpaso Mix) / Deeds And Thoughts – The World Is Made Up Of This And That (Fatboy Slim Remix) / Beats International – Echo Chamber / Beats International – Dub Be Good To Me / Jean-Jacques Perrey – EVA (Fatboy Slim Remix – radio edit) / A Tribe Called Quest – I Left My Wallet In El Segundo (Vampire Mix) / Beats International – The Sun Don't Shine / Shinehead – Start On Avalanche / Wildchild – Renegade Master (Fatboy Slim Old Skool Mix) / Lunatic Calm – Roll The Dice (Fatboy Slim Vocal Remix) / James Brown – Payback (The Final Mixdown) / Beats International – Tribute To King Tubby

I ∩D∈X